Assortment and Merchandising Strategy

"This book provides a comprehensive yet easy-to-read account of current knowledge related to assortment and merchandising decisions. It uncovers the interdependencies between these decisions from the shoppers' perspectives, and translates academic insights and experience-based evidence into practical guidelines. A strongly-recommended read for suppliers and retailers alike!"

—Els Gijsbrechts, *Professor of Quantitative Marketing, Tilburg University*

"A must-read for all retail professionals interested in taking the shopper experience to the next level.

Today, shoppers often struggle with endless assortments. Berkhout offers visionary shopper-focused solutions to tackle this so called assortment anxiety. The book provides both tactical and strategic approaches on how to create more variety without increasing complexity by utilising data-driven merchandising and assortment management."

—Ari Akseli, President, *Grocery Trade, Kesko*

"Berkhout does an amazing job bringing simplicity and clarity to the complex and often debated world of assortment and merchandising. He not only makes it relevant in the still large world of physical stores but also in the new and emerging digital world of online shopping. This book is a must-have guide to those wanting to grow sales and satisfy and delight their shoppers."

—Bob Nolan, Senior Vice-President, *Conagra Brands*

"Rapid changes in technology, online landscape and shopper expectations call for a new approach to assortment management that integrates decisions on brick-and-mortar and digital retail. *Assortment and Merchandising Strategy* provides practical frameworks and valuable insights that get you started straight-away. Best practices from Berkhout's vast retail experience and the wealth of academic insights on shopper decision-making make this book an essential handbook on assortment and merchandising."

—David Moore, International Retail & Development Director, Member of the Board, *SPAR International*

Constant Berkhout

Assortment and Merchandising Strategy

Building a Retail Plan to Improve Shopper Experience

Constant Berkhout
Rijnbrug Advies
Utrecht, The Netherlands

ISBN 978-3-030-11162-5   ISBN 978-3-030-11163-2   (eBook)
https://doi.org/10.1007/978-3-030-11163-2

Library of Congress Control Number: 2019932615

This Palgrave Macmillan imprint is published by the registered company Springer Nature Switzerland AG
The registered company address is: Gewerbestrasse 11, 6330 Cham, Switzerland

To

Henny and Miep, who converted their house into our home from where I could explore life, and who provided me a diversity of tasty cuisine, time to play handball every day, love for travelling abroad and enabled my education.

Opa, who had endless patience for me, and whose sublime furniture, wooden sculptures and drawings still beautify my world.

Foreword

I remember reading dozens of textbooks and articles in the past few years claiming that times are turbulent or changing faster than ever—and therefore defending the need for the ideas cited in these texts. No one can argue that retailing is going through what are probably its most turbulent times. Some of the macro and industry changes affecting almost every retailer are as follows:

- the rise of digital channels and how they impact communication, POS activities and delivery
- the still increasing importance of private labels in many industries
- the ease with which shoppers can compare prices and conditions across retailers
- category (or potentially industry) killers like Amazon
- changes in shopping habits and lifestyles (e.g. more going out or the increasing importance of rental versus purchase transactions)

It is such turbulent times that require taking a step back and reflecting about these changes to help practitioners understand what to change, what to adapt and what to continue. Have these changes made certain concepts obsolete? Which merchandising and pricing strategies need adaptation? How can we align our activities effectively across the various channels we want to play in?

Constant's book provides a most valuable resource to help managers think about these questions in a systematic way. He introduces a number of useful frameworks that help brand managers, category managers and retailers to assess the context in which they are competing, identify different pathways for action and make reasoned choices—from communicating with shoppers to understanding shopping missions or making smart merchandising decisions.

One particular strength of this book is its call for thorough understanding of the shopper-retailer-product triangle and how it impacts the shopping experience.

Constant emphasises that different shoppers have different expectations and that the same shopper changes expectations when shopping for different needs or categories and relates these expectations to information processing theories, willingness to search, price preferences and other attitudinal and behavioural concepts. The real leverage then comes from the author's decades of experience in the industry and thorough understanding of the scientific research in the field: He provides tailored hands-on advice, fuelled by numerous examples from various industries, all of which are also backed by academic work. This is a rare combination and provides an ideal source of advice for the manager who is interested in questioning his gut-feel decision-making approach.

Department of Marketing   Oliver Koll
University of Innsbruck,
Innsbruck, Austria

Acknowledgements

While it is commonly accepted that eye-level offers the best sales opportunities, I often found myself in conversations discussing whether the end of aisle was better than the centre of aisle and how merchandising guidelines had to be amended for online retail environments. After the famous jam study by Iyengar and Lepper, the belief of 'more is less' has stuck with retail practitioners; however, this seems difficult to align with a sheer endless assortment in stores like Amazon and the shopper preference for variety. I was intrigued by the fact that only few assortment and merchandising principles are universally applied in retail. I decided to plunge into the latest academic findings and was able to validate some of these myself in experiments when working as a consultant for retail clients. Therefore, I wish to thank all the academics whose articles were instrumental for building the arguments in this book, and all my clients and co-workers who inspired me with new learnings and challenges. The book project absorbed quite some family time and I am proud to be part of a family that allowed me to follow my curiosity: My wife Carola and our children Thomas and Isabel. A group of fantastic experts deserve special words of thanks because they were so generous to comment on an early draft of this book:

- Bas Bakker, Manager Private Label at Jumbo Supermarkten
- Els Gijsbrechts, Professor of Quantitative Marketing, Tilburg University
- Jeroen van der Kallen, Customer Experience Manager at Innogy
- Sean Raw, Director at Raw Management Solutions

The support of these people was great and any error or omittance is completely on me. I hope that this book provides you a clear route on how to delight shoppers with more variety without increasing complexity. Enjoy!

Contents

About the Author

Constant Berkhout is a passionate practitioner of retail marketing and shopper insights. He obtained a Master of Science in Economics Cum Laude with a major in Marketing at the Rijksuniversiteit Groningen in the Netherlands. His curiosity and career made him travel across the world and live in the USA, Argentina and the UK.

Constant is founder and owner of Rijnbrug Advies, a consultancy in the areas of retail marketing and shopper insights. With a passion for retail and building on more than 20 years' experience, Rijnbrug Advies finds new ways to grow categories and connect with the shopper. Clients include food retailers, non-food retailers and suppliers in Europe, the Middle East and Asia. His way of working is further detailed at www.constant-opportunities.com.

Before setting up his own agency, he gained broad experience across a large number of categories, functional areas and countries:

- At retailers De Boer Winkelbedrijven and Ahold, Constant got acquainted with the principles of retail and category management.
- For Kraft Foods, Constant set up the trade marketing practice and worked as customer manager for large supermarket chains.
- At Gillette/Procter & Gamble, he led business restructurings in commercial and value-chain departments in several European countries. Later he was given overall responsibility for the marketing at the business-to-business division in Europe.
- At PepsiCo, he first assumed the responsibility of consumer insights and innovation for Northern Europe. In his last role at PepsiCo, he was responsible for shopper insights and marketing in more than 45 countries in

Europe. He set up trade marketing in Eastern European countries such as Russia. For Western European markets, he increased customer intimacy with customers such as Carrefour, Casino and Tesco. He worked closely with colleagues in North America to apply breakthrough technologies.

Constant is married, and he and his wife have two children. In his free time he loves reading and travelling, and although he was a passionate handball player in the past, most time on the sports field is now spent watching his children play soccer and basketball.

List of Figures

List of Tables

1

Integration of Assortment and Merchandising

Learning Objectives

- Understand why organisations benefit from collaboration between assortment managers and merchandisers in an early phase.
- Learn when to take a common approach to online and brick-and-mortar assortment decisions, and when to differentiate.
- Get acquainted with a holistic approach to the decision on number and sort of products for online and brick-and-mortar stores.

Visual Merchandising Versus Traditional Space Management

When searching for sports clothing or navigating through a supermarket, I sometimes pause and wonder where all these products have come from. I imagine that my running shoes are designed in New York, produced in Bangladesh, shipped to Hamburg and somehow arrived in my favourite store. My tomatoes are perhaps harvested at a farm nearby or came by truck from Spain. All these products have made a long journey. And I also start imagining how carefully the category manager tasted and tried the products, made an incredibly complex spreadsheet to calculate the business potential and closed a deal with the supplier. With all the care given before the product arrived in-store, I am even more amazed by the fact that the placement of the product seems to be an afterthought. There are more products than the shelves can

© The Author(s) 2019
C. Berkhout, *Assortment and Merchandising Strategy*,
https://doi.org/10.1007/978-3-030-11163-2_1

hold. For example, boxes of toys are merchandised in such a way that the attractively designed front side is not visible. Or the perfume bay contains so many bottles and colours apparently placed without any logic that I do not know where to start the search. Products with similar colour are placed next to each other and they cannot be identified easily. The energy retailers spend before the product arrives at the store is completely lost if the shopper cannot conveniently search and select from the offer. This is where the space management and visual merchandising functions can help. The former seeks the most optimal location and visual stock for each product considering commercial and retail brand objectives. The latter supports the shopper decision process through merchandising material and store communication. Both functions ensure the category presentation fits the overall retail brand and the shopper is supported with the right inspirational and informative messages. It seems that retail functions for selecting and merchandising the assortment work too often in silos. When category managers involve the space management department only at the last moment just before launch, the role of a space manager is more like a strip cartoonist and the visual merchandiser becomes an artistic fortune teller: Both have great stories that one day might become true.

There could be several reasons for the late involvement. It has become a habit for category managers to deal with product sourcing and assortment development first before working on merchandising. This makes sense from the perspective that retailers first need to select and feel the product and decide what quality and how much of the product they source. Secondly, the category managers tend to dedicate more time to urgent daily duties like promotional planning than to considering the time constraints for ordering new shelf material or building the right online environment. Thirdly, the category managers sometimes determine the range and the order size of non-food products on overseas trips because competition and supplier negotiation leave them no other choice. At large online retailers, the focus on numbers and analytics is such and they have created work environments in which creative visual merchandisers do not feel understood and appreciated. Finally, starting with the product in mind is also linked to the fact that the category manager operates within the frame of the existing store environment. Investments in the store infrastructure are significant and are preferably made when considering several categories in their relationships. This takes time that the category manager feels is slowing them down. As a consequence, any amendments in store furniture or website infrastructure are postponed to a later moment, and to other people. Chances are nobody raises the question at a later moment as to what could have been the optimal way of merchandising the product. Considering the time, budget investment and the logical fear of disturbing current shopping habits, retailers often prefer to take the current merchandising as a given.

What If Merchandising and Assortment Decisions Are Made in Harmony?

Currently, product introduction is often supplier driven. Let's imagine a supplier of energy bars has developed an appetizing range of cereal bars filled with juicy fruits and delicious nuts and crispy cereals and they approach a high-street convenience retailer. The supplier promises a favourable promotional package and a satisfying price. The retailer already has some cereal brands available and after a quick analysis the category manager works out an assortment for one bay of energy bars. This could very well work. Alternatively, the category manager could have started with the shopper in mind and thought about the benefits of the cereal bar to the shopper. The cereal bar might be purchased for a healthy breakfast. The shopper may not want to decide between brands of cereal bars but rather make a choice among bars, yoghurt, apples and smoothies. Other cereal bars that are covered with chocolate could be placed together with snacks such as pies and potato chips for an afternoon indulgence occasion. In the first case, when the retailer places all cereal bars by product type together, it is more a case of re-organizing the existing bay. In the second case, the retailer needs to come up with an idea for equipment that holds both ambient and cooled products. The integration of coolers for yoghurt, metal shelves for the cereal bars and wicker baskets for apples should be designed such that the shopper perceives the assortment as a combined offer for a healthy breakfast. It sounds challenging as well as cool! Shoppers find the products according to their needs and the retailer differentiates itself through the way of merchandising, while each of the individual products and brands may be offered elsewhere. As discussed later in the book, when products are placed by benefit rather than by product type, shoppers are inclined to look more for similarities. They approach the assortment with the assumption that the products address the same need. As a result, the products are perceived to be more or less similar and therefore the benefit grouping allows the retailers to carry a less wide assortment. The same principles are applicable online. Shoppers often struggle with the almost endless assortments. While placement by product category reinforces comparison, online retailers may discover that organizing by benefit makes the number of products on the websites more digestible for shoppers.

Considering the way a product is merchandised at an early stage, perhaps even before selection of the product, offers both tactical and strategic opportunities. Making the merchandising decision before assortment may lead to new insights and innovative practices. I observe that the new thinking is not woven into the regular retail process. Indeed, merchandising is integrated at an earlier stage at times of major refits and repositioning of the retail brand. When retail formats and webstores are reconsidered is the time when merchandising does come first in retail. The big win is that category managers and merchandisers consider the context of shopping and shopper decision processing when building the assortment and designing space.

In addition to the strategic advantages of more shopper-focused solutions and holistic approaches which encourage innovation, the timely integration of merchandising aspects also has very practical benefits. For example, a retailer may develop a grey-silver packaging line for its private label that looks appealing in itself but becomes a dull, neglected spot when placed on a shelf or website. Or the supplier develops such shapes and sizes of Cornflakes boxes that only two flavours rather than three flavours fit the shelf. Both retailers and suppliers benefit when product packaging is developed in relationship to the store context it will be part of. When presenting products online, much time is spent on the best product image, but the role of packaging for shoppers is as important. Online players need to analyse the functions of packaging in each stage, from salience on the webstore to protection during shipment to convenient opening at home. The same product could be contained in a simple carton box or a colourful box that turns the ordering of a toy from a webstore into a playful unwrapping moment at home. Or the packaging displays the most important steps of the instruction manual of a closet. For retailers, there are opportunities for tapping into needs of both instruction and delight at the home moment. As a consequence, the same product may need different packaging for online sales and brick-and-mortar stores.

The early integration of merchandising decisions into the assortment management process pays off. From different angles this will generate more positive financial returns. First of all, when knowing and using the physical dimensions of products, retailers know at an earlier phase of the category development process whether products will fit on a shelf or whether they need to amend the composition of the assortment. This is what space managers describe as a 'space aware' assortment software and process. When space is created for the right products, the retailer can offer more variety and appeal to a wider set of needs. It also means that sufficient space is created, so that there are no lost sales as a result of out-of-stocks. Avoiding out-of-stocks could mean a higher frequency of store deliveries and therefore supply chain costs, and balancing the cost of refilling and out-of-stocks at an early decision moment should determine the optimal space. Finally, the term space awareness is used in the world of brick-and-mortar retail, but also the dimensions of a smartphone, tablet or PC set restrictions on the amount and size of products. The concept of space awareness focuses on the amount of space dedicated to products. Even more can be gained from the way of merchandising. As this book will demonstrate, the quality of merchandising is more important for sales than the quantity of merchandising. Amending the location of the worst to the best location could deliver 59 per cent increase of sales, whereas changing the amount of space by 10 per cent generates on average only 3 per cent more sales. The suggestion that quality of merchandising plays a more significant role than quantity of merchandising might be even more important for online stores. Online shopping is mostly a visual rather than a multi-sensory experience. What gets represented to shoppers and how depends on the search term they entered. Clever algorithms based on previous visits or similar visitors could deliver personalised search-based merchandising. The visual design of products and their arrangement become ever more decisive for both online product search and decisions.

Online Shopping Experience

The term store is used equally for brick-and-mortar stores and web-shops throughout this book. The reason is that many of the human biological features and psychological processes lead to the same effect. The focus is on shoppers, their behavioural biases and their needs. An example of a human, biological characteristic is the way people's eyes are cast in their heads. This results in a vision field with the shape of a diamond that is wider than it is high. This makes it easier for shoppers both in online and offline stores to browse through products when they are displayed horizontally than vertically (up and down). There are also all kinds of behavioural biases, and tapping into these works anywhere. For example, showing recommendations for certain brands from a well-known pop-star or TV doctor may provide a gentle push towards a brand at the final moment of product selection. In summary, there is not one underlying drive or motivation of the behaviour that conceptually takes the same shape in online and brick-and-and-mortar stores. This is not to say there are no differences in what they mean and offer, and how they are expressed. In this book, I look for common features and will point out where the differences in assortment and merchandising management are. Shoppers have started to expect the same experience and service levels across stores. The different types of stores are both used for the same shopping tasks such as information collection, product comparison and payment. Therefore, it is no wonder that stores offer the same functions and become woven into each other. This reflects the world in which shoppers may use a combination of digital and physical touchpoints on their shopping journey.

This book suggests that shopper psychology and behaviour is the same in these retail environments, but the expression of the principle may need to be adapted. So, the same shopper principles apply to both worlds. For example, one of the principles that will be discussed in much more detail is that shoppers enjoy those assortments which they can process more easily. And the smoother the process, the more variety they observe. A second principle says that an assortment with a large number of products creates more choice stress. Retailers could resolve this by reducing the number of products. However, under certain conditions they can maintain the same high number of products without a negative impact on the shopper's mind by giving the shopper tools to navigate through the assortment. The way this is actioned upon may be the same or different in brick-and-mortar and online stores. In the physical store, the retailer may use tactics as structured planograms or brands with salient packaging colour. In an informative paper on visual design, Kahn (2016) gives practical suggestions on how online retailers can practically translate the principle of easy processing of information into more pleasurable online shopping experiences. She suggests a range of tactics such as reduction of dissimilarity between products on the page, reduction of number of colours and contrasts, using images rather than text, applying high contrast of font type versus the page background colour and using symmetric rather than irregular and asymmetric shapes. These are crucially important suggestions for building a pleasurable online experience, but they should not draw away the attention from overlaying principles anchored in shopper decision-making and behaviour. Indeed, this book applies thankfully dozens of academic studies of which many were constructed with the help of online stores. Though the original reasons for research teams may be efficiency and the control of environmental factors, still the large number of experiments with the help of online tools provides good support and the academic results can be relevant for all types of stores, both online and brick-and-mortar. The new shopping journeys have made the stores become intertwined: Digital giants like Amazon open bookstores, and traditional grocery chains open click-and-collect points. Formerly traditional retailers want to capture part of the online market, and formerly pure digital players seek opportunities for additional services and excitement. Continuous switching between the two worlds is making a distinction less meaningful for the shopper, and therefore for professionals. The number of product alternatives for shoppers has increased, and though this seems contradictory, this forces retailers to think carefully about the role of digital versus physical outlets, the different impact they have and where and how the products will be sold most successfully and in a cost-effective manner.

The thought has run through my mind that if everyone applies the same set of merchandising principles, stores start to become organised in the same manner and look the same. However, assortment and merchandising management is not that simple. Each category and shopping context brings its own characteristics and challenges, and the number of possible combinations of the different merchandising guidelines is high. Retailers want to leave their signature in the way of merchandising. And though there are many similarities across shoppers that allow for universal merchandising principles, there are also differences in attitudes and behaviour that require a differentiated approach. For example, some shoppers like to scan all product options, whereas others are happy with the first product that meets a given minimum requirement. Therefore, apart from universal merchandising principles, retailers need to develop principles that fit their decisions on target group and assortment.

Focus on Space Decision

Retailers that decide on the amount and quality of space for a specific product know that this decision cannot be made in isolation. Whether the product can be listed depends on the amount of space available for the total category. And if the supply chain capabilities of the brick-and-mortar store put restrictions on the number of deliveries, each individual store needs to reserve more capacity. If the online store is not efficient enough for low-rotating products, it will need to rely on external vendors and possibly settle for less margin and slower delivery to the shopper. Cutting the assortment tail often leads to an acceleration of rotation of the remaining products, which needs to be addressed with either more space in-store and warehouse or more frequent store deliveries. Internally set financial targets may overrule shopper satisfaction: Supply chain cost optimisation could lead to fewer deliveries and more out-of-stock. In such situations, retailers hope that the shopper is sufficiently happy to switch to a substitute product from the category. These interactions show that product listings cannot be made without considering the available retail space and supply chain.

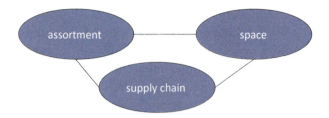

Image 1.1 Interaction assortment decisions

Another way of looking at the interrelationships is dividing the assortment decision into three smaller steps: Composition, amount of space and location. These steps are taken both on category level when building an (online) store layout and on product level when developing a category. The focus of the book is on the second type, so category-level decisions. Sometimes store-level factors are discussed because the various interrelationships make it hard to decompose cause and effect and identify the 'real' driver of change. With the rise of big data (technologies), this becomes more manageable, though there is still always a level of uncertainty, as shoppers do not always act rationally.

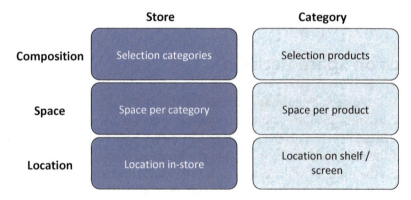

Image 1.2 Scope of book

With professionals active in retail and consumer products in mind, this book intends to help them make better decisions in the following areas:

- Improve insights and innovation programmes by integrating decisions on merchandising in an early phase of assortment management.
- Increase rotation of brands by applying universal visual merchandising principles.
- Apply marketing instruments more sharply by making a distinction between actual and perceived assortment variety.

- Make more effective planograms and online environments by enlarging knowledge of what shoppers see and how they behave.
- Invest marketing budget more wisely by carefully selecting those categories that matter according to merchandising role model.

This book also provides help for all shoppers, online and in brick-and-mortar, who exercise the power of choice every day through their habits and behaviours. They are the co-shapers and co-creators of assortment and merchandising strategies everywhere. The shoppers who gain more insight into their decisions and day-to-day shopping behaviour can more wisely achieve their personal happiness and in doing so give direction to future retail.

Structure of the Book

This book is built on a step-by-step structure. This first chapter introduces the scope. Chapters 2, 3, 4, 5, 6, 7 and 8 each represent a building block for selecting products that satisfy shopper needs and merchandising them in such a manner that they enjoy the richness of variety, while the costs of search and evaluation are minimised. Chapters 2, 3 and 4 have in common that they deal with products.

- Chapter 2: The number of products in the category and the amount of space allocated to the category create perceptions of variety and complexity.
- Chapter 3: These perceptions are dependent on the types of characteristics of the products available, or stated differently: Composition of assortment.
- Chapter 4: The same assortment can be displayed differently and the way the products are merchandised in the category has a high impact on shopper behaviour.
- Chapter 5: Apart from the products, characteristics of the shoppers themselves influence the assortment and merchandising preferences.
- Chapter 6: The same shopper undertakes a number of different missions, and each mission provides a new framing to the shopping decision.
- Chapter 7: On top of product and shopper considerations, the retailer has its own set of objectives which are reflected in the assortment and merchandising plan.

- Chapter 8: This is where it becomes very practical. The combination of certain human behaviour and retailer objectives will generate principles that are equally applied to all categories.
- Chapter 9: Some categories need more attention, some need less and the category role model in this chapter helps in making those decisions.
- Chapter 10: Often it is sufficient to let the product talk: The product itself communicates its function and makes itself both salient and informative through its packaging. At other times more communication is required, and the shopper communication model provides a clear structure for type of message and media.
- Chapter 11: The plans and frameworks in Chaps. 7, 8, 9, 10 and 11 are built on the insights derived before. The 11th and final chapter brings all the chapters together in what I consider as the ultimate retailer objective: Delivering shopper delight. This chapter concludes with a view on future developments in assortment and merchandising management.

Chapters 2, 3, 4, 5 and 7 are grounded in the latest academic research on shopper decision-making; however, I do not wish practitioners to get lost in the scientific work in the fields of vision, brain functions and psychology. The 'so-what' question is asked to make sure practitioners can apply the insights to the retail context. Examples are added to illustrate how CPG suppliers and retailers can act on the findings of this research. Students and academics will find an in-depth review of articles combined with an inter-pretation of how these are applied in the retail world. In Chap. 8 and further, I provide practical frameworks that practitioners can complete with their own data. They provide starting points for internal discussion on how these models can be tailored to their specific retail environment. The practical models allow retailers to tailor the findings from academic research and best practices on assortment and merchandising management to their own organisation mission, vision and brand strategy. There is not one answer, and the models will advise how to differentiate by shopping mission and category. Early inclusion of visual aspects of assortment, measuring shopper perception rather than counting the numbers, a holistic view on the shopper journey and integrated data and software solutions are key ingredients of this book. By applying learnings from behavioural economics, visual merchandising, eye-tracking studies and experimental (online) store tests I hope to improve decision-making in retail.

Image 1.3   Integrated assortment and merchandising model

Important Learnings from This Chapter

- The number of variables influencing assortment and merchandising decisions for retailers is so high and they have become so complex that it might have stopped practitioners from actioning on the insights at all.
- Assortment and merchandising are often treated as separate decision areas; however, retailers are more successful when considering the way of merchandising in an advanced stage and together with assortment decisions.
- Retailers that thrive only on data analytics and short-term focused decision-making create work environments in which space managers and visual merchandisers do not feel understood and appreciated.
- Shoppers love variety, and it is not so much the actual assortment but their perception that drives their behaviour.

Reference

Kahn, B. E. (2017). Using Visual Design to Improve Customer Perceptions of Online, Assortments. *Journal of Retailing, 93*(1), 29–42.

2

Assortment Size and Space

Image 2.1 Integrated assortment and merchandising model

Learning Objectives

- Indicate what the consequences are of changing the number of products from various perspectives.
- Understand how shoppers absorb and process information from the retail context.
- Successfully amend the number of products in a category.

© The Author(s) 2019
C. Berkhout, *Assortment and Merchandising Strategy*,
https://doi.org/10.1007/978-3-030-11163-2_2

Supplier Perspective on Assortment Size

When it is up to suppliers, any discussion on product introductions used to mean getting more of the supplier brands into retail. When working at consumer products companies (CPC) such as Kraft Foods and PepsiCo, my goal was to beat competition by having more of the company brands on shelf and by having more displays. Being responsible for trade marketing and customer management, my role was to identify slow-moving products of competition, use colourful graphs to show the retailer how much money they were losing every year and convince the retailer to list any of our own products. In addition to these so-called permanent listings, suppliers orchestrated 'display waves' to seize any available temporary location in-store. The magic word at many CPCs some 20 years ago was 'ubiquity': Making all of the supplier products available at as many locations as a shopper would visit. The objective of number of the locations was operationalised in the number of retail locations across channels, the percentage numeric distribution at a given retailer like Ahold Delhaize and the number of locations shoppers could find the product at the retail location. The more the better. And it worked. Getting the brand listed at large retailers like Carrefour could be the result of a broad range of factors, such as strong supplier-retailer account management relationship, (simply) paying the listing fee, consumer research identifying unknown needs and supplier advertising campaigns to activate consumer demand and pull the product through the value chain. As retailers became more sophisticated and powerful, large suppliers would invest more resources in finding the right product-listing argument. It could take months or even years until the retailer accepted the product extension. Sales directors would remind category managers of the 'missing' products after each visit to the 'difficult' or 'problematic' retailer. When the retailer finally agreed, a cake would be delivered to the retailer offices to celebrate the listing and good supplier-retailer relationship. And then it was up to the next, innovative product-listing project. Product launches form a playful, often predictable act in the retail theatre. However, over the years the discussions between supplier and retailer have become more insights driven. Indeed, finding the right argument to obtain a product listed at retail created new roles and new industries in themselves. Some of the activities to build up a good story are:

- Conduct econometric or so-called volume-metric studies that predict the rotation of new products based on the marketing investment in, for example, advertising and a database of comparable historic launches.

- Visualise the product potential on shelf through space management software. The supplier investment in building shelf proposals—not just for their own brand but also for competitive products—effectively means the retailer has driven out activities and costs to others.
- Tracking the shopper profile of competitive products with the help of consumer household panel data. The goal is to see if competitive products are serving the same shoppers, which means that some overlapping flavours can be reduced, or to convince the retailer that competitive products are cannibalizing the retailer's private label.

The mere fact of the size of investment meant the 'more is better' strategy was working from a supplier perspective. Although the success rate of product launches varied widely, the high number of initiatives to make them work resulted in supplier sales growth and funds to initiate the next product launch. This treadmill of product launches moves on the thought that from a consumption or demand perspective more product variety is better for shoppers.

Deeper Insight: More Variety = More Consumption

Studies in the 1980s by Rolls and her colleagues (1981) show that when people were offered yoghurt of three different flavours (hazelnut, blackcurrant and orange) but with the same appearance and texture, they ate some 19 per cent more yoghurt than if only offered one flavour. In addition, the decline of consumption over successive courses was slower when variety was offered. Studies like these gave confidence to suppliers that they were on the right track in promoting more product introductions.

The supplier way of working itself contained catalysers for more growth. Brands with striking colours like Cadbury could build large coloured brand blocks in the shelf displaying their dominance. Retailers became gradually more dependent on suppliers, making it difficult to decline listing new products and stop receiving the promotional contributions they were linked with. Higher volumes of brands gave higher economies of scale and lower production costs. Better margins and complementary incentives aroused new energy and search for new products. In summary, suppliers seek any opportunity for more distribution to maximise profits, they want to control the environment where the product is sold to protect the desired brand image, and propose new products to satisfy new shopper needs and stay ahead of competition. Their ambitions are not always aligned with those of retailers.

Retailer Perspective on Assortment Size

From a retailer perspective a wide assortment worked well. Retailers learnt that by expanding the assortment with new products or even entire new categories, their revenues increased. In grocery retail, the players often carry the same categories so that the level of variety should be measured on product level. A larger assortment increased the chances of serving a wider spectrum of shopper needs and attracting more people. Shoppers may perceive the assortment as unique, which helps differentiate the retailer from others. In surveys, shoppers point to assortment as one of the top three reasons to select a store, next to price and location. The assortment marketing instrument is more complex than the other two due to heterogeneity in shopper expectations. Everything else being equal, all shoppers love stores with lower prices or stores that are closer to home. However, offering more products may attract some shoppers but others might be deterred.

In addition, it is difficult to determine the importance of assortment compared to other retail instruments. Understanding the importance of retail instruments is important to ensure that retailers allocate their investments correctly. Because investments in pricing and promotions show direct impact, they may steal away attention from assortment decisions. For an assignment at a grocery retailer I relied mostly on shopper surveys. When asked about reasons to visit the store, the respondents mentioned factors including location, price, convenience/habit, assortment and emotional motives such as 'it feels fine'. The survey method depended on what shoppers claimed their behaviour was; however, it is better to look for more indirect manners that measure actual behaviour with regard to location, price and assortment. In one such study, Brown (1978) concluded that shoppers are prepared to visit more distant stores if the assortment is larger. In a more recent study, Briesch and his colleagues (2009) analysed thousands of shopping trips for ten grocery categories with the help of consumer panel data covering all types of stores in Chicago. In Briesch's study, the importance of location was measured by taking the actual road distance from the zip code area of the consumer panel member and the store address. They concluded that the convenience of proximity has a significantly larger effect on store choice than price and assortment, which is consistent with what shoppers would tell in a survey. More surprising is the fact that the store choice depended more on assortment than on price.

Deeper Insight: Assortment Is More Important for Store Choice than Price; However, This Depends on Type of Retailer, Shopper and Category

- Market shares of retail brands based on Every Day Low Price (EDLP) were more sensitive to the location, price and assortment than High-Low (HiLo) retail brands that discount and otherwise promote categories to drive traffic to their stores.
- Although the frequency of feature advertising did not affect store choice, the researchers concluded that the heterogeneity of shopper behaviour suggested that for some shoppers advertising played a crucial role in selecting their grocery store.
- Shoppers were more inclined to visit a store when they carried more brands and when they listed the most favourite, highly rotating brands. On the other hand, having fewer products per brand and fewer pack sizes per brand contributed positively to store selection. The researchers took the proportion of products uniquely sold by a store as an approximation for private label and concluded that higher private label penetration in categories like soft drinks, coffee, diapers and household cleaners resulted in lower probabilities of visiting the store.
- Correlations between the store traffic drivers were not significant apart from one: Shoppers make a trade-off between a store close to their home and a store farther away with a larger assortment. Alternatively stated, shoppers are prepared to overcome a large distance to a store as long as the assortment is large.
- The importance of assortment for selecting a store varied widely among shoppers, whereas responses to price and location were more uniform. Indeed, the researchers also identified a small but significant group of shoppers that preferred stores with more products per brand, more sizes per brand, more unique products but do so with fewer brands.

The study emphasises the importance of assortment for store choice, which may play a bigger role than retailers currently act upon. At the same time, it shows that the role of assortment depends on the (target) shopper and type of shopping trip. Often, for daily groceries the convenience of one-stop shopping deprioritises the price argument. However, the retailer may also target shoppers with a limited purchase power, in which case the importance of pricing may take over. The order of importance may also vary depending on the category: Shoppers may attach value to assortment variety of fresh vegetables and shop at the local vegetable shop, and for categories like condiments proximity and low transaction costs may take precedence. In other words, there is a difference between share of wallet and share of customers that a retailer can achieve.

Retailers have historically given much attention to location, which makes sense as shoppers only travel so far to buy daily necessities. Being first in a catchment area helps build market share as people who live there form habits. Indeed, the opening of a new store will make shoppers within the catchment area reconsider patronage, but until that time they will most likely continue to shop where they always have. The role of assortment variety has become more important. Stores have become retail brands and use assortment as a variable to differentiate them. Fierce competition and more transparency make it difficult to compete on price. Having the opportunity to order food from supermarkets or restaurants 24/7 has made the purchase location less relevant. Prioritising location strategy is understandable as long as certain areas in the country are not 'covered' with a supermarket by online or brick-and-mortar retailers. In Western countries, this is hardly the case anymore. Within a given catchment area, shoppers make a choice from the available food stores: That's when people make a trade-off between price and assortment and select the store that fits their shopping needs. Western countries that do show a growth in the number of stores are replacing larger stores in more remote parts of the city with convenience stores in urban areas. Indeed, time and travel have become more valuable to a shopper.

There are many arguments in favour of a large assortment; however, retailers may also find it beneficial to skim off their assortments in search for more sales and higher differentiation. At a certain moment, the costs of adding products to their value chain become higher than the incremental revenues. More products equal a larger product database to fill and maintain, more warehouse locations assigned, more warehouse handling and movement and more in-store merchandising. A reduced assortment gives more visibility for the remaining products. In addition, the focus on a selection of highly rotating products supports the ability to forecast and decreases overall level of out-of-stock products. A reduction of assortment puts category managers in a privileged position in supplier negotiations: When there are three brands and space is available only for two, the category manager will demand lower prices from the remaining two brand owners. While at first glance a larger number of products always seems to be a better option for retailers, they also have strong arguments to put a lid on assortment size.

In conclusion, more than ever retailers need a unique assortment to differentiate from competition as online sales has made location a less important retail instrument. Shoppers love this variety but it conflicts with supplier needs for economies of scale. Knowing what their desired retail brand is helps retailers set priorities by category. For this they need to know what their shoppers want.

Shopper Perspective on Assortment Size

For shoppers a large assortment has many benefits. First of all, it simply creates more opportunities for shoppers to find what they want in that specific moment, the perfect match so to speak. It also allows shoppers to keep their options open and tailor the product to a specific occasion. For example, shoppers may appreciate the convenience of a coffee capsule in the morning and take the time for grinding beans from their favourite coffee region on the weekend. Thirdly, even if the shoppers know pretty well what they want to buy, the knowledge that a retailer has a wide assortment reduces the uncertainty that elsewhere other and perhaps even better alternatives are available. When Amazon displays a total assortment of TV sets of 1800, the shopper may actually only be interested in 1 of the 25 TV sets with a small screen, but it feels good to the shopper that Amazon gives their utmost effort to offer all the alternatives. This explains why in the US some 50 per cent of all product searches start on Amazon—beating search engines like Google (Survata 2017). The fourth benefit is that some shoppers buy several alternatives from the same category to allow themselves the flexibility of selecting what they use at a later moment. For example, shoppers may buy several evening dresses for the same occasion and like to have several menu course options for the same special dinner. A larger assortment also makes things easier when the shopper buys for others and needs to cater their needs for a specific size or flavour. In a practical way, a larger assortment saves the shoppers time and energy as they can complete their shopping mission in one stop. Variety could be another reason: In categories like chocolate and desserts shoppers like to alternate flavours and taste new products. Finally, there is a deep, emotional driver that explains why large assortments appeal to shoppers. A larger assortment offers a sense of control that humans naturally seek. Imagine shopping for breakfast cereals and there is only one product available. Apart from the fact that shopping becomes less fun, shoppers feel forced to buy this cereal or leave the store empty-handed. Being able to choose from two, three and more makes shoppers feel in control of what they buy. Iyengar (2011) explains in *The Art of Choosing* that the need for control is deeply ingrained in humans. She illustrates this point with a study in which babies become sad and angry when they are deprived of their music options. She goes on to explain that Anglo-Saxon culture emphasises the right of individual choices in life, and that with its globally expanding importance in recent decades the awareness and importance of being in control has dispersed. In addition to the sense of control, shoppers just feel better. Offering variety is considered positively by shoppers and may put shoppers in a good mood. And once in a good mood, shoppers see other things in store more positively as well. They may also enjoy variety because this allows them to be (seen as) innovative and variety taps into their creative spirit. In summary, there are many aspects that shoppers look for in assortment: Variety for their specific need or occasion, inspiration from breaking the routine, sense of control and convenience from one-stop shopping.

Deeper Insight: Increased Variety Goes Together with Increased Complexity

A study by Scheibehenne and his colleagues (2009) sums up the benefits of a large assortment, but also shows some of the challenges shoppers face. They compared the same shoppers that in one shopping trip selected classical music from a small set of 6 CDs and in another trip chose from a large set of 30 CDs in an online environment. The results showed that:

- Fifty-five per cent of people perceived the large assortment as more attractive.
- The number of considered products (consideration set) increased from 2.6 for small assortments to 5.3 CDs for large assortments.
- The number of CDs for which shoppers sought detailed information increased from 5 to 16.

However:

- Eighty-three per cent of people thought the large assortment was more complex.
- Average time needed to pick a CD more than doubled to 64 seconds. Seventy-nine per cent of shoppers spent more time choosing from a large assortment.

The Impact of Assortment on Choice

Large assortments seem to work. This is one of the most discriminating features of online retail: Amazon is adding more products every day and shoppers can buy more than 562 million products in the US (Scrapehero 2018). The number of products available in brick-and-mortar stores is astonishing as well. For example, Walmart Supercentres sell more than 140,000 products in the US and Auchan hypermarkets in France offer more than 100,000 products. These numbers prove that an almost endless number of products can be offered, and the thriving existence of these retail formats illustrates that they meet shopper demands. This is contradictory with what we have learnt from academic studies, retail best practice studies and behavioural economists about the impact of large assortments on shopper behaviour. They point to two considerations that determine the way that shoppers perceive assortment size: Cognitive processing and human visual capabilities.

Cognitive Choice: How Shoppers Think

With their famous jam study Iyengar and Lepper (2000) opened the eyes of retailers to the fact that large assortments may attract many shoppers, but when it comes to conversion to actual purchase, shoppers prefer smaller assortments. Retailers like Carrefour, Walmart and Loblaws used the outcome of the study to cut assortments by some 15 per cent in the first decade of the twenty-first century. The initial success of these programmes for shoppers can be explained by what Schwartz (2004) coined as the paradox of choice: It seems great to be in control but learning to choose well in a world of unlimited options is hard, perhaps too hard. When making a purchase decision, people find it hard to decipher all relevant attributes like weight, region and production method, weigh these attributes and score each product accordingly. With all the different sizes of packaging it takes advanced calculating skills to determine the best price-value product. Traditional economic theories assume information flows are transparent and shoppers consider all relevant information in their decision. For too long retailers considered shoppers as rational decision-makers, while more often than not they take simple cues like brand or what popstars or best friends like as the most crucial purchase consideration.

Deeper Insight: Our Brain Likes to Keep It Simple

Nobel Prize-winning psychologist Kahneman makes a distinction between System 1 and System 2 thinking. The first thinking process generates impressions and emotions without much effort. System 2 thinking processes are considerate and evaluate several options at the same time. The most cognitive part of our brain is smaller and much of shopping follows System 1 thinking: When shoppers feel they are in a safe environment and make a routine decision from a category they know well, they rely on their automatic impulses. Sometimes the choice is hard, perhaps because much is at stake like a dinner for your would-be friend, or because the shopping aisle is crowded with colourful packaging, banners, staff and shoppers. In such cases, the considerate part of your brain may switch off and let the more emotional part of the brain make the decision. When it comes to assortment, this theory implies that with each new product the cognitive costs rise. Imagine a long soft drinks aisle with dozens of products and it becomes clear that each additional product will make the value of the category increase only marginally and each time slightly less. Amazon's supersize assortment raises expectations in a supersize manner, but it is unlikely that these are met due to shoppers' limited processing capabilities.

Human Visual Capabilities: What Shoppers See

Apart from the cognitive skills, the human visual capabilities shape the way in which shoppers perceive assortments because most sensory impulses come in through the eye. There are a couple of characteristics concerning human vision that are important to know in order to understand shopping behaviour better. Let's look at the working of the human eye. So-called photoreceptor cells in the retina convert light into electrical signals for the brain. Two types of photoreceptor cells contribute to sight directly: Rods and cones. The latter help us perceive great detail and differentiate colours if there is sufficient day or artificial lighting. They help shoppers identify the exact packaging they want and read the shelf label. The rods are very sensitive to light and enable us to see in the dark. The rods help shoppers navigate through the store and detect movements by other shoppers around them. Humans have far more rods than cones, 120 million rods versus some 6 million cones (Wikipedia 2018). Therefore, a small percentage of our sight is extremely precise. Most of the shopping environment is scanned, but not researched. Retailers can increase the level of focused reading through the size of the object and colour contrasts (which I will discuss later in the book). So, the amount of detail in our vision is very restricted.

When studying shopping behaviour, it is also important to remember that the range of vision in front of shoppers has a more or less oval shape and is far bigger horizontally. Simply put, the placement of the eye in the socket restricts what human beings see. Vertically, our range of vision is some 115 degrees, a bit more down than up. In the horizontal line, the nose limits the vision and the total field of horizontal vision is 140 degrees wide. Where the ranges of the left and right eye overlap, the brains melt the images together into 3D vision and this is called the binocular range of field. In practice, this is some 150 centimetres to the left and 150 centimetres to the right when the shopper is standing in front of the shelf. Where the eyes do not overlap, human beings see in 2D. The fact that the shape of our vision is oval and slightly more downward helps explain why shoppers do not perceive the shelf straight in front of them best.

This is also driven by a third characteristic of human vision: The human vision line runs down with an angle of some 15 degrees. The downward vision line is explained by the fact that human beings need to exert efforts to look in a straight line ahead. First of all, there are muscles in the neck that need to keep the five kilos of the head up. Second of all, looking straight ahead will require the six muscles to keep the eyeball in tension. Instead, humans are inclined to save energy when they can and keep the muscles relaxed. The resulting declining slope of the vision line makes some products more salient than others. It is helpful for walking around with a shopping cart and at the same time explains why narrow-casting TV screens and promotion material hanging from the ceiling are often a waste of investment. Putting the head backward is not comfortable for the neck muscles.

These are some general principles of vision. The exact shape and quality of the vision range are different per person because they are determined by the location in the eye socket and the rounding and quality of the eye. When the left and right eye do not collaborate well, the shape of the vision range changes. And although many imperfections of human vision can be solved also when human beings grow older, there are shoppers who have a vision limitation or are even blind. In a physical store, they will appreciate being assisted by staff or have the possibility to borrow glasses. For people with vision restriction, home delivery of groceries and other products is a great solution. When creating physical store environments, I often work with the average height of the shopper and reduce this number by some 10 centimetres to obtain the height of the eyes. From this point, the vision line starts with a slope of 15 degrees and will tell what the shopper focuses on when standing in front of a shelf.

Both the cognitive and visual capabilities of shoppers favour a small assortment. The preference for smaller and more personalised assortments is also a response to the faster pace of life. The drive of people to combine work, household duties, hobbies, social get-togethers and some sleep all in one day creates the context for how they shop. A study by Wiseman (2007) conducted in 32 large cities in 2006 showed that people walked 10 per cent faster compared to the early 1990s. And when they pop into a store they expect things to work and go quickly. Technologies such as those that enable cashier-less payments increasingly set new expectations from shoppers and new benchmarks for retail players.

So, assortment size may come at a cost: Shoppers find it more complex to find the product they want. In a similar way retailers experience a limitation: Large assortments are associated with costs from warehousing and diluting brand image. And also for suppliers there are constraints: They seek economies of scale and promote universal assortments; however, by limiting the size of assortment, they can invest more in advertising and innovation. Suppliers, retailers and shoppers need to find the right assortment size.

Deeper Insight: More Cities Means More Shoppers in a Hurry

Today, 55 per cent of the world population lives in cities. The United Nations (2018) expects this number to rise to 68 per cent in 2050, so more and more people enjoy the fruits of urban lifestyle and also bear the burdens. North America is the most urbanised part of the world with 82 per cent of inhabitants living in cities. Asia and Africa are still home to 90 per cent of the rural population, but they are catching up quickly: The United Nations forecasts that India will add 416 million urban dwellers, China 255 million and Nigeria 189 million by 2050.

Setting the Right Assortment Size: Actual Number Versus Perception

At this point, we know that suppliers, retailers and shoppers enjoy large assortments but also that there is a limit to what they can actually handle. The question arises as to what should the optimal size of assortment for the category or retail format be. In a moment it becomes apparent that this might not be the right question or, more to the point, the retailer should do more than determine the number of products. In current retail practice, the actual number of products depends on factors like:

- Available physical space, either in-store or in warehouse (less of a concern to pure online players)
- Retailer brand positioning as one-stop-shopping place versus more specialist provider
- Category role with one category being more important to attract shoppers and support the brand positioning than another
- Shopper appetite for variety and adaptation to personal needs
- Level of supplier innovation where novelty creates more attention from both retailers and shoppers

The actual number of products present drives the way shoppers experience the size and variety of the assortment; however, what people perceive might be different. Therefore, perception rather than actual number of products will build the experience of assortment variety and satisfaction.

Deeper Insight: Store Traffic Is Driven by Perception of Assortment

A study by Broniarczyk et al. (1998) illustrates the difference between actual and perceived assortment. The researchers built a store environment in test facilities and invited 229 people to shop for popcorn. Each shopper conducted two trips: They could buy from the full assortment on one trip and on another trip the researchers had reduced the number of products. In the latter case, space for the popcorn category was eliminated or the remaining products were given more space so that space dedicated to the category remained the same. The results were striking: Shoppers did not notice a 25 per cent reduction of assortment. The threshold for perceiving product reductions was between 25 and 50 per cent, which is still a rather broad range. This outcome implies that for shoppers the perception of assortment size is not always a direct function of the actual number of products. The researchers made another discovery: In case of a 25 per cent reduction of products, the perception of assortment variety even improved as long as the space for the complete category was held the same and as long as the shopper's favourite products were still present. Favourite products were easier to find because they received more facings.

In conclusion, retailers can improve assortment variety by reducing the number of products. While I showed earlier that assortment is the top driver of store traffic after location, this research points to the fact that the actual number of products drives store choice only in an indirect manner. The perception of assortment size is more important than the actual size.

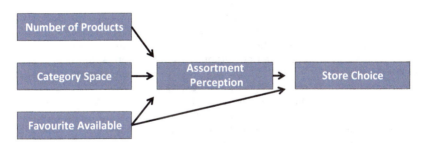

Image 2.2   Assortment perception as driver of store choice. Sourced and adapted from Broniarczyk et al. (1998)

In a rational world, there is a linear relationship between the number of products and variety. However, shoppers may draw conclusions about the assortment that are in contrast with reality. When determining their assortment strategy, retailers need to consider assortment size, composition and merchandising at the same time because all of the components interact with each other.

Deeper Insight: Practical Examples of Assortment Reductions and Their Impact on Shopping Behaviour

1. Reduction of more than 50 per cent of products results in more revenue

Broniarczyk and research colleagues validated their lab study in a food convenience store. They reduced the assortment in five categories that represented 80 per cent of sales at the same time. Fifty-four per cent of the products with low sales were taken off shelf, while total space for the five categories stayed equal. Results of two test stores were compared with two control stores where no changes were made. In-store intercepts before and after the assortment reduction revealed that shoppers perceived no difference in assortment variety. They thought the stores with reduced assortment made shopping easier. In terms of revenue there was an indication that stores with reduced assortment performed better (plus 8 per cent versus plus 2 per cent for the control store). I do not know what the stores looked like before they underwent the assortment reduction: Perhaps they were a total mess and a nightmare to shop in. Still, eliminating more than half of your assortment in a convenience store and maintaining the same perception of variety is an impressive achievement.

2. Less assortment results in less pilferage and more customer service

The outcome of this field study coincides with what I learnt in a project for a home décor retailer. From research I learnt that shoppers thought their assortment had become less trendy and they experienced difficulties obtaining an overview of the store. An important principle of the new store format was a reduction of the assortment of almost 50 per cent. The eliminated products were no longer fashionable, had low or no rotation at all or were part of a category that I eliminated entirely. Other principles of the new design were the placement of low fixtures to create open vision lines in the store and breaking aisles into smaller paths to stimulate browsing. The results were stunning. Shoppers maintained their perception of variety and one out of five shoppers actually thought the new format had extended their assortment. A significant minority said the assortment had become much nicer though at the time no new products had entered the store: The elimination of other products had merely made them visible for shoppers. Improved assortment perception was not the only positive outcome. The new design stopped pilferage as shop-lifters felt less comfortable in a more open store environment, impacted ordering and value chain because remaining products obtained more attention and rotation, and increased customer satisfaction as shoppers could more easily notice store staff in a less crowded aisle.

3. Shoppers may respond positively first but next start buying less frequently

A study by Boatwright and Nunes (2001) confirmed the overall positive effects of an assortment reduction. An average assortment reduction of 56 per cent resulted in an 11 per cent sales increase. The online grocer made assortment cuts between 20 per cent and 80 per cent and even large product reductions could deliver sales growth. In general, the shopper response to a cut in the number of products was very similar: 75 per cent increased the spend on the category. Despite the overall positive sales uplift, Boatwright and Nunes were convinced this would change. Their analysis showed that the probabilities of buying at the online retailer decreased. They found that some shoppers started buying less frequently but that the corresponding sales effect was compensated by higher purchase volumes from those who stayed.

4. Reduction of assortment impacts sales through purchase frequency

In designing new store formats with reduced assortment, the retailer may also find that store revenue declines. Setting the percentage of assortment reduction is difficult and, among other factors, depends on the current size of assortment. I hope that the example percentages provided here give inspiration to retailers' own pilots. One of the questions retailers need to ask themselves when they aim for higher revenue despite or thanks to assortment reduction is whether this is derived from new shoppers, higher visit frequency and/or spend per basket/customer. In the case of the home décor retailer that I mentioned earlier, the main objective was to increase traffic among existing shoppers. Apart from the assortment reduction and improved vision lines in the store layout, this was achieved by, for example, creating an open window front, lighting that made the store stand apart more from neighbouring stores and more communication of (the already existing) free wrapping service. As the scope was limited to a few pilot stores in the beginning, it was unrealistic to expect many new customers from the small and local communication campaigns. More could be expected in the form of higher basket size from promotional bins that, although reduced in number by 50 per cent as well, were more visible than before. The question is whether there is a general principle on the source of revenue increase after assortment reduction. A study conducted by Borle and his colleagues (2005) provides part of the answer: Their experiment gave insight into the importance of purchase frequency and basket spend as sources of revenue after an assortment change. They reduced the assortment offer for a sample of 840 households shopping at an online grocery during at least six months and compared their shopping behaviour with that of others who still received the regular, full assortment offer. The assortment cut appeared to have a stronger impact on the purchase frequency than on the basket spend. They observed that the so-called inter-delivery time, the time between two purchase moments for a category, increased on average by 25 per cent. This means that shoppers purchased less frequently in the store with reduced assortment. Purchase frequency was affected more often than basket spend: In 74 per cent of the categories the purchase penetration decreased, while in only 36 per cent of the categories the purchase amount declined. The average purchase volume declined by 4.8 per cent. What makes the above study interesting is that the method was based on observing real shopping behaviour rather than surveys. In addition, the scope of the experiment was broad. While previous research focused on assortment changes with a limited number of categories, they investigated the effects of assortment reduction on customer loyalty across all categories and within individual categories. In contrast with many other reported experiments, Borle found that overall store sales declined after the assortment reduction. The online retailer might have gone too far and shoppers started missing variety: Some categories were reduced by 91 per cent. In addition to a well-considered decision on the percentage of reduction, the online retailer learnt that shopper response depended on the type of category: Categories like produce, milk, bread, cereals and soft drinks that had high purchase frequency were affected less than categories like frozen bakery and aluminium foil. A final consideration for retailers working on assortment reduction is that there is a relationship between the frequency and basket volume in Borle's study. The delay in purchase was likely to increase the purchase amount on the next shopping trip. Doubling the time between two purchase moments was expected to lead to a small increase of 5.3 per cent of purchased volume.

Taking Assortment Decisions in Relationship to the Amount of Space

So far the focus of the discussion has been on the number of products in the assortment of a given category or complete store. An important finding was that shoppers construct their satisfaction with the assortment more on their perception than on the actual number of products. Therefore, I suggest that retailers determine what type of assortment perception they envision and think of ways to create the desired assortment variety. In the experiment I discussed, Broniarczyk and his colleagues not only looked at the perceived and actual number of products but also considered whether the most favourite product remained available or not, and whether filling the space left by the reduced product made a difference. They concluded that both factors impact the outcomes of assortment reduction. Strictly speaking, filling the space left behind by eliminated products is a space effect rather than an assortment size effect: The moment that the number of unique products is reduced, and total space dedicated to the category remains, the amount of space per product or, put differently, the number of facings, increases. Decisions on assortment size affect decisions on space allocation. Retailers need to include two aspects with regard to space dedicated to the category in their decision:

- More space for products generates minimal sales.
- More space enhances the product image.

Space Elasticity Is Low: More Space for a Product Generates Minimal Sales

It is self-evident that more space for a product or brand generates more visibility and therefore a higher chance of success. A space extension provides additional bonus effects: Less risk of out-of-stock and the fact that shoppers tend to believe that products with more space are more authoritative and popular. Many CPG suppliers have a firm belief that their brands derive great sales from more facings and attempt to influence the decisions that retailers make on the planograms in-store. Some years ago, I facilitated category management projects between a national Dutch retailer and their top ten suppliers such as P&G and Unilever. In one of the workshops, a supplier asked for three facings for their products. I could not bring home the exact number of three and asked for the reason. The answer was a vague reference to a study conducted somewhere in Europe that unfortunately was never shared. Then I asked the supplier if the retailer would fare well with four, five or even more facings of the supplier brand, which received a solid confirmation: The more the better. From my perspective, the supplier had lost credibility by not considering the effect of such a decision on other brands and total category revenue. The biased view was not my only learning from this workshop. It appeared that retailer staff from several departments had left the meeting with opposite views and I found out their interests could be very different in the same retail company. When I later caught up with the retail brand department, they weren't too excited about the workshop due to superficiality of advice and lack of insight into the category dynamics. To my surprise, the buyers appreciated the supplier presentation thanks to the exact numbers and the concreteness of the advice. Their responsibility was to increase sales and profits and they took on board any advice to achieve this. Though stakeholders in the retail organisation have different roles and objectives, they can of course come to a solution that meets those of all. In another category workshop both the retail brand department and the buying group agreed with a brand block of an energy drinks brand that received far more share of space than the brand deserved based on its volume and sales. Both the buying and the retail brand department agreed that a significant cash payment made the unbalanced space ratio a good deal for the retailer. In this discussion, the interest of the supplier and the different stakeholders in the retail organisation prevailed. One could argue that the objective of the retailer was to maximise their profit from a given amount of space: In this example, it was more profitable to charge for the additional space than to award the space to another brand. They thought they were not losing sales of other brands so, by inherence, their existing shoppers were happy. If they actually were happy, I did not know. Perhaps over-spacing one brand of energy drinks stopped listing of small brands with unique target groups or took away space from more profitable or differentiating propositions in other categories.

Academic Evidence of Low Space Elasticity

Indeed, academic research shows that adding space has only a small effect on revenue. In addition, it is not productive to add facings infinitely: Each new facing generates each time fewer additional sales. Evidence for the limited effects from space is best explained in an extensive meta-analysis by Eisend (2014) for which he gathered the space elasticity ratios from a set of studies. Space elasticity is a multiplier that tells by what percentage the revenue will change if the amount of space is amended. Eisend concluded that on average, a 10 per cent variation of space delivers a mere 1.7 per cent change of sales, which is expressed in a space elasticity of 0.17. This average is based on 1268 space elasticities in 57 different store contexts measured from 1960 to 2012. In order to give a better sense of whether a space elasticity of 0.17 is high or low, it can be compared with the elasticities of other marketing instruments. For example, other meta-studies found a price elasticity of −2.62 (Bijmolt et al. 2005), 0.30 for personal selling (Albers et al. 2010), 0.24 for advertising in the long term (Sethuraman et al. 2011), and 0.24 for electronic word of mouth (You et al. 2015). A variation of space has about the same impact as an investment in advertising in the short term (0.12 according to Sethuraman et al. 2011), which also tells a lot about the low effectiveness of advertising.

It can be concluded that a change in space generates much fewer sales than other marketing instruments. Of course it all depends on the retailer starting point. Stated in an exaggerated way: Zero facings deliver zero sales, so adding one facing will lead to at least some sales. The point is that adding facings for one product is likely to produce fewer sales than introducing another variety or investments in other retail marketing instruments. The limited size of an expansion of facings should make suppliers wonder to which extent they are prepared to pay retailers for space in their store. Apart from a direct negative effect on the brand itself, the space expansion could also hurt other brands. Moreover, Eisend found that in 30 per cent of the situations, the space elasticity was negative, which meant that more space resulted in fewer sales. Apart from the low absolute size effect, Eisend made two more important conclusions.

A second finding from the meta-analysis was that on average price elasticities for space decreases were lower than those for space increases, 0.06 versus 0.32. So, shoppers respond more to a space expansion than to a space decrease. It seems that space reduction of a product hurts some of the shopper purchase intentions; however, they are prepared to make an additional effort to search and find the product despite the lower visibility. Eisend concludes that shoppers have grown accustomed to the previously chosen products. On the other hand, a space expansion comes with a bonus effect of better visibility, a reduced chance of out-of-stock and a signal to the shopper that products with more space are more important. Indeed, this is good news for retailers and suppliers. Imagine if the retailer starts a merchandising process whereby they add assortment and next systematically take out facings. First, the space expansion has a positive effect, while the following space decline has a much lower effect.

A third important finding by Eisend is that the size of space elasticities is smaller when the space expansion is larger. A space expansion of 30 per cent generates 2.3 per cent, an expansion of 60 per cent gives 2.1 per cent and a duplication of space generates a mere 1.9 per cent more sales. The implication of this finding is that a large make-over planogram may not be worth the effort. If the retailer wishes to create more space for a brand, it is more effective to increase space in smaller steps. A phased expansion of 40 per cent more space delivers a better return than a space expansion in one large turnaround.

Deeper Insight: Impulse Products Benefit More Space Additions

The effects of space elasticity depend on the shopping context. When retailers or suppliers conduct space reviews with significant changes, there are more detailed aspects to consider, such as difference by type of category:

- Impulse products such as ice cream, confectionery and salty snacks have a larger space elasticity. Purchases for these products are often unplanned and they benefit from a better visibility as a result of marketing activities. The lowest space elasticities are found for commodities like sugar and salt. These products are bought when you need them, when supplies at home are almost or completely finished. There is a third group of products, staples such as canned vegetables and cereals, that have an elasticity in-between. Shoppers are still prepared to make a bigger effort for staples because they feel they cannot do without them.
- Apart from the difference by type of product, there is variation in space elasticities by size of store. In small stores a shopper will notice an expansion of space for a brand to the same extent as that for a whole category. In large stores, space elasticity on category level is larger. The explanation is that in large stores shoppers are less likely to notice an expansion on single product level. Expansion of category space in large stores could be attractive for shoppers because assortment variety grows, and the expansion offers the opportunity to bring more structure and clarity into the planogram.
- Having more facings of a brand could lead to all kinds of side effects. Van Nierop et al. (2006) found in a large study for the canned soup category that an increased number of facings also led to a lower promotional elasticity. More facings also meant higher regular price elasticity. Apparently, more facings led to more visibility for the brand, which in turn resulted in a higher price consciousness and price elasticity. When there were 1 or 2 facings, price elasticity was low.

The relatively low impact of space variation is in contrast with popular belief. Eisend found no change in space elasticities over time or differences by country. In unpublished academic articles, elasticities are even lower. There must be an explanation that justifies the time and effort that retailers and suppliers invest in shopper-marketing projects to achieve more space. The best justification is the type of category as impulse categories do benefit significantly from space expansions. In summary, investigating the amount of space for a brand or category might be worthwhile, but perhaps not to the extent practitioners were expecting. It becomes clear that changing the amount of space for the category is no guarantee on the financial outcome. Therefore, the practice of some CPG companies of paying retailers for space may only have a positive return on investment for impulse products with larger space elasticities. The importance of space in physical stores will reduce more if more purchases in the category move to online channels.

Space-to-Product Ratio: More Space Enhances the Product Image

So far the discussion has covered a mix of assortment changes on product, brand and category level. A specific scenario is when retailers increase the space for the total category but keep the assortment and way of organising the same. As a result, the space-to-product ratio (or product density) is impacted. This is interesting for online retailers that need to decide on the amount of white space versus products and also for brick-and-mortar retailers selling non-food categories that have a high financial return per square metre and are less concerned about minimum rotation levels. Creating space around the product changes the perception of the product, which is an effect on top of the quantitative space elasticity effect. This is illustrated in a series of retail experiments by Sevilla and Townsend (2016). Not so much the quantitative impact was the focal point but more so the type and relationship among several psychological shopper responses. Their conclusion was evident: Giving more space between products resulted in a more positive product evaluation.

Deeper Insight: More Space Around the Product Makes Shopping Less Complex, the Products More Beautiful and Shoppers Willing to Pay More

They based their conclusion on an experiment in which they collaborated with a locally known jewellery retailer that regularly participated in open-air events. The jeweller operated with different dimensions of the table for displaying the products at several events. In this way, the jeweller could compare the effects of doubling of space and different space-to-product ratios. Apart from the positive product evaluation, Sevilla and Townsend observed a duplication of conversion from stand visitor to buyer and a duplication of spend per buyer. Sevilla and Townsend explain the positive effect of high space-to-product ratio by pointing to an aesthetic response by shoppers. They describe aesthetic response as an appreciation derived from our primary sensory perception. Such response is automatic, non-deliberative, enduring, holistic and the result of a combination of intertwined aspects. Higher space-to-product ratio makes the aesthetic response more positive: Shoppers consider products more beautiful when the additional space around products makes the perception of the products in the visual field feel more seamless. More space isolates the product and makes it easier to recognise in the context, and therefore processing this information is perceived as more pleasurable. Once Sevilla and Townsend discovered that shoppers appreciated the increased space positively, they tested this effect under a range of conditions. For example, it could be that the positive result from the higher space-to-product ratio is caused by the type of product, jewellery, which is a hedonistic product. Therefore, Sevilla and Townsend set up an online store and invited shoppers to select Marks & Spencer moisturising hand cream under different conditions. Shoppers read an introductory description of the hand cream presented as either a utilitarian (analgesic and pain relieving) or hedonistic (silky, smooth and moisturizing) product. However, regardless of whether participants shopped under the utilitarian or hedonistic condition, a higher space-to-product ratio led to higher purchase intent, a more positive product evaluation and a higher estimation of a fair price for the cream. This means that shoppers also appreciate a comfortable space around functional products like pasta sauces and toilet paper.

Implementing More Space for Products in Retail

Online retailers can play with the number of products shown on a page view: They enhance the shopping experience with more white space around products whereas crowded online shopping environments create more stress and a lower willingness to pay. For brick-and-mortar retailers, return on investment on space is more of a concern, and therefore retailers that carry categories with high margins are in a better position to allocate more space around a single product than those that depend more on rotation from the product. For supermarkets it is too costly to create much space around each pack of cereals, whereas Nike stores allow themselves to place each pair of shoes on a separate shelf on the wall. It makes them seem more exclusive and special. Changing the space-to-product ratio can be achieved in the most literal sense by changing the amount of space in a webstore, in a fixture or in a promotional area. For example, by increasing product density in power aisles retailers attempt to improve price perception of the store. However, the product aesthetic response is grounded in perceptions; this effect could also be created with, for example, mirrors in a physical store. The impact of space on product ratio depends on the price positioning of the store. Sevilla and Townsend asked shoppers to buy earrings online at Tiffany & Co (premium retail brand), Forever 21 (low-end retail brand) or in 'a store' (used as control scenario). A higher space-to-product ratio led to a willingness to pay a higher price in premium and control stores, but not in discount stores. More space per product generated better perceptions of product aesthetics and store price-quality image for both the premium and control stores.

More space for each product produces a positive, aesthetic effect on products in an automatic response by shoppers. In addition, more space for products results in higher appreciation of the store environment; however, Sevilla and Townsend were able to demonstrate that this effect was more considered. And the latter effect may disappear in certain situations.

> **Deeper Insight: Shoppers Cannot Help but Have a Positive Response to More Space Around Product**
>
> Sevilla and Townsend invited shoppers to buy hand cream in an online store. For some shoppers, they simulated a so-called high cognitive load, which represents situations when shoppers have much on their mind before entering the store or, for example, if the store is full of advertising and other communication stimuli. They did so by asking shoppers to remember a 12-digit number before browsing. Other shoppers had to remember a 2-digit number, which is less stressful. Because the effect of space-to-product ratio on product aesthetics perception remained no matter the cognitive load, the researchers concluded that aesthetic product perception was a more automatic response to the space-to-product ratio. Sevilla and Townsend showed that when shoppers were under cognitive load, the effect of additional space for a product on store price-quality image disappeared. Therefore, the researchers concluded that the space-to-ratio effect on store perception is a deliberative process. Later in this book, the topic of scarcity is discussed, and therefore it is important to state here that the researchers found no impact of the extent to which the product was perceived as scarce or factors such as the preference of shoppers to shop in discount or premium stores, popularity of the product and way of organising the assortment.

Actual Versus Perception of Assortment

We now know that assortment is an important driver of shopper pleasure and therefore retailer patronage, but that too much of it will keep them away or postpone their buying decisions. The actual number plays a much less important role in shopper stress than we think. Shoppers enjoy variety, not the assortment size as such. That opens broadly two paths for retailers: They keep the assortment size small but give the perception of high variety or they create a large assortment and make this easy to read. If retailers find ways to increase assortment without pushing the stress levels of shoppers, they can increase sales by meeting as many shopper needs as they can physically offer. This will be the question that I want to answer in the next chapters: What context and which retail strategies offer shoppers the pleasure of variety without the pain of size and other features of the assortment? Retailers should avoid choice overload for shoppers whereby the complexity of a purchase decision exceeds the cognitive resources of the shopper. In such situations they are likely to delay or make no decision, switch to retail environments with smaller assortments, and in general feel less satisfied and happy with their decisions.

Important Learnings from This Chapter

- Perception rather than actual number of products creates the experience of assortment variety and satisfaction.
- When determining their assortment strategy, retailers need to consider assortment size, composition and merchandising at the same time because all of the components interact with each other.
- Distance to the store is the most important criterion in store choice; however, shoppers consider first assortment, next price. The exact ranking of assortment compared with price and location depends on the (target) shopper and type of shopping trip.
- Assortment cuts have a stronger impact on revenue through purchase frequency than via spend per visit.
- Despite significant assortment reductions, the perception of assortment variety can improve as long as the space for the complete category is held the same and as long as the shopper's favourite products are still present.
- A change of amount of space has only a limited effect on revenue. The average elasticity of space amendments is 0.17, which is low compared to elasticities of other retail marketing instruments.
- A high space-to-product ratio generates positive, aesthetic effects: Shoppers consider products to be more beautiful. The additional space around products makes the perception of the products in the visual field feel more seamless. More space isolates the product and makes it easier to recognise in the context, and therefore processing this information is perceived as more pleasurable.

References

Albers, S., Mantrala, M. K., & Shridhar, S. (2010). Personal Selling Elasticities: A Meta-analysis. *Journal of Marketing Research, 47*(5), 840–853.

Bijmolt, T., Van Heerde, H. J., & Pieters, R. G. M. (2005). New Empirical Generalizations on the Determinants of Price Elasticity. *Journal of Marketing Research, 42*(2), 141–156.

Boatwright, P., & Nunes, J. C. (2001). Reducing Assortment: An Attribute-Based Approach. *Journal of Marketing, 65*, 50–63.

Borle, S., Boatwright, P., Kadane, J. B., Nunez, J. C., & Shmueli, G. (2005). The Effect of Product Assortment Changes on Customer Retention. *Marketing Science, 24*(4), 616–622.

Briesch, R. A., Chintagunta, P. K., & Fox, E. J. (2009). How Does Assortment Affect Grocery Store Choice. *Journal of Marketing Research, 46*(2), 176–189.

Broniarczyk, S., Hoyer, W. D., & McAlister, L. (1998). Consumers' Perceptions of the Assortment Offered in a Grocery Category: The Impact of Item Reduction. *Journal of Marketing Research, XXXV*, 166–176.

Brown, D. J. (1978). An Examination of Consumer Grocery Store Choice: Considering the Attraction of Size and the Friction of Travel Time. *Advances in Consumer Research, 5*, 243–246.

Eisend, M. (2014). Shelf Space Elasticity: A Meta-analysis. *Journal of Retailing, 90*(2), 168–181.

Iyengar, S. (2011). *The Art of Choosing: The Decisions We Make Every Day of Our Lives, What They Say About Us and How We Can Improve Them*. London: Abacus.

Iyengar, S., & Lepper, M. (2000). When Choice Is Demotivating: Can One Desire Too Much of a Good Thing? *Journal of Personality and Social Psychology, 79*(6), 995–1006.

Kahneman, D. (2011). *Thinking, Fast and Slow*. London: Penguin.

Rolls, B. J., Rowe, E. A., Rolls, E. T., Kingston, B., Megson, A., & Gunary, R. (1981). Variety in a Meal Enhances Food Intake in Man. *Psychology & Behavior, 26*, 215–221.

Scheibehenne, B., Greifeneder, R., & Todd, P. M. (2009). What Moderates the Too-Much-Choice Effect? *Psychology & Marketing, 26*(3., Assortment Structure and Choice), 229–253.

Schwartz, B. (2004). *The Paradox of Choice: Why More Is Less*. New York: Harper Perennial.

Scrapehero. (2018). [Online]. Retrieved February 14, 2018, from https://www.scrapehero.com/many-products-amazon-sell-january-20198/.

Sethuraman, R., Tellis, G. J., & Briesch, R. A. (2011). How Well Does Advertising Work? Generalizations from Meta-analysis of Brand Elasticities. *Journal of Marketing Research, 48*(3), 457–471.

Sevilla, J., & Townsend, C. (2016). The Space-to-Product Ratio Effect: How Interstitial Space Influences Product Aesthetic Appeal, Store Perceptions, and Product Preference. *Journal of Marketing Research, LIII*, 665–681.

Survata. (2017, December 20). [Online]. Retrieved September 30, 2018, from https://www.survata.com/blog/amazon-takes-49-percent-of-consumers-first-product-search-but-search-engines-rebound/.

United Nations. (2018, May 16). 2018 Revision of World Urbanization Prospects. [Online]. Retrieved August 1, 2018, from https://www.un.org/development/desa/en/news/population/2018-revision-of-world-urbanization-prospects.html.

Van Nierop, E., Fok, D., & Franses, P. H. (2006). Interaction between Shelf Layout and Marketing Effectiveness and Its Impact on Optimizing Shelf Arrangements, Erasmus Research Institute of Management, ERS-2006-013-MKT.

Wikipedia. (2018). The Number of Photoreceptor Cells. [Online]. Retrieved February 18, 2018, from https://en.wikipedia.org/wiki/Photoreceptor_cell.

Wiseman, R. (2007). International Experiment Proves Pace of Life Is Speeding Up by 10 Percent, Press Release British Council, Issued 25 March 2007.

You, Y., Vadakkepatt, G. G., & Joshi, A. M. (2015). A Meta-analysis of Electronic Word-of-Mouth Elasticity. *Journal of Marketing, 79*(2), 19–39.

3

Composition of Assortment

Image 3.1 Integrated assortment and merchandising model

Learning Objectives

- Understand that an increase of variety is associated with a rise of complexity.
- Mention the aspects that increase the perceived variety of an assortment.
- Recognise the rational and less rational shopper decision strategies.

The size of the assortment offers shoppers a higher chance of buying everything they need in the same store and a feeling of being in control of their

© The Author(s) 2019
C. Berkhout, *Assortment and Merchandising Strategy*,
https://doi.org/10.1007/978-3-030-11163-2_3

decisions. The actual number of products in combination with the availability of the most popular products and category space determine the number that the shopper perceives to be available. And in turn, this perception of assortment size drives traffic to stores. The perceived available number of options is important, but of course also which products are on offer. The effects of composition of the assortment are the topic of this chapter. Stores can vary assortments in numerous ways such as in terms of the flavours, the brands and the levels of customisation. From a strategic perspective, retailers may even use assortment composition as an instrument to differentiate themselves from composition. Which products are actually part of an assortment is the result of a commercial process in which the retailer makes trade-offs on the attractiveness among aspects such as profits, level of incrementality (or uniqueness) to the category, (financial) incentives from suppliers and retailer strategy with regard to either a narrow or wide assortment. Listing an apple juice in a SPAR convenience store in Ireland is different from composing the baby food range on Alibaba's webstore TMall.com. It is impossible to discuss each category specifically but fortunately there are general principles that help retailers analyse and understand the composition of assortment better.

Why Variation Is Important from Retail Perspective

Imagine this experiment: Shoppers are taken blindfolded to a store for do-it-yourself products (DIY), health and beauty or daily groceries. When the shoppers are allowed to open their eyes, do you think they will be able to recognise instantly in which retail brand of DIY, health and beauty or supermarket they are? They may find it difficult as many use identical iron fixtures, flooring, colour schemes and often the same assortment. If retailers offer the same brands and products, shoppers start wondering what reason they have to visit one store over the other. If shoppers perceive little difference, the price starts playing a more important role. The same is true online, which is one of the reasons why comparison sites are so popular and successful. In order to keep the category attractive to shoppers, retailers may find themselves forced to win hearts with lower prices and price promotion. The pricing instrument is addictive for retailers because it is easy to implement and because they can observe an immediate impact on sales after the price change. In contrast, sourcing and building the right assortment is complex because many functions are involved, and shoppers do not express their needs clearly.

However, the pay-off is worth the effort: A retailer with an assortment that shoppers cannot find somewhere else offers shoppers an additional incentive to shop for these unique products. At the same time, shoppers add non-differentiating products to their basket. The selection of unique products entices shoppers to visit the retailer and contributes to a differentiating image in the market place that is more enduring and more difficult to copy than price tactics and promotional campaigns.

Large online retailers are primarily successful through their guarantee that products are available, not so much as a result of their expertise in the categories they operate. Their positioning evolves around very functional shopper benefits such as delivery slots, accessible customer service and ordering convenience. Mind you, these are hugely challenging to achieve one by one, certainly at a healthy profit level. However, only one player can be objectively the best in these functional areas and this makes the remaining online players more interchangeable. At the same time, the competition on functional rather than emotional benefits among large online players offers opportunities for both specialised webstores and brick-and-mortar retailers.

The previous chapter shows us that mere assortment expansion does not automatically lead to more sales. Shoppers are restricted in what they actually perceive and process in their brains. They show a waning interest in large assortments: They are short of time and experience choice stress even for simple commodities. Retailers can make a difference for shoppers by keeping the depth of assortment shallow but wide. The rise of discounters like Lidl and Aldi is in part the result of their low overall pricing but increasingly the well-earned outcome of their pre-selection of diverse, high-quality products and related trendy image. Still, some retailers find it worthwhile to position themselves on a large assortment. Hornbach's DIY assortment in the Netherlands contains some 55,000 products and is twice as large as two large players, Praxis and Gamma, offer. This provides an incentive for the shopper to exert more effort to reach the store, though 20 minutes is about the maximum time of driving without becoming annoyed.

Finally, when designing an assortment, I encourage retailers not to feel restricted by the current design of their store. The benefit of borderless assortments that come naturally to online players can be integrated into physical stores. Best practice is the traditional, brick-and-mortar hypermarket Carrefour in Belgium which provides a digital ordering point for books that happen not to be available in-store and a digital wall to order heavy groceries such as washing powder and soft drinks that can be picked up conveniently in a car drive-thru.

British grocery Sainsbury's launched the non-food retail brands Habitat and Argos, which were previously owned by the Home Retail Group. These brands were brought in as shop-in-shop brands in supermarkets as a way to differentiate their offer versus other grocery retail brands, as well as to win back market share from online retailers. Reversely, traditionally online players seek ways to demonstrate they are not like the other online players. Examples are Amazon's brick-and-mortar book stores and Alibaba's Hema stores that combine the functionalities of supermarket, restaurant and wholesale for online deliveries.

Destination Categories: Unique Products Drive Traffic

Unique products provide a great starting point for shoppers to visit and explore the category. The unique products may change the way the shoppers perceive the complete category. Next, the associations that shoppers hold for the complete category at the retailer help build a credible and different retail brand image. As a result, a retailer may decide to compete on par with regard to other marketing instruments such as price. Take the example of the German DIY retailer Bauhaus. They offer everything shoppers expect when it comes to maintaining house and garden. In addition, they created an exciting nautical category with any related product the shopper can think of like anchors, digital fish finders, life vests, outboard motors and boats themselves. Because DIY retail stores of Bauhaus and competitors like Hornbach and OBI are located in industrial areas not far from each other, the nautical category provides a stimulus in itself. Perhaps this category brings Bauhaus an image of being sportive and adventurous that it can leverage in other categories.

The nautical category has become a destination category for Bauhaus, a primary reason to visit the store that differentiates this retailer from others. Destination categories leverage the intrinsic power of a category: The capability of a category to attract shoppers without the support of promotions or price reductions but purely based on the fact that the category meets their needs. Briesch and his colleagues (2010) conducted research on grocery shopping trips in the US to find out whether retailers could create destination categories in such a highly competitive market. As a measure, they took the extent to which shoppers bought the same category in various grocery retailers. For this they used consumer panel data with regard to eight grocery chains in the US including Walmart, Food Lion and BI-LO and looked into shopping behaviour of 80 categories for 2 years. It seems strange for a market place with high competition, large formats and convenient access; however, they found out that 16 per cent of the shopping trips were made to two or more grocery chains on the same day. The trips were not of equal size: Shoppers spent four times as much and purchased four times more categories in one store versus the other. However, there was more to the fact that people shopped at two grocery stores on the same day. The shopping trips to several supermarkets on the same day were predictable and had become a shopper habit. The probability to visit the same two supermarkets on the same day on a next shopping trip was 35 per cent, for three supermarkets 61 per cent and for four or more supermarkets 82 per cent. In addition, little overlap in categories was seen when shoppers visited several stores on the same day or in the same week. More than 90 per cent of the categories were unique. All this indicates that shoppers habitually chose to shop in specific stores because of a category they considered unique.

Briesch and colleagues formulated a number of guiding principles to identify and create destination categories. First, the intrinsic attractiveness of a category increases if the retail brand carries more unique brands, which could be private label or A-brands. Secondly, chances of creating a destination category decrease if retailers offer more brands and list more products per brand. This sounds counter-intuitive, but the key take-away is that actual number is less decisive. Finally, the number of size formats and promotion frequency do not impact the extent to which the category becomes a destination category for shoppers. In summary, attractive assortments are not so much characterised by the number of brands and products. Shoppers are more interested to know if their favourite products are available, and if the products, whether private label or A-brand, are available only at the respective retail brand.

Deeper Insight: Categories with Only One Category Help Predict Which Category Drives Traffic

If a shopper is perfectly loyal to a retail brand, the convenience of one-stop shopping would predict all categories are purchased at this retail brand. As further evidence of destination categories, Briesch and his colleagues looked at shopping trips in which the shoppers purchased only one category. If shoppers visit the store especially for one category, it is an indication that the retailer offers a unique product and/or destination category.

- The probability that a category was purchased at the shopper's favourite supermarket was 38 per cent; however, the probability that the category was purchased at the retailer with the highest category market share was 58 per cent, so much higher than expected. A final remark is that only on a minority of the shopping trips was one category purchased.

Shoppers bought the products on their single category trips at the retailer with category expertise rather than at their store which they visited most often. It has become clear that the reputation of a certain category can drive traffic away from the regular, favourite store.

Identifying Unique Products

The recommendation sounds straightforward: Listing unique products or, even better, a highly intrinsically appealing category will draw shoppers to the retail store. The big dilemma is that having more products not only improves the perception of variety but also raises the perception of complexity, and the latter will reduce the probability of purchase. For a retailer the challenge is to balance these two aspects. So far, I discussed how the size of the assortment influences the perceived variety (and complexity) of the assortment. This chapter discusses how the products themselves may make the search and selection process more difficult. For example, what is more challenging for a shopper, having ten flavours in the category or ten jars of jam of one flavour but each different in terms of size, packaging, country of origin, brand and other variables? Categories differ significantly in their complexity. Take, for example, the bottled water category. A small set of variables is sufficient to describe the products: Still/sparkling, brand, mineral/spring. In addition, the products themselves are large. In contrast, the category of deodorants is composed of a wide variety of small products with many different colours begging for attention. The dozen or so brands invented their own names to describe the scents and active ingredients. Sometimes it is difficult for shoppers to figure out what really matters to them: Making sure they select the deodorant that works best for them. Retailers can help shoppers by carefully (pre)selecting the products. Variety and complexity are two sides of the same coin. When composing an assortment, these opposite powers derived from functional attributes of the products need to be balanced. Maintaining variety needs attention across all scenarios:

1. Building assortments by analysing density and entropy of assortment
2. Adding assortment in an alignable way
3. Finding the right attributes through assortment reduction

Building Assortments by Analysing Density and Entropy of Assortment

Measuring the degree of variety and complexity is a challenging but essential task. This is where the concepts of assortment density and assortment entropy are helpful in deciding which product generates incremental value for the category and which one does not. The concepts may take some time to fully absorb but they are worth it. They are exploited at maximum scale when the retailer comprises of an accurate product database with many descriptive fields and some analytical tools, but even when making simplifications retailers can build a model to assess their products on the degree of density and entropy. So, what are they?

Lower Density: Select Attribute Levels That Are Farther Away from Each Other

Density is the difference in value (attribute level) of a product compared to its closest neighbour on one given characteristic (attribute). Let's take the dairy category as an example. If all yoghurt products contain more or less the same percentage of fat, the assortment density increases and the choice for the shopper becomes more complex. Higher density means less attribute variability, resulting in more complexity. Imagine a horizontal line on which the fat percentage of the yoghurt products is marked. If one yoghurt contains almost 0 per cent fat and the other yoghurts differ widely on fat percentage, the distance among the products increases, whereas if all listed yoghurts contain almost 0 per cent fat, the distance among the products is small. When explained in terms of flavours, it means that three different chocolate flavours have a higher density than an assortment of chocolate, vanilla and strawberry. Shoppers find it easier to make a choice between two yoghurts with 1 per cent versus 10 per cent fat than between two yoghurts with 1.5 per cent and 2.0 per cent fat respectively. When increasing assortment size, chances are that the products occupy more spots on the horizontal line; however, larger assortments do not automatically lead to higher densities. Density should be analysed independently of assortment size. For example, a small assortment of wines specialised in one region or one type of grape generates high density. Secondly, if the existing range of yoghurts has fat content between 0.5 per cent and 5 per cent, the assortment expansion of a yoghurt with 10 per cent fat will not lead to a higher density, but the addition of a 2 per cent fat yoghurt will.

Entropy: Look for More Attributes and Uneven Distribution of Products

Entropy is a measure for the amount of information of a set of products. In relation to assortment analysis, entropy is composed of two factors. First of all, entropy counts the number of characteristics (attributes) of products such as fat content or country of origin. In addition, entropy measures if each attribute value (e.g. 5 per cent fat) occurs with the same number of products, or if some attribute values (3 per cent fat) attract more products than other attribute levels. If each attribute level has a different number of products, the distribution is uneven and the complexity for the shopper is higher. When analysing entropy for two attributes, let's say packaging size and sugar content of ice cream, entropy can be displayed as dots corresponding to a vertical and a horizontal axis. When all dots are clustered, the distribution is even. When the dots are scattered across the object, the distribution is uneven. In summary, entropy increases when the number of attributes is higher and in case of uneven distribution of products on a certain attribute level. A higher entropy results in more variety but also more complexity.

Deeper Insight: Entropy Is Different by Type of Category

Researchers Fasolo and his colleagues (2009) calculated the level of density and entropy for 12 categories such as jam, pasta, toilet paper and butter and included two supermarkets in Germany, one with a large and one with a small assortment. They arrived at the following outcomes:

- With respect to assortment density they found that categories with large assortments have high levels of density, so these are more complex for shoppers. The large assortment also generated a higher entropy.
- Each new product that was added to the assortment made the number of attribute levels rise by 1.76. This suggests that product expansion adds attribute levels on more than just one attribute. Although the large supermarket carried seven to eight times more products than the small supermarket, the entropy was only four times larger. This means that the smaller supermarket, most likely it concerned the discount supermarket brand Aldi, covered consumer needs quite efficiently.
- Entropies varied widely among the 12 categories. A category like soluble coffee had a very low entropy: Three attributes (brand, price, packaging size) explained 94 per cent of entropy. In contrast, the yoghurt category is very complex. The top three attributes (flavour, kJ, brand) explain 39 per cent of entropy.

The concepts of density and entropy are helpful in building assortments. They ensure that retailers keep a close watch on the type of attributes (e.g. packaging size) and attribute levels (e.g. 200 grams) that come with each product. The next step is determining the importance of the attributes. At this stage, measurement of density and entropy allows construction of an assortment that fulfils as many shopper needs as possible but at the same time not to select too many so that retail operations run smart and smoothly.

Measuring the Level of Substitution

This study on entropy and density demonstrates that shoppers become happier from selecting from different types of product. Retailers are encouraged to identify the extent to which products are interchangeable. If shoppers easily switch between two brands of vanilla ice cream, the retailer could take out one brand. There are various approaches to establish whether products are interchangeable or even complete substitutes. In the most optimal situation, the retailer can establish the level of loyalty by tracking shopper behaviour over time through, for example, loyalty card programmes or website cookies. Consumer panel data may also indicate that products appeal to the same shopper segments or consumption occasions. In the absence of such data, they may find out the impact on the demand of one brand if they change the price level of another brand. When the retailer has different compositions of assortments across stores or runs with different assortments for different web-store shoppers (A-B testing), they obtain a thorough understanding based on actual shopper behaviour. Webstores may analyse which products are taken out of the shopping cart just before the shopper signs the deal with the ulti-mately chosen product. This may suggest that the products are perceived as very similar. A variation of this approach also happens in physical stores: Whenever you see a jar of Italian pasta sauce left behind on the shelf of Indian korma sauce, one may conclude that the shopper was more interested in the convenience of a quick meal than in truly cooking an authentic Italian meal. Finally, and this is unfortunately one of the most frequently applied approaches, if a product runs out of stock, the retailer suddenly sees other products picking up demand.

Adding Assortment in an Alignable Way

When brand managers and category managers have the choice to list a few more products in the category, they wish to avoid any confusion for shoppers; doing so in an alignable manner reduces complexity for a shop-per. Alignability refers to the combination of attributes such as flavour, type of packaging and percentage of certain ingredients of one product in relationship to the others. In a so-called alignable assortment of jams—apart from price—the jams differ on one dimension like flavour; however, brand and pack size are equal among the flavour alternatives. In case of a non-alignable assortment of jams, an attribute is associated with one alternative but not with the other. For example, one jam has a QR code and the other an easy-open jar opening. Gourville and colleagues (2005) showed the role of alignability in a choice experiment with microwaves. At the start there were two brands, Panasonic and Sharp, with both an equal alternative. In their alignable scenario, they increased the number of alternative microwaves of Sharp whereby each added product offered more capacity (and a higher price). Other attributes than capacity of the brand Sharp remained the same and also the Panasonic option did not alter. The share of preference in favour of Sharp went up from 53 per cent to 77 per cent until it reached a certain level of saturation. This was different when the researchers expanded the assortment in a non-alignable way: Each addition came with a new feature such as adjustable speed, moisture sensor and programmable menus, again with different prices. Now the preference share of Sharp initially rose when one product was added to a level of 63 per cent. However, the preference share quickly faded away until it reached a preference of 40 per cent when the total number of Sharp products was five. If shoppers would respond in a fully rational manner, retailers should expect a higher market share for the brand with the highest number of options: There is only one product available from Panasonic and much more offers from Sharp. However, in a retail context things do not always work out in that way. Even if an assortment is small but with many differences in type of dimensions, it takes more effort for shoppers to make a choice.

Finding the Right Attributes Through Assortment Reduction

The opposite of assortment building is the elimination of products from the category. Using the density and entropy concepts retailers find products that represent duplications of attribute/attribute levels. For example, the effect of reduction of number of brands can be balanced by maintaining the right mix of brands and sizes. For example, when the soft drinks assortment contains a Pepsi of 1 litre, a Coca-Cola of 0.5 litre and a Cola-Cola of 1 litre, the Coca-Cola bottle of 1 litre is the first candidate for delisting because alternatively the shopper will miss the Pepsi brand or the 0.5 litre format. This mechanism is what Boatwright and Nunes (2001) found in the shopping data of an online grocery retailer that had reduced their assortment in 42 categories for some shoppers, while keeping the assortment more or less stable for others. They found that a 10 per cent reduction of brands resulted only in a reduction of 4 per cent of brand-size combinations.

Deeper Insight: Some Attributes Are More Important than Others, and Elimination of Products Makes This Salient

Boatwright and Nunes zoomed in on the shopping behaviour after eliminating certain attributes. A reduction in options does not mean the same for everyone. The reduction of sizes evoked very different responses among shoppers: Some became very upset and stopped buying, others welcomed the reduction. As a result, the average effect of a reduced number of sizes was zero and smaller than the impact of reductions of brands. They also zoomed in on shoppers who had bought only one brand or one size or one brand-size combination. How would they react if exactly that option were eliminated from the online store? The researchers compared them with other shoppers who also bought just one option before the assortment reduction but in which case the option was not taken out. If the size option was eliminated, 51 per cent kept buying in the category compared to 68 per cent whose size option remained. So apparently they were satisfied with another size. For brand-size combination and brand, the numbers are 53 per cent (vs 67 per cent) and 39 per cent (vs 69 per cent). Apparently, brand is more important for most shoppers than size of packaging. Through the elimination of options, they established generic principles on the relative impact of attributes.

Working with Attributes May Not Work: Shopper Decision Strategies

Analysing the attributes and attribute levels in such a detailed manner helps practitioners understand the contribution to the category and value of the product; however, it is easy to forget this is not such a rational process for shoppers. When shoppers enter the aisle or open the product page online, they absorb and process the information coming from the products themselves and communication signs in the most optimal manner given the circumstances. For some categories like cars and mobile phones, they put in more energy than for others and on Sundays they may feel less stressed than on weekdays. More clarity about how attributes are processed in the shopper decision-making process helps us understand why some categories are successful and others are not and enable any amendments to the assortment strategy. According to Bettman and his colleagues (1998), the processing of attributes and attribute levels can be described in terms of four aspects:

- The first aspect makes a distinction between processing of attributes of an alternative before they move to the next alternative, or the comparison of alternatives on one attribute before they examine the next attribute.
- The second aspect states that shoppers may use little or much information.
- The third aspect concerns information processing: Shoppers take into consideration the same information for each attribute/alternative (consistent approach) or process different amounts (selective approach). In the latter case, they may stop searching for information after having analysed the first one or two alternatives.
- The fourth aspect deals with an irrational heuristic: Shoppers compensate a good score on one attribute for a poor score on another in a high-quality trade-off, or in a less rational way opt for a product with a positive score on one attribute, while the remaining attributes are far below average.

The various combinations of these four aspects on the way shoppers select attributes and alternatives generate a wide range of shopper decision strategies, six of which I will discuss here.

1. One of the most rational decision strategies is when shoppers consider one product at a time, weigh each of the attributes against the importance of the attribute, and when all of these utilities are summed, reach a decision. This is called the weighted adding strategy: Shoppers use much information in a consistent manner and compare alternatives.
2. In contrast, according to the lexicographic decision strategy, the product with the best score on the most important attribute is simply chosen. So little information is used in a very selective manner, and there is a focus on attributes and no compensation of scores.
3. In a third type of strategy, the satisficing strategy, products are considered sequentially and the first option that passes the cut-offs for all attributes is selected.
4. A fourth strategy, the elimination-by-aspects strategy, assumes the shopper eliminates products from the decisions that do not meet a minimum value for the most important attribute. This is repeated for the other attributes of decreasing importance until one product is left.
5. In a fifth strategy, called the equal weight strategy, the shopper ignores all information about the importance of attributes. Though all attributes and alternatives are considered, the decision-making is simplified by summing up the value of attributes in an equal manner.

6. A sixth strategy, named the confirming dimensions strategy, also assumes extensive information processing but simplifies the decision-making by processing products in pairs. The winner from the first comparison is retained and compared to the next alternative.

Talking about attributes makes it almost feel as if shoppers approach the shopping task fully rationally and as if retailers have full clarity about how their shoppers approach the decision task. All these decision strategies might be mixed into one effort to fulfil the shopping goal. They describe how shoppers attempt to maximise the degree of correctness of decision, minimise the effort and avoid negative consequences and emotions. The framework of decision strategies enables us to recognise situations, for example, when the shopper restricts the information search. The emphasis of these decision strategies is on the weighing and comparison of attributes. Theoretically they also include situations that are highly complex and emotional. For example, the decision strategy could include the pain felt when eliminating options from the choice set. Each time a shopper makes a trade-off between two products, they have to let go of an option and they feel a loss. And a loss is felt at least twice as heavily as a gain, which is described in the prospect theory by Kahneman and Tversky. However, shoppers may avoid difficult trade-offs among alternatives by applying heuristics such as choosing the middle alternative or selecting what a well-known chef recommended on TV. Or they may be confused as the starting page of the website framed the information in such a way that only one product seemed to qualify. However, how do you define what is good? In traditional economic models, this is described when the utilities of the products are perfectly known and weighted, but it is impossible to know when this is true. Shoppers themselves may lack clarity on which preferences for attributes they have. Self-explanations of behaviour may sound perfectly reasonable but only in hindsight. The degree to which shoppers use information and weigh all attributes depends on their personal characteristics, shopping goals, the category and other aspects of the environment.

Apart from reasons of restricted rational shopping behaviour, the fact that retailers carry often thousands of products makes it impossible to analyse and act on decision strategies for each of these categories by shopper (segment). For me the value in the framework of decision strategies is deducting in hindsight conclusions from various, actual compositions of assortments how shoppers made decisions. Retailers will not have the time and resources to do so on individual product level and here a trial-and-error approach is more realistic. For more important categories, my suggestion is to play with the descriptors and types of decision strategies when mapping out the shopper journey. For example, from online shopping behaviour the retailer may discover that shoppers set cut-off levels on price first, after which all products are carefully examined, and information via drop-down buttons is accessed. Knowing if they start the decision process by comparing alternatives or by comparing attributes helps in laying out the products in the online store. Shoppers may first prioritise the organic nature and deselect all non-organic yoghurts from the decision set, after which they compare the alternatives. Perhaps retailers could offer tools aligned with the decision-making strategy: If the shopper has to make many comparisons and engages many computations, perhaps a tool that lets the shopper assign weights to the attributes makes the decision process go more smoothly.

A final remark on composition of assortment. When making a trade-off between available space and operational costs on the one hand and the desire to meet all types of shopping needs on the other hand, retailers could investigate whether they can offer personalised online offers or create local (individual store or clustered groups of stores) assortments. Perhaps the retailer could make 85 per cent of the assortment identical and only make 15 per cent of the assortment flexible. Shoppers think of themselves as more unique than they really are so creating the perception of personalisation might be more important than the actual degree of (local and personal) adaptation.

Summary Principles for Optimal Assortment: REDUB

Perceived complexity and variety depend both on the number of products and the complexity of the assortment. When it comes to composing an assortment, a retailer should ensure the category

- contains the best Rotating, most favourite products
- offers some 'Extreme' choices that facilitate the selection process
- creates a Depth of assortment that mirrors the category-dependent attributes such as flavour, packaging size and brand
- attempts to offer Unique variety versus competition
- carries a selection of Brands

To remember these characteristics of a well-composed assortment, I use the acronym 'REDUB', which is short for Rotating Extreme Depth Unique Brands. More of these will help drive shoppers to stores.

Important Learnings from This Chapter

- Shoppers are interested to know if their favourite products are available, and if the products (whether private label or A-brand) are uniquely available in the respective retail store.
- At the same time the perceived variety increases the perceived complexity from searching and selecting in the category.
- Density and entropy are measures to determine the level of assortment variety. Density is the distribution of values on a given attribute. Higher density means less attribute variability, resulting in more complexity. Entropy increases when the number of attributes is higher and in case of uneven distribution of products on a certain attribute level. A higher entropy results in more variety.
- Shoppers experience less complexity in case of an alignable addition of products whereby the added option only brings new attribute levels and not new attributes.
- Shoppers apply a wide range of rational and less rational decision strategies to process the attributes and attribute levels of the available products.

References

Bettman, J. R., Luce, M. F., & Payne, J. W. (1998). Constructive Consumer Choice Processes. *Journal of Consumer Research, 25*, 187–217.

Boatwright, P., & Nunes, J. C. (2001). Reducing Assortment: An Attribute-Based Approach. *Journal of Marketing, 65*, 50–63.

Briesch, R. A., Dillon, W. R., & Fox E. J. (2010). Destination Categories and Store Choice. Retrieved March 11, 2018, from http://www.cemmap.ac.uk/resources/scanner_data/sd10_briesch.pdf.

Fasolo, B., Hertwig, R., Huber, M., & Ludwig, M. (2009). Size, Entropy, and Density: What Is the Difference That Makes the Difference Between Small and Large Real-World Assortments? *Psychology & Marketing, 26*(3), 254–279.

Gourville, J., & Soman, D. (2005). Overchoice and Assortment Type: When and Why Variety Backfires. *Marketing Science, 24*(3), 382–395.

4

Ways of Organising Assortment

Image 4.1 Integrated assortment and merchandising model

Learning Objectives

- Describe several ways of organising assortment and their impact on perception of variety and complexity.
- Allocate the optimal location to products both online and in brick-and-mortar stores.

© The Author(s) 2019   **55**
C. Berkhout, *Assortment and Merchandising Strategy*,
https://doi.org/10.1007/978-3-030-11163-2_4

Quality of Space Is More Important than Quantity of Space

Category managers often find themselves in a situation where the amount of space allocated to their category is a given and slow and difficult to amend. As a result, the number of products is more or less fixed. Once they have chosen the products and have chosen a level of variety they think is important for their target shopper, they tend to get distracted by other tasks such as the weekly feature and price adjustments in response to competitive actions. However, the time they spend on the location of the product on screen or on shelf is as important as or even more important than the selection of products themselves. Both quantity and quality of space count. To emphasise the significance of quality of space, I refer to a large experiment by Drèze and his colleagues (1994). They measured the impact of each single replacement of products on the shelves in Dominick's Finer Foods, a leading supermarket chain in Chicago.

Moving a Product from the Worst to the Best Spot Delivers 59 Per Cent More Sales

Based on historical performance of products in each cluster and with the help of suppliers, they changed planograms of 10 categories in 60 stores whereby planogram alternatives were benchmarked with unaltered planograms. The type of amendments they made related to eliminations of the product, the number of facings, shelf height and precise positioning on shelf. Adherence to the planograms was frequently checked through store visits to make sure the data could be interpreted reliably. Based on these precise data, the researchers concluded that the location of a product in the planogram had a stronger effect on sales than the amount of space for the product. Moving a brand horizontally on the planogram could improve its sales by 15 per cent. Outcomes were not consistent on the direction of the horizontal movement, so whether centre or edge of the planogram was better. In terms of vertical positioning the study confirmed a widely known principle: Eye-level was by far superior to other shelf heights. Moving products in a vertical direction proved to be more impactful than horizontal movements: Relocation from the worst to the best vertical position can improve sales by 39 per cent. The combined impact of relocating a product from the location to both vertically and horizontally best spot delivers the brand owner 59 per cent more sales. The study claims that changing the quality of space is more important than that of quantity of space. This is consistent with the findings of low space elasticities that I described in Chap. 2. A more recent field experiment by Hansen et al. (2010) validates the superior role of the quality of space. Hansen and his colleagues changed planograms in the health and beauty section in 12 stores of a large US retailer and looked at the effect on profits. They found that each extension of facings led to a decreasing amount of profits, a vertical change in position had twice the impact of a horizontal change, and the effect of a change in the number of facings was smaller than the position effect.

Need to Become More Fact-Driven in Approach on Shelf and Store Layout

Over the years I have come to realise that I spent too much effort in my shopper marketing approaches on the amount of space for a certain brand. Shopper marketing and account managers at suppliers are given objectives to increase the number of facings of the supplier brand and to extend the number of secondary placements in-store through double placements or temporary displays. The instructions they receive are less specific on the location of the product on shelf or the location of the secondary placement. This is understandable: It is easier to count and reward on the number of displays than to check adherence of each product to specific merchandising principles. Some suppliers have taken this to the extreme: They create so-called Perfect Store programmes in which they prescribe retailers the experience shoppers should have (for the supplier brands) in-store, and in which—unfortunately for the shopper—they meet an almost endless number of branded second placements. This happened to me as well. When I was end-responsible for the European shopper marketing and insights initiatives at PepsiCo, one of the major objectives was to obtain transaction-level scanning data of all categories from customers such as Tesco. A specialised team of data scientists crunched the numbers and investigated which products shoppers were inclined to purchase together on the same shopping, trip. For example, knowing that lemons are typically purchased together with crustaceans helps the retailer be reminded that these should be placed together. This contributes to convenience of shopping, though the cross-merchandising of these products might be in conflict with a functional and product-driven way of organising stores. By reconfiguring all products without amending the type of product or number of products the retailer carried, these store refits could deliver real store growth of 5–8 per cent in saturated, developed (Western) markets. With the help of so-called affinity scores between categories I could recommend retailers the optimal combination of salty snacks displays with other categories, to the extent that it appeared completely logical to place salty snacks at the butcher's counter in Spanish hypermarkets of Carrefour, which staff at the butcher's absolutely disliked but did result in more sales. With their own scanning data as evidence, it made sense to have ten or more displays of salty snacks throughout the store. And though a good amount of thinking and hard work went into the data analysis and the recommendations for locations were very specific, in hindsight the focus was more on the number than the quality of placement. Still, this experience proved to be very insightful and positive: Evidence from large datasets of actual shopping behaviour challenged many of my beliefs on the effectiveness of certain store locations. Some 20 years ago, I advocated the placement of low-rotating but high-margin products in the first bay of a store aisle. This is good for profits but requires shoppers walk further into aisle. Increasingly, the busy lifestyles of shoppers make their shopping trips shorter and they would rather not exert too much effort.

Irrationality of Retail Marketing Decision-Makers

As practitioners, we talk a lot about the irrationality of shopper decisions and their applications of heuristics to simplify their lives, but we should consider our own decision-making as well. Is it sufficient to rely on simple rules of thumb such as image size for online retailers and minimum stock levels by space management for brick-and-mortar stores? Or is more research on shopper decision-making in the retail-specific context required? The minimum that good merchandising needs to achieve is to go beyond the reliance on historic principles. Often practitioners use rules of thumb whereby the share of shelf of products equals the share of sales or share of profit. This may deliver poor results. Van Nierop et al. (2006) compared the application of simple rules of thumb with assortment modelling. Using real store data, they achieved 6–20 per cent more profits with their models. They also noted that success depended on the selected key performance indicator. A shelf position may not generate the highest sales, but still profit could be optimal thanks to a low price sensitivity of the product.

Large Assortments Do Work, If Organised Well

Organising the assortment helps to overcome the choice stress that may happen if shoppers browse a large number of products. An important extension to the original conclusions from the jam study of Iyengar and Lepper is that shoppers do enjoy variety; however, assortment needs to be presented according to some kind of structure. Kahn and Wansink (2004) substantiated their claim that large assortments may work for shoppers with an experiment in which participants were offered jelly beans as a snack while rating TV commercials. The researchers tested four different trays of jelly beans that differed in the number of colours of jelly beans (6 or 24) and the level of structure (all colours in one compartment or all colours mixed). People loved variety and ate the highest number of jelly beans when offered 24 colours; however, the level of structure needed to be high, so each compartment contained only one type. On average they ate 12.7 jelly beans when the variety was low and presented in a structured manner, and 28.3 jelly beans when having many options in a structured presentation. It seems that structuring a small assortment makes the offer boring to the shopper. Merchandising is not an afterthought to assortment building. Taking into account effective structuring measures will help retailers to offer a large assortment both online and in-store without confusing and complicating things for shoppers. Category managers are encouraged to include functions that impact the quality of space early in their decision-making on assortment. Ensuring the early inclusion of space managers who build planograms, concept developers who design merchandising material and IT designers who build online shopper interfaces widens the potential of offering a large assortment and high variety to shoppers.

Having discussed in the previous chapters the effects of number of products, the quantity of space and the composition of the assortment on shopping behaviour, I will now show the effects of different ways of organising assortment. A well-known principle of organisation with both professionals and shoppers themselves is the placement of the products the retailer wishes to sell on eye-level. However, there are so many ways in which the same assortment in an equal amount of space can generate a wide spectrum of shopper responses if displayed differently. Below are a set of guidelines that apply to both physical and online retail. They may not be relevant for all retail environments and practitioners are encouraged to experiment with what works best for them. The guidelines are supported by academic studies and experiments. Sometimes these studies cover various guidelines at the same time such as the effects from products blocks based on complementarity, horizontal height and vertical distance to aisle. In such cases, I also discuss the cross-effects among the guidelines.

Guidelines for Way of Organising Assortments

Vertical Positioning

One of the best-known organising principles is placing the target products on eye-level in brick-and-mortar stores. What target products are depends on the retailer and category objectives. If the retailer wishes to facilitate the search process of most shoppers, the highest rotating products are placed on eye-level. However, if the retailer needs more margin, they may decide to create a block of private label on this level. Placement on eye-level is most favourable as a result of the way people physically hold their heads and the automatic desire to absorb and process information in an efficient manner as explained in Chap. 2. However, physical aspects are not the only explanation. Shoppers have a biased belief that the quality of products runs higher from low to high location and at the same time the assumed price level goes up as well. Placing the product more or less in the vertical middle of the assortment therefore feels like a satisfactory trade-off between low and high quality for shoppers and forms an additional reason to focus attention on products on eye-level.

Deeper Insight: Shoppers Assume Products Placed Higher Are Better
- Valenzuela and Raghubir (2015) researched the price and quality associations that shoppers have for each level of height. They asked shoppers to imagine themselves as tourists buying a bottle of wine in another country. The shoppers could select from five brands from five vertical positions without any description or price tag presented. First they chose the wine; next, they assessed the price, quality and popularity of the brand. The results showed that shoppers expected both price and quality to decrease from the top shelf to the bottom in a linear manner. However, the distribution of shopper choice and the perceived popularity of brands ran in an inverted U-shape. Shoppers most often selected wine from the second highest shelf, while the top level and other levels were chosen less. Shoppers assessed the middle level as the most popular. Apparently, shoppers expect to find the product with the best price/quality relationship in the middle of the shelf or somewhat higher.

- The assumption that higher is better is deeply ingrained in our way of thinking, not only when it comes to shopping. People picture heaven in the sky, and the Greeks placed the destiny of the dead in the underworld. Such clues are also found in our language: People speak of higher as being better in expressions like the top of the organisation or having a high opinion of someone. Importantly for online marketers, people recognise positive words more quickly on top of the screen and negative words on the bottom (Meier and Robinson 2004). According to Nelson and Simmons (2009), the term north is associated with going up, more efforts and higher quality, while the term south is associated with a lower willingness to pay.
- The belief that higher is better is reinforced in retail practice. Retailers tend to place higher-quality and more premium-priced products on higher shelves, a custom that shoppers have come to expect to see even before knowing the category or having visited the store. In a twist to the original research design, Valenzuela placed a premium, high-quality wine on the bottom shelf. As a result, shoppers stopped applying their rule that the best wines are on the top shelf. In such situations, shoppers are aware that they apply the vertical quality/price rules and are aware of shopping contexts that are inconsistent with their shopping rules. Shoppers associate the vertical height with a certain price range and respond differently to a price change.
- Using data with regard to the soup category that Drèze and his colleagues collected at Dominick's Finer Foods stores, the academics Van Nierop and his colleagues found that a higher vertical placement is correlated with a higher price elasticity. So, when prices on the top shelf change, they have a stronger effect. In contrast, products on the bottom shelf offer great promotional opportunities. Products that are placed low have a high promotional elasticity, most likely because without a promotion mechanism they are not salient in the planogram. The study localised the optimal shelf height for sales in the soup category, which unsurprisingly was the fourth shelf (out of five). Sales opportunities rise from the bottom shelf to the fourth shelf. Simply put, retailers are encouraged to place their target products on eye-level and non-strategic products on the bottom shelf. The top shelf above eye-level has a more promising sales outlook than the bottom shelf, but it is connotated with premium pricing.

Horizontal Positioning

The confidence that I have in the recommendation for eye-level or just above the centre location in vertical direction is not that strong for placement in horizontal direction. Academic studies do not all point in the same direction. This is among others the result of difference of underlying methodologies and criteria. The arguments for whether a placement to the left, in the centre or to the right is best are mentioned below and I will conclude with advice for horizontal placement depending on retail context.

Centre Offers Optimal Price/Quality Balance with the Most Popular Products

In the same previously discussed wine study, Valenzuela and Raghubir also investigated whether shoppers had the same type of assumptions in horizontal direction as they had for merchandising in a vertical way. And shoppers do! Shoppers assumed that both price and quality increased going from the left of the aisle to the right end of the aisle in a straight, linear way, if confronted with a planogram they did not know. This bias seems to come from the automatism in which people let number series run up from left to right, like a tape measure. Therefore, this principle is assumed to occur everywhere, regardless of which language shoppers speak. People apply the left/low to right/high principle of the tape measure unconsciously to other situations. It feels comfortable for shoppers to apply this rule in a shopping context even though they are not consciously aware they do.

The conclusion from the researchers is that if shoppers aimed to buy the most popular product, they chose the middle option. Valenzuela and Raghubir point to the middle position as the best position on shelf and use strong arguments based on brand inferences and price/quality expectations that shoppers have.

Deeper Insight: Shoppers Are Unaware of Their Bias Towards Horizontal Placement

The negative connotations for things on the left and positive connotations for things on the right are also mirrored in language. For example, left-overs, having two left feet or being in left field are not positive or hopeful for someone, whereas right is associated with being right, having the right or getting off on the right foot. As in the case of vertical placement shoppers chose the middle option as most optimal when balancing price and quality. In a similar way, as with perceptions on vertical positioning the curves for choice and perception of popularity have inverted U-shapes where the middle scores are highest. There is, however, an important difference between the vertical and horizontal assumptions that shoppers make. Apart from building planograms that are consistent with the left/low–right/high associations, Valenzuela and Raghubir also tested a planogram in which high-quality wine was placed on the left. In such cases, shoppers stuck to their belief that prices run up from left to right and selected from the middle, which represented the optimal price/quality for them. In other words, shoppers are conscious of the fact that they apply a vertical rule, but they are unaware that they apply a price/quality heuristic on the horizontal placement of products.

Centre Attracts More Attention Through More and Longer Eye Fixations, Because the Centre Is the Most Efficient Landing Spot to Discover the Rest

There are also strong arguments for placement in the horizontal centre as a result of attention studies. So, while academics who study the way our eyes register products and merchandising take a more biological perspective and consider attention as a distinct concept from recall and brand associations, they do arrive at the same conclusion. Apart from quality-price inferences also attention is a second explanation for the success of middle position: Shoppers are inclined to pay more attention to the centre.

Deeper Insight: Shoppers Look at the Horizontal Centre of the Aisle, Regardless of Where They Stand

- Eye-tracking has become an increasingly popular methodology in academic studies. In one of them, Atalay and his colleagues (2012) researched the way shoppers search and buy from two categories, vitamins and meal replacement bars. For both planograms, they used three fictitious brand names to exclude any effects from brand preference. Each brand had three facings. Shoppers could carefully review and then select the product they would like to have. While they watched the brands on the screen, a discreet infra-red camera located below the screen recorded the participants' eye gaze unobtrusively. The researchers found that brands in the horizontal centre received 25 per cent more eye fixations, and these fixations lasted 20 per cent longer. Forty-five per cent of shoppers selected a product from the horizontal centre, 18 per cent more often than from the sides. There was only a small difference between the number of times shoppers chose from the left or right side. Atalay and colleagues found no relationship between the preference for the central position and aspects like perception of quality and popularity on which Valenzuela reported. Still, Atalay's study supports the preference for the central position, and points to arguments of visual attention.
- Over the years, I noticed that the results of eye-tracking studies showed more eye fixations in the centre and I wondered whether this significant attention to the horizontal centre was influenced by the fact that respondents were placed with their eye-tracking glasses right in the centre of the screen. The natural initial response to look at the centre is called central fixation bias. To make sure the preference for the centre was not the result of the position of the shopper, Atalay and his colleagues set up a second study whereby the planogram was either at the left or right side of the participant. The researchers found that participants did indeed gaze for 0.5 seconds at the centre to orientate themselves. This initial fixation on the middle before they looked somewhere else served as an efficient location on the shelf to obtain a maximum of information. However, the initial fixations on the brands in the middle did not increase the probability that people select a brand from the

middle. Shoppers have the tendency to allocate their last few fixations to the product they select just prior to their choice. This is the so-called gaze cascade effect. For products in the middle this effect is even stronger. Shoppers are inclined to look even more often to a brand placed in the centre in the last few seconds, the so-called central gaze cascade effect. In Atalay's study, the last fixations on brands in the centre made the chances of selecting the brands increase. These results were confirmed in an experiment with real units of energy drink rather than a screen in such a way that participants were asked to stay at either the left or right side of the planogram. The conclusion is that the effect of centrality is caused by the visual attention preference for the middle rather than the experimental set-up whereby participants happen to stand in the middle of the planogram. Visual attention to the middle is high because unconsciously the middle is perceived as the most efficient landing spot to explore further information, and we have a born preference that keeps our pupils in the middle and that makes our eyes look straight ahead, the so-called orbital reserve.

Centre Feels as Safe Heuristic

The preference of people for choosing the middle alternative has been demonstrated across various contexts. Christenfeld (1995) demonstrated that people tend to choose the alternative in the middle from making a choice for public bathrooms, arbitrary symbols and products in a supermarket. Shaw and colleagues (2000) asked people in an experiment to sit on a chair among a row of chairs. Participants preferred the middle option. To rule out any effects of symmetry, they tested whether the placement of a backpack on a chair on either end made a difference, which was not the case.

Beginning Attracts Most Traffic and Is More Sensitive to Price Changes

Based on sales data from the soup category discussed in the previous section on vertical positioning, Van Nierop and colleagues reach a different conclusion than Valenzuela and Atalay. They found that products that are placed farther away from the middle have higher sales. Secondly, if products were placed at the side opening to a high-traffic aisle ('the race-track'), sales were higher as well. The researchers concluded that the beginning of the aisle is preferred. The next option is the other end of the aisle, and finally the horizontal middle of the planogram. In addition, they found that products placed at the beginning have a higher price elasticity and lower promotional effectiveness.

From their study, I conclude that thanks to the mere effect of traffic the chances of finding a product at the outer ends of the aisle are higher, because these can be observed from other store paths. Because retailers use end-gondolas often for promotional activities, shoppers seem to associate these with products placed at the outer ends of the aisles and respond more strongly to price changes at the outer ends of the aisle. The higher promotional uplift for products in the centre could be a result of the fact that shoppers do not enter so far and do not observe the product that often, and when they observe the centrally placed product is in promotion, they take their chances relatively more often versus products at the outer ends. From a sales perspective placement at the outer ends is preferred, though brands placed in the horizontal middle benefit from less price-sensitive shoppers and higher promotional effectiveness.

Summary of Practical Guidelines on Horizontal Placement

In summary, academic studies do not come to a uniform judgement. It is difficult to overlay the different studies. Valenzuela and Atalay used fictitious brands so the preferred location at the outer ends in the real store study by Van Nierop could be a brand effect or the result of shoppers having to exert greater physical effort to walk to the middle of the aisle. Often stores do not have fixed walking patterns that are uniform for all shoppers and that determine that shoppers always enter an aisle from either the left or right. That leaves us with a choice between the middle and the outer ends. Practitioners are encouraged to consider various aspects that might impact the horizontal placement and come up with hypotheses for their categories and store environments:

- As people shopping online do not need to walk down an aisle, a central position in the middle might be preferred online. The outer ends might attract more sales in a brick-and-mortar store.
- For a routine category that a shopper needs to check off from the shopping list and for high-involvement products, people are prepared to go to the centre, whereas impulse and low-involvement products are better placed at the outer ends.
- If shoppers are not loyal to a brand, the retailer may benefit from placement at the outer ends.
- Stores that make the centre of the aisle appealing for shoppers, for example, with a protruding merchandising element for exclusive wines, may take shoppers further into the aisle.

Of course, horizontal and vertical placement cannot be treated independently. Valenzuela et al. (2013) wondered what perceptions shoppers have when it all comes together and what they believe which type of product is stocked in each position. They told shoppers to act as consultants and optimise the sales of 8 brands in a planogram with 25 positions (5 rows × 5 columns). Each brand was described in a different way: Premium brand, price leader, popular, slow-moving, promoted, private label, well-known and a new brand. Associations of shelf positions are shown in Image 4.2. It becomes clear that the middle position from both a vertical and a horizontal perspective is preferred. The outer ends and bottom shelves were less popular and the left side next to the gondola was attributed to promotions.

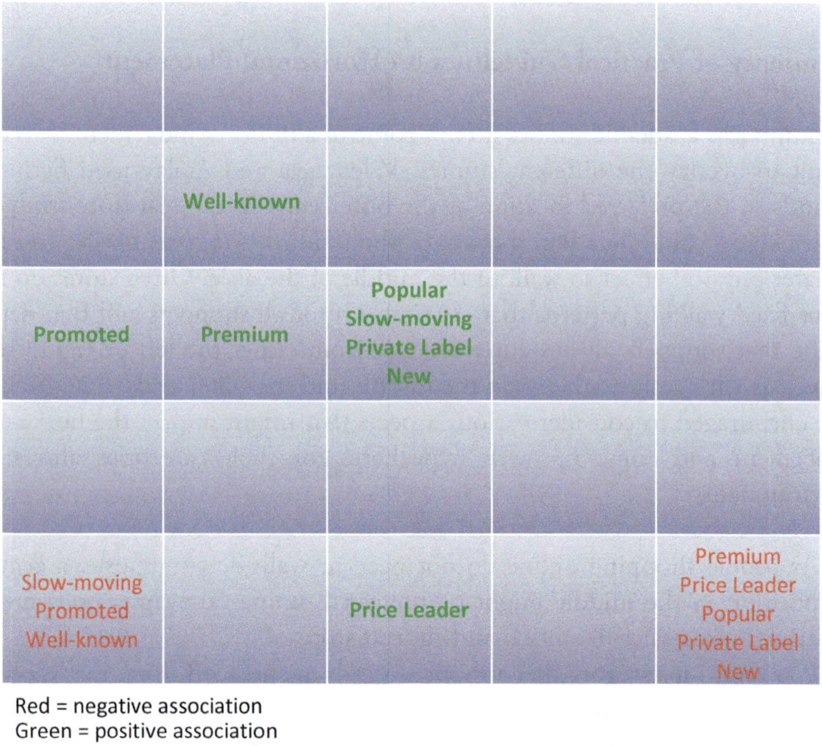

Red = negative association
Green = positive association

Image 4.2 Shopper associations with positions. Based on Valenzuela et al. (2013)

Vertical Versus Horizontal Stripe

When the retailer has determined the location within the aisle, products that make up the category could be placed horizontally over a shelf of let's say 1 metre, or products that belong to the same segment could be distributed vertically. I get the impression that French supermarkets increasingly build planograms according to the latter principle whereby the brands are displayed as thin, long, vertical stripes occupying several shelves. The question is what is more effective, merchandising products belonging to the same brand horizontally on one shelf or giving two or more facings and creating a vertical brand block? Fortunately, there is conclusive evidence here. A horizontal placement goes well with the horizontally shaped binocular vision field and encourages shoppers to select more than one variety. Should shoppers make a trade-off, a vertical stripe of products is beneficial.

Deeper Insight: Presenting the Brand on One Horizontal Line Works Better

- To obtain more clarity on how people process information in case of vertical or horizontal stripes, Deng et al. (2016) conducted several experiments. In a first field study, they worked together with a retail chain in the US for personal care and home fragrances. Displays of a hand sanitizer, a type of soap, were placed at different locations in-store. The 32 trays each with a different scent were either merchandised horizontally on a table or the same 32 scents were presented in a vertical, more tower-like construction. Shoppers were observed, and the researchers checked where they walked and shopped. After the purchase, the shoppers were approached to collaborate with a small survey. Deng and colleagues found that shoppers bought 61 per cent more units and 54 per cent more types of scents from the horizontal presentation.
- In a series of subsequent experiments, they tried to know why this happened. Shoppers were asked to select chocolates from ten sorts that were either presented in two rows of five (horizontally) or two columns of five (vertically). The participants were given 3 or 15 seconds to make a choice. In case of the horizontal presentation, the processing speed (or ease of processing information) was similar in both time frames; however, in case of the vertical presentation, processing speed was lower when participants were given little time. The horizontal merchandising also influenced variety: In the horizontal scenario, shoppers selected more unique types of chocolates and perceived a higher variety. In short, the shoppers needed less time to look at all available options in the horizontal set-up, which allowed for an increased perceived variety and higher number of selected varieties.
- In an eye-tracking study, the researchers investigated how eye movements of shoppers differed between the two scenarios. Participants browsed at either a vertical or horizontal presentation of 35 lollipops for 10 seconds. Next, they

could indicate how many they would like to buy and could look at the assortment as long as they wanted to answer some questions. The type of presentation made a difference: In case of a horizontal presentation, the eyes moved more often horizontally, and a vertical presentation led to more vertical eye movements. Shoppers needed less time per lollipop and fixated their eyes on more options in the horizontal presentation. The advantage of number of options per second (or processing efficiency) disappeared when given more time. They included on average 7.11 lollipops in their consideration set in case of horizontal displays, while selecting only 3.18 lollipops from the vertical display.

- Finally, the researchers tested the hypothesis that the dominant direction of eye movement of people in the West is from left to right, like reading a book; however, this remained unproven.

The studies show that horizontal presentation works better than vertical presentation and there are a number of explanations for this:

- The binocular vision field of human beings is wider in horizontal direction than it is vertically. This makes processing of information go much more smoothly.
- Studies on reading behaviour have shown that the span or reach of an eye fixation is twice as large in the horizontal direction as the vertical span width. This facilitates horizontal eye movements.
- The muscles that support horizontal eye movements are stronger than the muscles that control vertical movements.
- The heads of people hang forwards slightly in a natural manner; however, as a result it takes more muscle power to lift the eyes and browse and scan in a vertical direction.

From another experiment by Deng and colleagues, an important limitation came to the surface. Shoppers visited an experimental mini-store in which they were asked to shop for their favourite chocolate such as KitKat and Twix, or select more types of chocolates. When shoppers browsed for more options, the outcomes of previous studies were confirmed, and the horizontal presentation made people buy more: 3.00 versus 2.36 chocolate bars. However, in the single-option scenario, there is no difference between a vertical and horizontal presentation. In such context, shoppers purely focus on finding their favourite option. Variety is not relevant at such moments. The researchers recommend horizontal presentation for categories in which it is common or desirable that shoppers buy more products. Horizontal presentation seems less relevant where people make a trade-off among alternatives and buy one product. In such situations, a vertical presentation might work better because shoppers are guided by the (perceived) hierarchy of price/quality. A summary of the impact of presentation mode is given in Image 4.3.

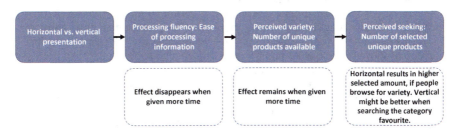

Image 4.3 Effect of horizontal versus vertical presentation. Sourced and adapted from Deng et al. (2016)

The Number of Category Labels

Some retailers litter their stores with product and category signs whereas others preach a 'clean floor policy', a belief that the focus is on the product. Therefore, product packaging should attract and speak to the customer. Sometimes showing the product is not sufficient. When buying a coffee machine or laptop, shoppers appreciate a list of the main features and the product specifications enhance the perception there is much to choose from. In addition, category signs or labels referring to a group of products have been found to prompt a profound effect on shopping behaviour: Indicating to shoppers there is a subdivision to be found in the category increases the perceived variety as Mogilner et al. (2008) showed. They conducted a series of experiments with the magazines category in grocery stores. They investigated how the number of category names such as Health & Fit and Fashion & Beauty affected the perception of assortment variety. For this they conducted exit interviews among shoppers in 10 stores that varied widely both in the number of category names, from 18 to 26, and the number of magazines, from 331 to 664. They concluded that the number of individual titles did not affect the perception of variety. However, a larger number of category names increased the perception of variety and was directly linked to shopper satisfaction.

Deeper Insight: The Category Labels Are Most Beneficial to Shoppers Who Are Unfamiliar with the Category

Mogilner and colleagues wanted to find out if some shoppers would benefit more from the category labels than others. If the shopper pays an occasional visit to the magazines aisle to buy a title as a present, they will surely show different search behaviour than shoppers who buy the same title every week. And as Mogilner and colleagues found out, there was. They considered the extent to which shoppers felt familiar with the category, in this case magazines. The first group of shoppers who were familiar with buying magazines were called preference matchers. For them selecting a magazine should take less effort and be more straightforward because selection equals finding the favourite from the past or identification of the best match to the shoppers' ideal combination of attributes. On the other hand, the so-called preference constructors are unfamiliar with the selection of magazines and shape their preferences during the decision process. The researchers gave shoppers 3 minutes to browse and select a magazine, the average time it takes in a grocery store. Preference matchers were asked to pick a magazine they read on a regular basis whereas preference constructors chose a magazine they did not read frequently. To explore any differences in shopping behaviour the researchers used two types of category labels, so in total there were four scenarios. They divided the same number of 144 titles by 3 generic category names (Men's, General Interest and Women's) or placed the title with one of the 18 specific category labels such as Music, Craft and Business. The study highlighted that labelling effected one group more than the other. The preference matchers perceived no difference in variety and were as satisfied in both store set-ups. Apparently, the happiness of shoppers who are familiar with their decision process for the category is independent of category clues. This was different for the preference constructors. Their perception of variety and satisfaction was significantly lower in case of the three generic names compared to 18 more specific names. In addition, their satisfaction score in case of three names was lower than that for preference matchers. The researchers concluded that if shoppers are unfamiliar with the category, they recognise the assortment variety based on external hints. A higher number of labels that are more specific will drive satisfaction and assortment variety for shoppers who are unfamiliar with the category.

The Sort of Category Labels

In addition to the number of labels, Mogilner and colleagues started playing with the type of labels. They took the example of coffee shops that invent the craziest names for coffee flavours. They wondered what impact the type of label had on shopper behaviour: Do shoppers perceive a difference in variety when they select from coffee types with fancy names or with more descriptive labels?

They set up an experiment in a food court whereby all participants were given exactly the same coffee (Ethiopian Fancy from Peet's Coffee and Tea) but were asked to make their choice from one of the four different menus. Each menu offered 50 types of coffee under 10 different labels. The first menu carried informative labels such as complex, spicy and nutty. The second menu contained somewhat more informative labels following names of fabricated coffee shops such as Java Joe's, Coffee Time and The Living Room. The third menu had non-informative labels with letters (category A, category B, etc.). And in a fourth scenario no category labels were displayed at all. The food court visitors were given 1.5 minutes to make a choice. After some 5 minutes the researchers returned with a cup of coffee with the flavour written on the cup. As mentioned, the coffee actually was the same for everyone to ensure that their evaluation would not be actually influenced by the coffee itself. Surprisingly, there was no difference among the types of label with regard to satisfaction and perceived variety; just the fact of applying a categorisation changed the perception of shopping context. The outcomes did differ by amount of category experience people had. If people were familiar with coffee, the preference matchers, having a category label made no difference in their perception of variety or satisfaction. For the preference constructors, there was no difference between type of labels. However, satisfaction and perceived variety were much lower if there was no categorisation, so any category label was better than having none. It will strengthen their belief they make their own decision, which in turn will increase their satisfaction with their decision process.

Deeper Insight: Shoppers May Prefer a Smaller Assortment If There Are No Category Labels

In a somewhat altered version of the food court experiment, the researchers came up with a number of alternative menus whereby they investigated both the actual number of coffee types and the effect of categorisation. Because, surely, the type of label should make a difference if shoppers are offered an abundance of coffee types? The researchers created four scenarios: 5 types of coffee without categorisation, 50 coffee flavours without categorisation, 50 flavours grouped into 10 informative categories and 50 flavours applying one of 10 slightly informative labels (coffee shop names). Experience with the category still mattered. Preference constructors presented with 50 uncategorised flavours were less satisfied with their choice than the preference matchers with 50 uncategorised flavours. Preference constructors would rather have an option from 5 flavours than a large choice from 50 coffee flavours without labels. Again, the mere presence of category labels aided preference constructors in perceiving more variety and becoming more satisfied, no matter how informative the label was. For preference matchers the perceived variety and satisfaction increased when they were offered 50 flavours versus 5 flavours, both without any labelling.

The mere categorisation effect may help retailers that struggle with their assortment variety. When shoppers evaluate the retailer's category much lower on variety, instead of sourcing and adding new products, it might be worthwhile to consider subcategory labels. The categorisation signals there are different alternatives available and raises the perception of variety.

Asymmetries

At the beginning of the chapter, a study by Kahn and Wansink was discussed from which they concluded that shoppers can handle a large number of alternative options as long as these are structured well. They set up a nice experiment whereby people thought they were rating TV commercials but instead the researchers observed under which circumstance they ate more jelly beans.

- In an altered version they offered M&Ms instead, and this time they looked at the so-called asymmetry effect in an assortment. This may sound odd, but the concept of asymmetry is easily translated into the retail context. Think of colour blocks of confectionery brands such as Milka and Cadbury and or the stain remover brand Vanish that take a dominant share of space. A group of products with the same shape and/or colour may form a great landing point for the shopper's eyes in both online and in brick-and-mortar stores to explore the remainder of the assortment. If an assortment is composed of the same number of units for each product, an assortment is called symmetric. If on the other hand one product is available in a relatively large number of units, the same assortment is called asymmetric. Respondents rating the TV commercial were offered either seven or ten colours whereby the number of colours was either evenly distributed or one colour was more dominant than the others. The researchers found a significant effect of symmetry. In the symmetric scenario, the consumption was not different when either seven or ten colours of M&Ms were offered. In case of the asymmetric, large assortment of ten colours, the consumption of M&Ms almost doubled compared to an asymmetric assortment of seven colours.

The reason that people ate more when variety went up is that the dominant items offer convenience as a starting point in the search process. This is true for online and in brick-and-mortar stores. Shoppers examine and process these dominant products first, after, which the remaining products can be identified. In case of a symmetric distribution, this heuristic is not possible. Indeed, if the assortment is really small and not complex at all, introducing asymmetry may very well raise the perceived variety. Even if the shopper is not interested in buying the brand or even the subcategory, the signal of asymmetry to the shopper is strong: Here is where you can find a (chocolate) snack or (stain) cleaning agents. Shoppers may then save time by clicking on other pages or keep on walking to the next aisle. When working as end-responsible for shopper marketing at PepsiCo Europe, I did not mind that retailers gave a prominent location to the Coca-Cola brand at the beginning of the aisle in countries where they had a far superior market share versus other brands. I believed that in such situations the shopper would benefit more from navigation to the category than from following the category shopper decision tree in a strict sense.

Double-Facing

It is common practice for suppliers to attempt to increase the number of facings, shelf placements of the same product, for their own brand. The idea behind it is simple: The more product of one brand, the more chance the shopper's eye will be caught and the less space there is available for competition. In addition, for sales-driven organisations this is an easily measurable performance indicator. Provided they have sufficient space available rather than double-facing one brand, retailers could opt to carry out this measure for all available alternatives. As children are believed to be more sensitive to structural dimensions, Kahn and Wansink set up an experiment with M&Ms and spider toys with children. They offered M&Ms or spiders in 6 colours to the children in either a small tray of 6 sections or in a large tray of 12 sections. The products were either neatly organised by colour or randomly distributed across the tray. Children were told they could take as many M&Ms or spider toys as they liked. Interestingly, when they were randomly presented, the consumption did not differ between a large or small tray. The highest consumption was found when the spiders and M&Ms were offered well-organised on a large tray with products double-faced.

Filtering

The filtering concept entails that alternatives from the assortment are shown gradually to the shopper. This is a technique often applied online. For example, the shopper searches for watches and may find out that the retailer carries some 40,000 items. Large images then invite shoppers to choose from watches for men, women and children. After clicking on one of them, a slider will let the shopper filter on a specific price range or type of watch band. By applying several selections (or filters), the elusively high number of alternatives is brought down to a comprehensible and tailored offer. The filtering technique can also be applied in brick-and-mortar stores. For example, a jeweller might offer shoppers first two or three very different bracelets to better understand which style they like best. Next, the jeweller zooms in on the chosen style. Large hypermarkets may offer most of their wines next to the main aisles; however, after entering the wine department the shopper discovers an opening of a cave that leads to more exclusive premium wines. Optical retailer Warby Parker smartly applies this technique in a combined online and offline manner: Shoppers may order five pairs of glasses and can try them out for free during five days at home. Applying filters may make things easier but it will change the shopper's perception of the assortment.

Morales and a team of researchers (2005) found out more on the impact by asking shoppers to buy backpacks online in three different scenarios:

- No filter applied, and all backpacks were visible to the shopper straightaway;
- No filter applied, and all backpacks were visible to shoppers; however, this time the products were given a certain subsegment description;
- Filter applied to website whereby all names of subcategories and links were visible, and after clicking on a link shoppers browsed the desired subcategory.

Shoppers of the backpacks differed significantly in their assessment on how many backpacks had been available to them in the store. When a filter was applied, shoppers estimated they had been shown 17 backpacks and participants who shopped without a filter reported 21 to 22 bags (in reality they got the opportunity to browse 32 bags). The two scenarios without filters result in the same level of perceived variety and satisfaction. So, the no-filter option letting shoppers understand more about the structure of the assortment by providing a label did not make a difference.

In conclusion, when the shopper path is filtered in subsets, they perceive a lower variety and they are less satisfied with their choice. However, if no filter is applied, shoppers experience a higher cognitive effort or even overload. Therefore, the researchers recommend retailers to implement maps and guides that encourage shoppers to browse the store before the actual buying starts. Large stores could help shoppers in an intuitive manner to encourage the phased browsing, for example, by introducing a comfortable landing zone after the entrance, creating wide paths between the different departments and marking the zones for moving and browsing in different colours. Though the forced walking direction in IKEA does not make shopping comfortable for shoppers, at least the circuitous paths that allow shoppers a good view on what each department offers enable shoppers to process the assortment in a smoother manner. Some retailers disguise the filtering mechanism as a personal service. Movie producer and streaming company Netflix promotes its personalisation service as a great way to fine-tune their offer to the viewer's personal taste. However, if viewers trust more the recommendations and pre-selected movies from Netflix, the less they browse for different (types of) movies and the less chance there is they find out that the assortment variety is actually low.

Text Versus Images

When displaying assortment online, it is a challenge to find the right balance on the amount of information with each product image. Providing long descriptions makes the page come across as cluttered. Striking images with little text enable navigation but may be seen as too distant or empty. Online retailers invest much time in getting the images right, which makes sense because as a general principle shoppers prefer the assortment options presented in images. This is because shoppers process images in a holistic manner that takes less effort, while words are processed in a more considered way and piece by piece. Still, working with images to present the assortment does not always work better for the shopper.

Townsend and Kahn (2014) set up an experiment in which they asked shoppers to select crackers online. In their online store, the crackers were either described completely in words or displayed in images and they looked at differences between a small assortment of 8 crackers and a large assortment of 27 crackers. So, a cracker could be circle shaped, taste like pumpernickel and be topped with salt and another was square shaped, of wheat flavour and had no topping. The researchers found that when the assortment was small, there was little difference between the visual and the textual way of merchandising, although shoppers spent more time per cracker in case of the presentation in words. When a large assortment was presented in images, shoppers spent less time viewing a certain cracker, skipped crackers all together and browsed in a less systemic manner than when the assortment was presented verbally. In contrast with common belief, text works better for very large assortments than images. Shoppers remembered more of their decision process when the large assortment was presented in words. For a small assortment memories were better when images were used.

The lower effectivity of working with images in case of a large assortment could be explained by the fact that visual merchandising of a large number of products not only results in a sense of greater variety but also causes a sense of larger complexity. Merchandising a low variety in the form of images makes browsing go quicker and effortlessly; in case of high variety, a verbal presentation mode works better. The research outcomes entail food for thought for online marketers. Images are not the Holy Grail that makes any size of assortment work more efficiently. If filtering is applied and the number of products is still high A/B testing is suggested to determine the number of alternatives shoppers still view systematically and where they make quick choices. In a brick-and-mortar environment, the text versus images principle is relevant for restaurants. Quick service restaurants like KFC help shoppers select fast from their relatively small assortment with the help of images. Chinese restaurants describe each option from their extensive menu in words. They do so because the Chinese menus typically offer a very large variety and when working with images shoppers might not notice the difference between duck and chicken in the written meal options.

Information

The above principle on text versus image gives direction to the number of alternatives that shoppers can easily grasp and process. This sounds like a completely black and white trade-off whereas they might work perfectly well in combination. When taking the intrinsic qualities of the holistic comprehension of images as a starting point, it is more a matter of what type of information is added, in which style and detail. The manner in which retailers offer information about the products influences the learning process and the satisfaction with the final choice.

Huffman and Kahn (1998) studied the impact of different ways of delivering information per product, and first compared information delivery per product and that per product attribute. In the latter case, shoppers were asked to indicate for each product attribute (e.g. colour of sofa) which value (blue, yellow, etc.) they preferred. When information was provided per product, each product attribute was fully described, and values were randomly given to product alternatives. Both approaches are used by online retailers, but they differ in impact on shoppers. The researchers concluded that in case of a presentation by attribute shoppers were more satisfied with the shopping process, felt readier to decide and perceived the choice as less complex.

In a second study, Huffman and Kahn varied the extent to which the shopper had to actively learn about their own preference. And they tested the effect of engagement both for the attribute and for the product alternative approach. Whenever shoppers were given more information on the attribute or product alternative, half of the respondents received the question which attribute level (of a certain attribute) or which product alternative got their preference, and the other half was asked which product attribute or product alternative they recognised. The first approach required a much larger effort from the shopper, but this was paying off: The shopper was more satisfied with the decision process and experienced the choice as less complex.

By presenting the information in the shape of product characteristics and by seeking manners to actively engage shoppers, they get to know their preferences better and are more satisfied with the purchase in the end. There is also a risk when giving shoppers information by attribute or by alternative: It may lead to too many details in a retail context because there is a thin line between seeking engagement through information and overwhelming the shopper resulting in choice stress.

Grouping by Attribute or Benefit

When building planograms, retailers can group the products based on attributes like flavour and weight or based on a benefit such as weight loss. Take cereals. In an attribute-driven presentation, all products of the same flavour or with same ingredients are placed together. This will facilitate the choice of shoppers who have a specific flavour or ingredient like oats in mind. In case of a benefit grouping, the relationship among the products is more abstract. In a benefit grouping for cereals, a shopper may find all products together that address the need for products with low calories, a breakfast on the go or an efficient, nutritious morning meal. A benefit grouping feels a bit more aspirational. The retailer likes to prove to the shopper they can solve an issue and satisfy shopper needs with their product range.

Deeper Insight: Shopper Solutions Connect More Categories Together

The focus of discussion in this chapter is on grouping by attribute or benefit for one category. When retailers take this one step further and go beyond assortment management of a category, they speak of building 'shopper solutions' whereby products from different categories are placed together that fit a certain consumption moment or need for shopping efficiency. Retailers that bring together fruit, drinks and sandwiches inspire shoppers with a tasty lunch box and when tomatoes, beef and a pint of milk are placed together the shopper will save time in making the shopping trip. These types of product groupings address certain shopping goals like 'today's evening meal' in a food context or 'buying a present for a friend' in the context of home décor.

When building the assortment for a single category, retailers often wonder if they can make shoppers satisfied with a grouping by benefit or by attribute. Products that are placed by benefit make shoppers look for similarities and help shoppers answer the question why these should be bought. On the other hand, merchandising by attribute gives shoppers clear pointers: They make shoppers look for and investigate differences between products and in essence answer how the product satisfies the need. So, what will make shoppers more satisfied with their decision?

- The researchers Lamberton and Diehl (2013) created a number of online retail environments and found out that a grouping by benefit or attribute significantly changed the way people perceived the same assortment. In their first study, shoppers made a choice either from an online shelf of nutrition bars which had rows labelled by attribute (fruit, nuts, chocolate) or from an online shelf which contained rows labelled by benefit (muscle building, energy boosting, fat burning). All products carried the same brand name Bumblebar with which shoppers were unfamiliar. After making their choice, the participants carried out a test that measured their level of abstract thinking at that moment. The outcome of the study was that shoppers who were offered the benefit-based grouping were thinking on a more abstract level. So, a benefit grouping generates a more abstract mindset with shoppers.
- In a second study the researchers reversed the causality. Through a range of questions, they moved people into either an abstract or a concrete mindset, and next they were tasked to pick a Bumblebar nutrition bar from a shelf without any merchandising structure. Shoppers with a more abstract mindset reported a higher similarity among the nutrition bars, which is a characteristic of looking for benefits.
- For a third study the researchers selected garden plants because the shoppers most likely had no organising principles in mind before the study. The same 16 garden plants were presented in an online store either by attribute (begonias, carnations, petunias, zinnias) or by benefit (attracting birds, butterfly magnets, colourful additions and fragrant favourites). They were asked to select their favourite garden plant and asked what they would do if it was out-of-stock. Again, participants reported higher similarity in case of the benefit grouping. The difference of satisfaction between their favourite and second choice was significantly lower in case of the benefit grouping than in the attribute scenario. So, in the benefit scenario there seemed to be more similar options. In addition, they were more satisfied with their choice.

- A fourth study extended the hypothesis a bit further. Now they tried to find out whether shoppers would buy more premium-priced products in the benefit or attribute scenario. Shoppers were selected for having no specific belief on the organisation of the hot tea category. They received a $5 budget to select a tea, after which they could keep both the tea and the remainder of their budget. The online store merchandised the 32 tea products either by attribute (black, green, mint, rooibos) or by benefit (weight loss, energy boost, cardio-health, stress relief). The benefit grouping not only induced a higher perception of larger similarity than the attribute grouping, but as a result made shoppers select less expensive products. What is important to add to this conclusion is that participants in the study were told explicitly that price was indicative of the quality of the tea.
- In their final study, Lamberton and Diehl set out to investigate what happens if shoppers enter the store expecting a specific grouping (benefit or attribute) and find out the store is organised differently. So, the shopper seeks a tea boosting energy but is faced with a presentation by flavour such as mint, green and black tea. The researchers brought shoppers into an abstract or a concrete mindset through a specific test. Next, they were tasked to shop for a Bumblebar nutrition bar in an online store organised either by attribute or benefit. Shoppers selected their favourite after which they were asked what they would choose in an out-of-stock situation. For shoppers in the concrete mindset—so looking for a comparison of the attributes nuts, chocolate and fruit—it worked out negatively when they faced a planogram that was merchandised differently from what they hoped for. When faced with the different benefit-based planogram, the drop of satisfaction between the first choice and second choice was much larger than the drop that shoppers in the abstract mindset experienced when they were shown an 'unexpected' presentation by attributes. The shoppers who looked for an attribute thought that a benefit-based planogram contained more similar products, while for benefit seekers there was no difference in similarity between an attribute and benefit-based planogram. Their abstract mindset made them take a step back and see the relationship between products in the same manner.

Online store environments offer the great advantage of being able to tailor the same assortment to different shoppers based on their preferences. However, taking all these above studies together it seems that when retailers have to make a choice between either a benefit-based or an attribute-based merchandising, they are better off with an attribute-based grouping. Shoppers who look for a grouping by attribute experience a drop in satisfaction, whereas benefit seekers are more comfortable when the presentation is not according to their preference. When grouping products by benefit, retailers should consider the fact that benefit groupings also induce more similarity among the products compared with an attribute grouping and their perception of variety may decrease. This impact might even be stronger for shoppers who are more price sensitive. The influence of the benefit versus attribute decision might dilute when the assortment contains strong private label or supplier brands and when shoppers hold more or less fixed beliefs and preferences. The more unknown the brands, the larger the impact of the shopping context.

Contamination

A newspaper that people pick up from a seat in a train feels differently than a newspaper 'freshly' delivered to the mail box. People are anxious in an unconscious way what the previous reader might have done with it. This fear of contamination also plays a role in retail. If shoppers think that a piece of clothing in a fashion store has already been tried on, that the online delivery is repacked, or that oranges in the grocery store have been touched and pinched by others, the products are experienced differently. In extreme cases, shoppers may fear food contamination by poison. On a conceptual level, contamination could actually make the product better. For example, if the same piece of clothing was worn by popstar Rihanna and becomes available in a second-hand fashion store, fans will happily pay more than it would normally cost. Food blessed by a religious leader or a hamburger shared with your new boy/girlfriend tastes better. Here the focus is on negative contamination. Shoppers hope for the freshest and best product. When people see a crate of apples delivered from the storage area into the store, they feel they are fresher and better than the apples already available in-store. On the other hand, shoppers want to avoid any contamination: Open magazines that have been flipped through and candy offered in jars for self-service. It does not matter if other people actually touched the product: It is the perception shoppers have. Therefore, retailers are encouraged to create freshness cues in the shopping environment and avoid any negative perceptions of contamination. The way of organising of merchandising makes a difference as studies by Argo and colleagues (2006) in a fashion store show. They invited people to buy a T-shirt and investigated three clues that shoppers use to determine contamination: Proximity between product and 'contaminator', elapsed time between contamination and moment of purchase and number of 'contaminators'.

1. Higher proximity generates more perceived contamination

In the first study in the fashion store staff told shoppers that their T-shirt was in stock and (a) another client is trying it on. The shopper was asked to wait at the dressing room and saw someone leaving the dressing room, leaving the T-shirt behind (b) or the T-shirt was this last piece on the returns rack or (c) the last piece was just over here on the rack. In the first case, when shoppers see someone leave the dressing room, proximity between previous shopper and product is highest. As a matter of fact, in none of the three scenarios did the clients actually touch the T-shirt, at least not that the shopper could see. The study showed that the lower the proximity, the higher the product evaluation scores and purchase intentions of the T-shirt. In addition, the researchers found out that high proximity leads first to disgust and this in turn leads to low product evaluation.

2. Fear of contamination lower when more time elapses

A second clue shoppers apply to find out if a product has been contaminated is the time elapsed between the assumed contamination and the moment they see the product. Actually, in the first study results might have been influenced by the perception that there was little time between the moment the other customer touched the product in the dressing room and the moment of entering the store compared to the other scenarios when the T-shirt was hanging on a (return) rack. Therefore, the researchers maintained more or less the same research set-up but now compared the scenario of a T-shirt on the return rack with that on the regular rack. The perceived elapsed time was created by the sales assistant who either told the shopper the T-shirt had just been tried on or said the T-shirt had not been tried on for a few days. Again, shoppers liked the product less when it was hanging on the return rack compared to a regular rack. And they were also less satisfied in the scenario when they were told the T-shirt had just been tried on. The researchers showed that product evaluation on the return rack was lower if the T-shirt was assumed to be there a little while ago versus having stayed there for a few days. This means that the effect of contamination disappears over time.

3. The more people, the more contamination

The third clue of contamination is when shoppers try to discover how many people have touched the product before. Shoppers love to taste, smell and touch products themselves but are far less happy if they think other shoppers were in contact with the product before. Argo and colleagues also tested the third clue in a fashion store and this time the sales assistant either told them another shopper had tried on the product or told them that many people had tried on the T-shirt. As expected, product evaluation went down if they were told many others had tried on the T-shirt. In the third and last study, the researchers looked into willingness to pay. The amount that shoppers were prepared to pay decreased in the scenario where many shoppers had tried on the T-shirt (versus one) and if the T-shirt had been on the return rack (versus the regular rack).

So, the financial incentive to retailers is clear. Retailers can address the (perceived) contamination through both their operational and merchandising guidelines. Brick-and-mortar fashion stores are encouraged to let staff collect the returns and take them back into the store in an efficient manner and as if they were fresh deliveries. Online fashion retailers like Zalando that face costly return rates ranging from 30 per cent to 50 per cent should do everything to avoid any clue the product was touched by another shopper before, for example, by repacking the product or even cleaning the product. There are extreme cases known in which online customers order a couple of dresses or suits, wear them at parties and return them for free within the guaranteed return period. Such cases may lead the online retailer to decide to destroy the clothing as it cannot keep its promise of a 'new, fresh' product. In order to avoid fears of any type of contamination, online retailers should present any product as 'fresh' to the shopper and communicate its operating principles for returns online. Shoppers may be seen selecting fruit and vegetables uncomfortably bypassing other produce to reach out to the far end of the crate. In order to promote continuous freshness, grocery stores could actually replenish the produce at the first row rather than at the back where shoppers search first. Regular replenishment from the storage area enhances the perceived freshness.

Scarcity

Sometimes the shopper is informed of zero or low availability of a product: The retailer has placed a banner in the webstore informing the shopper it struggled with its supply chain or the shopper has learnt from news media the retailer has banned a certain brand as a result of a halt in negotiation with the supplier. The shopper perceives these situations as incidental and bad luck. This becomes different when the shopper does not know the exact cause of low availability and the shopper believes the product is truly scarce. Traditional economic theory predicts scarcity will raise the price. Human desire for unicity makes the product more in demand. It becomes clear that if shoppers think the alternative is truly scarce, so not as a result of incidental reasons like trade wars and supply chain hiccups, the product is more preferred because shoppers think this scarcer alternative is more popular and of higher quality. The difference in availability does not have to be that high and 25 per cent difference in availability could trigger the scarcity effect. The role of scarcity becomes prominent if the brands have no strong pre-existing bias and price promotions are absent. It may get more attention in non-food categories because scarcity of food items may trigger fears the product is near its expiration date. Retailers that wish to promote categories without any investment in advertising have the opportunity to tamper with the replenishment. However, this is a risky strategy, because the scarcity effect disappears if shoppers think the scarcity is manipulated. Reducing availability may also result in complete out-of-stocks in which case there are no sales of the scarce product at all of course.

Deeper Insight: Scarcity Helps Selling More Expensive Products

In a series of studies, Robinson and her colleagues (2016) confirm that people are prepared to pay more for products that are perceived to be scarcer. Scarcity may also move shopper preference away from mid-tier price ranges to the premium price ranges. In three experiments they show that shoppers are attracted to products they think have low availability.

- First, they confirmed predictions from traditional economic price theory. They offered customers of a high-end beauty store a nice-looking French soap as a free gift. The shoppers could pick from two glass jars, one filled with linden-scented soap and the other with bergamot-scented soap. The shoppers had a strong preference for the scarcely filled jar. In another experiment, participants were asked to buy sun protection cream with either 15 or 20 products available. In case of the relatively scare availability of 25 per cent less products, participants were willing to pay 13 per cent more.
- In the next experiment, scarcity and price ranges are combined. The researchers invited shoppers again to buy sun protection and defined scarce as 15 products and 5 more as abundant. This time the assortment was split in three price segments. Three retail scenarios were played:

  - All products were abundant;
  - Products from the high-price tier were scarce, the other two price segments were abundant;
  - Products from the low-price tier were scarce / the other two price segments were abundant.

- In the first scenario with equal abundancy across price segments, the price provided strong guidance: 70 per cent of the shoppers chose the safe mid-tier segment, and the majority of the remaining shoppers preferred the high-tier segment. When the high-tier segment was scarce, it gained popularity: It won 15 pp buyer share compared to the first scenario. The mid-tier segment suddenly became the least popular. Finally, when the low-priced products were scarce they won two-thirds of the shoppers. The mid-tier segment obtained the remaining one-third of shoppers.

- In a third experiment, the group researchers investigated the role of brand name by imitating the replacement decision of a processing chip for a laptop. A pre-test showed that shoppers were more familiar with the brand name Intel than Turion. The buyer share of the unknown brand Turion rose from 5 per cent when it was abundant with 22 units to 39 per cent when Turion was scarce with 10 chips.

So, brands that are relatively unknown and are premium priced can suddenly pick up demand as a result of scarcity. Studies by Parker and Lehmann (2011) shed more light on how the scarcity influences the shopper decision processes and how scarcity can turn out positively for a brand. They show that scarcer products are perceived as more popular and higher quality.

Deeper Insight: The Effect of Scarcity Depends on the Type of Category and Works Differently for Food Products

- In a first experiment, Parker and Lehmann asked shoppers to imagine themselves buying wine for a friend's party in a store abroad. They shopped from a large supermarket assortment. Products were equally priced; however, one was relatively scarce. The shoppers believed that the relative scarcity originated in strong demand rather than incidental or supply chain reasons. As expected, the scarcer wine was preferred. The scarcity left the impression on shoppers that the scarcer product was more popular, and therefore of higher quality, which then led to a higher preference share.
- Parker and Lehmann wondered what would have a stronger impact on preference: Scarcity or letting shoppers know the sales ranking. Shoppers were asked to buy wine for a picnic. The most preferred wine was when it was both scarce and the sign on the shelf showed it scored high on the wine region's sales list. They also found out that the positive effect of a high sales ranking was much stronger than the effect of implied scarcity.
- Though the wine is of low quality, it may still attract a significant group of buyers. To make sure the quality level was clear to all, the researchers informed shoppers on the quality by showing the wine's ranking in the Wine Spectator, presented as a well-respected publication on wines. This is often used in retail when shoppers have difficulties determining the quality themselves. When both wines had high quality or when both had low quality, the scarce alternative beat the abundant quality. When the scarce wine was also of high quality, it obtained almost all buyers (93 per cent). Even when the quality rating was explicitly low, the scarce option still got 27 per cent share. The researchers concluded that because the impact of scarcity was present even if the quality was explicitly described as equal, the preference share is not only mediated through quality perception in the shopper decision process.

- In low-involvement categories such as shampoo and paper towels where shoppers do not commit much time and effort to make a choice, the impact of scarcity is much smaller. Shoppers were tasked to help a friend from abroad to choose among brands with varying availability. The branded option that was scarce drew away some 10–20 per cent of shoppers. This makes evident that branding in low-involvement categories reduces the scarcity effect; however, for brand managers in these categories such a buyer shift may still be significant to their profits.
- In another study, the researchers simulated a real store environment where shoppers received $6 to make a purchase of well-known brands and could keep the change as a reward. Each brand received a maximum of eight facings and three slots deep. When abundant the brand had 2 open slots and when scarce there were 14 openings. The scarcity effect was significant despite all other possible effects such as different sizes, ingredients and prices, though only in the non-food categories such as toothpaste. Most remarkable was that in the food category (canned soup) the brand was more preferred in the abundant condition. Apparently, there is a fear with shoppers, even for canned food, that the product is a left-over and near expiration.
- The final study by Parker and Lehmann looked into strong brand preferences and promotions. Shoppers were invited to buy motor oil whereby the brand Mobil 1 was either scarce or abundant and the other three brands were abundant. And Mobil 1 was either at regular price or a sign at the shelf communicated the discount from $3.99 to $3.19. The outcome will please brand managers and advertising agencies: When shoppers already had a strong preference for Mobil 1, both scarcity and promotional discount had no effect. Among people who had no strong brand preference, the discount and scarcity did make shoppers switch. This group ignored the scarcity when Mobil 1 was in promotion and the discount became more important. Scarcity did become significant again when Mobil 1 was not in promotion.

Complements or Substitutes Together

For many people lobster tastes better with freshly squeezed lemon, but because fish and fruits are separate departments in a supermarket or appear separated after applying an online filter, shoppers may easily forget to purchase lemon on their shopping trip. Retailers may comfort the shoppers by placing a basket of lemons in the fish department as a gentle reminder. They are then faced with new challenges. Will shoppers better like the Eureka type of lemon with strong flavour and scent or will they rather choose the juicy and less sour Verna type? And once the variety is chosen, should the retailer offer this both at the fruits and fish departments, or only at the fish counter? Brick-and-mortar retailers could solve the lobster/lemon challenge with double placement of products but will not have sufficient space to replicate this solution too many times. This is where online stores thrive. Online stores could be seen as stores with an infinite number of entrances where selection of a product (lobster) can induce the appearance of the five most commonly purchased products that go along well with the first purchase. Unfortunately, the endless number of entrances also comes with the same high number of possible exits. In addition, online retailers need to answer the question whether their shoppers like the products better grouped by complements (lemon with lobster) or by substitutes (varieties of lemon at the fruit department).

The discussion on attribute versus benefit seems to be associated with that on complementarity versus substitution. However, the first theme is related to intrinsic benefits derived from the product such as energy from cereal bars or attraction by butterflies from garden plants. The complementarity theme concerns the association with other product categories. This complementarity could be based on a number of arguments:

- The products are consumed in the same consumption context such as lobster and lemon in one meal or tables and chairs in one dining room. Co-merchandising of lunch items like salads, bread, drinks and yoghurts falls in the same category.
- The products appeal to the same aesthetic style. Home décor stores tend to differentiate among style groups with fancy names like traditional family and urban luxury. Items from different product categories like sofas, cushions and curtains are placed together in one style group. Cushions that are purchased for different usage contexts such as living room and bedroom, but belong to the same style group, are placed together.
- Retailers may also find out about shopping-related affinities. These do not have to go along 100 per cent with consumption affinities. Shopping goal affinities could be women buying hair colour for themselves and shaving gel for their partner, or a mid-week fresh quick stock-up grocery trip of tomatoes, milk and beef.
- Products may also be placed together because they address the same target group. Baby products are a good example. Baby milk and toys are merchandised conveniently in the same aisle or same web page, though parents may purchase them on different types of shopping trips.

Grouping by complementarity seems to make a lot of sense. The shopper is informed how to use the product and is inspired to combine products that go together well. However, it may also slow down the decision process. When comparing products from the same category, for example, cushions, the shopper needs to physically walk more or click and compare more web pages. The information derived from each product needs to be memorised, while switching among the cushions. Though it seems inspirational at first to browse through the same style of curtains, tablecloths and so on, if the shopper is really only after a nice cushion for the living room couch, the shopper exerts more energy and in such a case the presence of other categories is just an annoying distraction.

Deeper Insight: Grouping of Products by Complementarity Is Better for Hedonistic Categories

A series of experiments by Diehl and colleagues (2015) show how the difference between complimentary and substitute merchandising influences both shopper decision-making and assortment perception. They asked women to select a shirt from paper catalogues in which eight shirts were presented together (by substitute) or in which each shirt was accompanied by seven other, complementary categories like skirts, pants and bags. The researchers constructed an indicator of perceived effort which consisted of difficulty of choosing a shirt, amount of time required for decision and amount of effort. Assortment perception was measured as a mix of satisfaction, attractiveness and degree of feeling invited. The women thought the substitute placement took them less effort to select; however, the perception of assortment was less positive. In short, merchandising by substitute is easier but less inspiring. This is the general principle, but the researchers looked for nuances and restrictions in a range of studies.

- They invited women to an online store to buy a pair of pants. Their shopping behaviour was observed, for example, when they clicked on an image, more information on price and available sizes were made available. The researchers designed three scenarios:

    - A web page containing eight pairs of pants
    - A website with one pair of pants per page
    - A website where the pants were part of an outfit

- The difference between the first two scenarios allowed the researchers to measure the effort shoppers invested to click for more variety. Though time in-store was longer when each page showed only one pair of pants, there was no significant difference in terms of perceived effort and number of views. The difference in scores between the second and third scenario represents the complementarity effect. Here there was a significant outcome: Total time spent on the webstore when the pants were part of a complimentary outfit was much higher than in other scenarios: 83 seconds when considering all items and 80 seconds excluding non-pants items. This was double the amount of time for eight pants on a webpage (40 seconds) and also more than a web page with each time one pair of pants (52 seconds). This implicates that not just the physical separation and necessary click movements, but already the presence of complimentary items themselves lead to more shopping time and complexity.
- The degree of variety that shoppers seek was the subject of a third experiment, again involving women on an online clothing shopping trip, this time

for a job interview. The female shoppers could either select the pair of pants out of five options (and browse through pages of jackets, etc.) or view the pair of pants as part of an outfit from five complimentary-grouped categories. After making their choice, they completed a questionnaire and were asked to shop again but this time in the reversed scenario. Sixty-seven per cent of the shoppers preferred the complimentary-based merchandising and the remaining group liked the grouping by substitute. This positive outcome for complementarity was strongly linked to feeling better about the assortment. Complementarity encourages shoppers to consider information of the same product and restricts search to other products. Substitution-based merchandising stimulates comparison among alternatives based on an attribute. When the store was built up by complementarity, the shoppers searched in a different way compared to merchandising by substitute:

- They investigated a lower number of unique pairs of pants, so less broadly.
- They clicked less often on pairs of pants for more information, so less deeply.
- After clicking on a product for information, they searched further for other types of information of the same products. When merchandising by substitute, shoppers searched by attribute when they clicked on information for different products.
- Perceived effort of shopping was higher.
- Perception of assortment was more positive.

• Organising the assortment by substitution or complementarity might suit one category better than the other. A popular category distinction is between hedonistic and utilitarian type of products. Hedonistic products derive much of their value from the sensory observation, the aesthetic beauty or emotional attachment to the product, whereas utilitarian products are defined by an emphasis on functionality. Diehl and team of researchers invited shoppers to select a sofa for a friend that should either be a more utilitarian, practical sofa or a more hedonistic, pleasant one. They could select online by substitute or from complementarity-built rooms. In this study, participants recommended the substitution-organised store more than the alternative. This might be the result of the fact that shopping was experienced as less effortful. Organisation by substitute created a more positive assortment perception when the shopper focused on utilitarian aspects and the complimentary structure delivered better assortment perception when the shopper focus was directed at hedonistic aspects. It seems that the symbolic and aesthetic value comes across better in assortment perception when organised by complementarity.

The outcomes of the studies do not point to one universal principle: Both stores organised by substitution or complementarity could be liked. Complementarity creates a more positive assortment perception for shoppers with a hedonistic shopping focus and/or buy hedonistic products. Organisation by substitutes improves the assortment perception of utilitarian products. It also becomes clear that presenting by complementary products distracts shoppers from their mission, takes more processing time and results in more shopping time. This may work well for hedonistic products and whenever the retailer wishes to discourage the comparison by attribute and likes to make price comparison less evident.

Important Learnings from This Chapter

- The way products are merchandised has a higher impact on sales than the amount of space.
- Relocating a product from the worst to the best position delivers the brand owner up to 59 per cent more sales.
- The centre location attracts more attention through more and longer eye fixations, because the centre is the most efficient landing spot for the eye to explore the rest.
- A horizontal stripe of products of the same brand goes along well with the horizontally shaped binocular vision field of people and encourages shoppers to select more than one variety.
- The perceived variety increases if more category labels are used. Category labels that are more specific will drive satisfaction and assortment variety for shoppers that are unfamiliar with the category. Having experience in the category helps shoppers overcome the stress from choosing from a high number of alternatives, even if no label is applied. So-called preference constructors with little category experience will greatly appreciate labelling, no matter how informative or fancy the labels are.
- An uneven distribution of assortment types (asymmetry) helps overcome choice stress as the dominant type offers a convenient starting point in the search process.
- Filters as often applied online make the decision-making less complex; however, they reduce the perceived variety and may result in less satisfaction of shoppers with their choice.
- Presenting options with the help of images makes the processing of information work more holistically and faster. However, in case of a large assortment a verbal presentation may result in more systematic processing and less perceived complexity than images.
- Providing information on the product attributes and/or seeking manners to actively engage shoppers requires more effort from the shopper but the pay-off could be higher satisfaction with the shopping process and less perceived complexity.

- A grouping by product benefits induces the perception of larger similarity among alternatives than an attribute grouping and therefore shoppers select less expensive products. Shoppers who look for a benefit grouping are thinking more abstractly and experience less stress with an attribute grouping than people who look for an attribute structure do when they are not confronted with the grouping they had hoped for.
- The fear that other shoppers touched the product before reduces satisfaction and willingness to pay.
- Scarcity may increase shopper preference in non-food categories for (a) the assortment layer with premium price or (b) brands that are relatively unknown or have low preference.
- Merchandising different categories by substitute is easier than presenting these by complementarity but also less inspiring for shoppers. Complementarity encourages shoppers to consider information of the same product and restricts search to other products. It seems to go well with hedonistic types of products. Substitution-based merchandising stimulates comparison among alternatives based on an attribute.

References

Argo, J. J., Dahl, W. D., & Morales, A. C. (2006). Consumer Contamination: How Consumers React to Products Touched by Others. *Journal of Marketing, 70*, 81–94.

Atalay, A. S., Bodur, H. O., & Rasolofoarison, D. (2012). Shining in the Center: Central Gaze Cascade Effect on Product Choice. *Journal of Consumer Research, 39*(4), 848–866.

Christenfeld, N. (1995). Choices from Identical Options. *Psychological Science, 6*(1), 50–55.

Deng, X., Kahn, B. E., Unnava, H. R., & Lee, H. (2016). A "Wide" Variety: Effects of Horizontal Versus Vertical Display on Assortment Processing, Perceived Variety, and Choice. *Journal of Marketing Research, 53*(5), 682–698.

Diehl, K., Van Herpen, E., & Lamberton, C. (2015). Organizing Products with Complements versus Substitutes: Effects on Store Preferences as a Function of Effort and Assortment Perceptions. *Journal of Retailing, 91*(1), 1–18.

Drèze, X., Hoch, S. J., & Purk, M. E. (1994). Shelf Management and Space Elasticity. *Journal of Retailing, 70*(4), 301–326.

Hansen, J. M., Raut, S., & Swami, S. (2010). Retail Shelf Allocation: A Comparative Analysis of Heuristic and Meta-Heuristic Approaches. *Journal of Retailing, 86*(1), 94–105.

Huffman, C., & Kahn, B. (1998). Variety for Sale: Mass Customization or Mass Confusion. *Journal of Retailing, 74*(4), 491–513.

Kahn, B., & Wansink, B. (2004). The Influence of Assortment Structure on Perceived Variety and Consumption Quantities. *Journal of Consumer Research, 30*, 519–533.

Lamberton, C. P., & Diehl, K. (2013). Retail Choice Architecture: The Effects of Benefit- and Attribute-Based Assortment Organization on Consumer Perceptions and Choice. *Journal of Consumer Research, 40*, 393–411.

Meier, B. P., & Robinson, M. D. (2004). Why the Sunny Side Is Up: Associations between Affect and Vertical Position. *Psychological Science, 15*(4), 243–247.

Mogilner, C., Rudnick, T., & Iyengar, S. S. (2008). The Mere Categorization Effect: How the Presence of Categories Increases Choosers' Perceptions of Assortment Variety and Outcome Satisfaction. *Journal of Consumer Research, 35*, 202–215.

Morales, A., Kahn, B. E., McAlister, L., & Broniarczyk, S. M. (2005). Perceptions of Assortment Variety: The Effects of Congruency between Consumers' Internal and Retailers' External Organization. *Journal of Retailing, 81*(2), 159–169.

Nelson, L. D., & Simmons, J. P. (2009). On Southbound Ease and Northbound Fees: Literal Consequences of the Metaphoric Link between Vertical Position and Cardinal Direction. *Journal of Marketing Research, 46*(6), 715–724.

Parker, J. R., & Lehmann, D. R. (2011). When Shelf-Based Scarcity Impacts Consumer Preferences. *Journal of Retailing, 87*(2), 142–155.

Robinson, S. G., Brady, M. K., Lemonc, K. N., & Giebelhausen, M. (2016). Less of This One? I'll Take It: New Insights on the Influence of Shelf-based Scarcity. *International Journal of Marketing, 33*(4), 961–965.

Shaw, J. I., Bergen, J. E., Brown, C. A., & Gallagher, M. E. (2000). Centrality Preferences in Choices among Similar Options. *Journal of General Psychology, 127*(2), 157–164.

Townsend, C., & Kahn, B. (2014). The Visual Preference Heuristic: The Influence of Visual Versus Verbal Depiction on Assortment Processing, Perceived Variety, and Choice Overload. *Journal of Consumer Research, 40*(5), 993–1015.

Valenzuela, A., & Raghubir, P. (2015). Are Consumers Aware of Top-Bottom But Not of Left-Right Inferences? Implications for Shelf Space Positions. *Journal of Experimental Psychology: Applied, 21*(3), 224–241.

Valenzuela, A., Raghubir, P., & Mitakakis, C. (2013). Shelf Space Schemas: Myth or Reality? *Journal of Business Research, 66*, 881–888.

Van Nierop, E., Fok, D., & Franses, P. H. (2006). Interaction between Shelf Layout and Marketing Effectiveness and Its Impact on Optimizing Shelf Arrangements, Erasmus Research Institute of Management, ERS-2006-013-MKT.

5

Shopper Characteristics

Image 5.1 Integrated assortment and merchandising model

Learning Objectives

- Learn more on how characteristics of shoppers themselves influence the choice of products.
- Apply the phasing of shopping trips (landing zone, navigation, product search, product selection) to online and brick-and-mortar store environments.
- Differentiate between maximisers and satisficers.
- Take into consideration the expectations and beliefs of shoppers so that they are congruent with the assortment.
- Differentiate between shopper decision tree and shopper search tree.

© The Author(s) 2019
C. Berkhout, *Assortment and Merchandising Strategy*,
https://doi.org/10.1007/978-3-030-11163-2_5

It is not difficult to imagine that characteristics of the shopper like income and age or characteristics that relate to the past experience with the category will influence the shopping decisions. For example, mothers who select nutrition for their baby are much more careful in the first months of their child's life than after six months when they have become more self-confident. In the first months, they undertake great effort to understand all ingredients of the nutrition for their children and will generally seek trust in well-known A-brands. When I researched shopper-specific transaction data of the baby food category of a Dutch supermarket chain, I saw the A-brand effect wear off after 3–4 months and shoppers slowly adopted private label products in their basket that previously were perceived as too risky. There are things in the lives of shoppers that apply to all of us because they are bounded to who human beings are. Some merchandising principles will hold no matter the type of shopper: Products on eye-level attract more attention and creating labels for subcategories results in a higher perceived variety. In such cases, the information-processing and visual capabilities lead to more or less the same shopping decisions regardless of who the individual shopper is.

This chapter will start a description of what and how shoppers look and perceive the store context. Knowledge in this area is building up fast with the help of academic eye-tracking studies. Next, this chapter looks into the beliefs of the shopper and what happens if these perhaps subconscious preferences are not answered in-store. The retail contexts may not address the preferences and characteristics of the shopper because the retailer is not aware of them, or does not have the physical, technical and financial capabilities. Even in online stores when retailers have more possibilities to tailor and personalise assortments to their customers than in a brick-and-mortar store, this holds true. The discrepancy between what people expect and what they find is what researchers describe as the level of congruency, and the impact on assortment and merchandising decisions is discussed. At the end, we quickly review differences between shopper groups as literature reports with regard to assortment and merchandising.

Generic Customer Journey with Four Phases on How Shoppers Search and Select

In the chapter on assortment size, it became clear how cognitive and vision capabilities guide assortment decisions, and everything else equal, favour a smaller size of assortment. Human physiology results in a horizontally shaped rectangular vision field of some 115 degrees high and 140 degrees wide, a vision line with a downward angle of some 15 degrees that makes 2 per cent of what human beings see very precise and lets them to a large extent on movement, shape and colour. On top of this, the human cognitive capabilities are slowed down by a comforting reliance on our first, emotional impressions. Or they are the result of a shutdown of the human's most rational, but unfortunately relatively small, part of the brain due to stress or information overload. These characteristics set the boundaries for how people shop. On a high level, the customer journey can be divided into three phases:

- Planning, including need recognition, channel selection and planning of store visit
- Shopping, including landing zone, navigation, product search and product selection
- Consumption, including opening of packaging, actual use, sharing of product and of the consumption moment, evaluation and recommendation

Observing and describing these smaller steps helps a retailer to identify obstacles and triggers for shopping. What they look like very much depends on the retail context and whether the activity is performed online or in a physical store. Below is a description of what the second phase with regard to shopping could look like.

Landing Zone

Regardless of whether shoppers are switching webstores or popping in and out of stores on a high street, as they enter the store environment, they face a different context. They need to shift their mind from considering to buying to investigating the retail store offer. This implies that people literally need to slow down on a sufficiently large landing zone. An example from a brick-and-mortar grocery store illustrates how the shape of the entrance determines the first shopping behaviour and the importance of a resting moment at the beginning. For a store routing and layout study, I once placed video cameras in several supermarkets. When the results came in, I noticed that in one store shoppers hardly visited the first 50 square metres of the store and slowed in their pace later. After comparing the shape of the entrances, I found out that the shoppers entered the store through a small path between handrails that subconsciously made them walk faster and only slow down after 10 metres inside the store. In another example from a leading petrol operator, I observed how shoppers entered the convenience store to pay for their petrol. They were so absorbed in securing their car keys, finding their wallet, looking through the window at which gasoline pump they had parked that they only came to rest just before the checkout. As a result, they missed the signage for lunch deals and the first metres of impulse snacks. Therefore, retailers are encouraged to work on 'softer' landings through the shape of the entrance and locations of their fixture. Alternative approaches are a welcome mat that makes the shopper shift mindsets, a reception desk or a people greeter that Walmart worked with to welcome shoppers to their stores. Webstores could provide engaging images in their landing zones without too much background noise from text, videos and moving images. The challenge for them is that they have many potential landing zones.

Navigation

Navigation is mostly about what shoppers do not see: People who visit a store mostly deselect the information around them. The stimuli come from everywhere: Other shoppers, in-store and website signage, the shape and material of fixtures, products themselves, staff interaction or chat invitations. In contrast with these overwhelming messages, shoppers mostly seek only one product no matter if this concerns fashion, furniture or household goods. Even when it comes to grocery the most frequently occurring shopping trip contains only one type of product. And at the same time, most time on a shopping trip is spent on navigation. Let's imagine a grocery trip on which people buy 30 products in-store for 20 minutes. Assuming an average picking time per product of 5 seconds, product selection absorbs some 13 per cent of time and 87 per cent of the shopping trip is spent on activities like trolley pickup, waiting at the checkout and navigation through the store. In neuro-research studies, shoppers showed a drop in stress level of 22 per cent when signage to the right aisle was found (Storm 2018). There are a number of ways in which retailers attempt to facilitate a natural and easy-to-understand navigation:

- Placing filters (mostly applied online).
- Grouping product by shopping trip (sometimes called 'worlds').
- Placing product categories by target group if there are several store levels because shoppers unconsciously or consciously stay on the floor level they enter.
- Avoiding narrow aisles.
- Creating comfort and relaxation moments through, for example, 'white' space online or low merchandising and open vision lines in brick-and-mortar stores.

- Using signs to pull shoppers to a certain place: Faces of people, icons that are a symbol of the product group, or through words, colours and images. The overall principle is to keep the navigation signs simple, because shoppers want to know at this stage where to go rather than knowing all the details:

  - Text messages for navigation are best delivered in single words rather than complete sentences. They should be short and in large fonts.
  - If using an icon, the meaning should be immediately clear rather than resulting in ambiguous interpretations.
  - Colours of signage material should be salient rather than blend in with the remaining context. On the other hand, the colour code of the category or that of the leading brand steers shoppers in the right direction.

- Giving a prominent role to products, for example, by enlarging a star product online or stocking sample product high against the store wall that makes shoppers see them from far away though they are not in reach for picking
- Using different colours by department
- Emphasizing the difference between traffic and navigation aisles versus department areas by giving different colours or drawing lines on the flooring
- Applying lighting and bright colours (versus darker colours) that grab attention
- Giving shoppers control of which direction to go. Online retailers could place the same products on several pages and allow access to content through various search functions. In brick-and-mortar stores, retailers can use free flow store layouts that allow shoppers access from all directions. When a forced routing is used such as at IKEA shoppers walk against their natural inclination and use shortcuts wherever they see them.

In brick-and-mortar stores, retailers face the challenge to pull shoppers into aisles. From brain research studies I worked on, I learnt that shoppers are hesitant to enter long aisles of 13 metres and longer, especially when the merchandising is high so that shoppers have the idea of entering a tunnel. The appeal of the aisle can be improved by first of all applying round gondola ends as shoppers have an unconscious inclination to stay away from sharp edges and less occurring, unnatural shapes. Next, visits are further increased by designing some kind of interruption in the middle of the aisle such as a protruding shelf or display so that the aisle feels less long to the shopper. Starting the aisle with the leading brand helps shoppers quickly understand what they are likely to find in that area. And referring to the earlier discussion on asymmetries, if the brand or product segment has a unique shape or colour, it will help the shopper decipher quickly where to go. In my experience there is not one side, left or right, that attracts more attention, though perhaps individual shoppers may have a certain preference. What I did find in shopper studies is that once shoppers start shopping on one side they finish that aisle before they turn around.

The Magical Number 7 Tells How Much People Remember

Once the shopper has entered the aisle or found the offer of products online that address the shopping need, it is smart to keep the number seven in mind. In a paper on human information processing, Miller (1955) even called this number seven magical as for some reason people have used this number to categorise and remember important concepts like the seven deadly sins, seven wonders of the world and seven days of the week. Miller points to studies that conclude human beings have a span of attention that fits about six objects at a glance, a span of judgement that can distinguish about seven categories and a span of immediate memory of objects of about seven.

> **Deeper Insight: Shoppers Remember 7 Chunks of Information (in a Range from 4 to 10)**
>
> Before applying this concept to the retail context, let me first tell more how Miller arrived at the notion 7 is more than a random number. All sorts of experiments from tasting the intensity of salt to discriminating levels of loudness showed that people get confused at a certain point. Their capacity to absorb information levelled off after being presented 7 similar alternatives and it ranged from 4 to 10. In these experiments, only one dimension alternated in various levels. When more independent dimensions, for example, sounds, faces or words, were added, the capacity to process information increased, but at a lower rate. This presented one explanation for how people can still accurately identify hundreds of faces and thousands of objects. In addition, Miller said that people could absorb more information by recoding the original set of data: They re-grouped the data into larger sets of data which Miller called chunks of information, applied new names and then remembered the new names rather than the original bits of information.

When applied to a retail context I think of a shopper who quickly differentiates about seven sections in a brick-and-mortar store or webstore. Of course, four sections are much easier to absorb and process instantly, but ten different sections might be too much. Most of the shopping trips are likely to be one-dimensional as the shopper has one mission in mind like a book for a loved one or Sunday morning breakfast. Making sure that the store is divided into about seven departments will make navigation much easier. Next, once the shopper arrives at the aisle or on the category webpage, it makes sense to divide any category (coffee, jeans for men, etc.) again into about seven sub-categories for convenience of shopping.

Product Search

This is the moment that the shopper stops in front of the shelf or focuses online to select the right product. There are of course many differences between what shoppers see on a 4.0-inch smartphone screen versus in a multi-dimensional real store environment. However, conceptually the shopper takes the same steps. After conscious and subconscious deselection of products and irrelevant communication, the shopper weighs the importance of the attributes of the available product selection.

Shopper Decision Tree

This is where the so-called shopper decision tree comes into play. This is a schematic representation of the choices that people make in a buying mode and shows the order of importance of category attributes. It all starts with a careful definition of what the category entails; this could be 'on the go lunch' but could also be as simple and product descriptive as 'soup' and 'jeans'. If the flavour of soup is what the shopper cares about most, the soup category could be divided into vegetable, tomato and a mixed group. Each of these flavour segments could be split further, for example, the vegetable soup segment is further split by brand and the tomato subsegment is subdivided by the type of packaging. When visualising this, a tree appears upside down. The idea behind the shopper decision tree is that shoppers are not more or less inclined to switch between segments, certainly not on a high level in the tree. In the soup example, shoppers who love vegetable soup are not likely to buy tomato soup. If their preferred brand of vegetable soups happens to be out-of-stock they are more likely to pick up another brand of vegetable soup than tomato soup. In this fictitious case, the flavour attribute is more important than brand. The highest one or two levels in the shopper decision tree are also called walking levels: Shoppers walk away when the product segment is not available. The lower levels in the hierarchy are called switching levels as shoppers are more likely to substitute products. In brick-and-mortar retail, there is most often one shelf for the category, and therefore the shopping decision tree that is followed reflects how most shoppers behave. Shoppers tend to recognise only three or four attributes in one category, so it is important to identify the most important ones. Online retailers have the opportunity to adapt the shopper decision tree to individual preferences, which is a great way to make shoppers comfortable and delighted with their choices. Another area where online retailing provides a great advantage is in the relative ease of collection of data and measurement. This allows them to measure the shopper decisions accurately, but also when there are almost no data there are sufficient methods available to identify shopping decision trees.

Deeper Insight: Methods for Identification of Shopper Decision Tree Depend on Data Availability

- In a conjoint survey, shoppers are asked to select their favourite option from two products that are described with a range of attributes and values. The pairs change during the survey so that the researcher can identify which attribute and which value is more important.
- MaxDiff looks a bit like the conjoint method. Here respondents are asked to rank the attributes that are most and least important to them.
- Far from perfect, but retailers get a hint on the importance of products and the attributes that go with them, if they ask in surveys what shoppers would choose if a certain product is out-of-stock. This helps them find substitutes. A more anecdotal way of doing this is when retailers find a product unpurchased and left behind at similar product groups, for example, frozen pizza left with pizzas in a fridge or organic lettuce left behind with regular lettuce. Apparently, the shopper found the product they really wanted and did not take the effort to sort them carefully. In a similar manner online retailers can track the filling and emptying of shopping carts while they link these to the pages shoppers visit.
- Identifying decision trees is easier when retailers have some kind of system to track individual shopping behaviour over time. An example is a loyalty card number that is registered with each transaction. The way this works is that retailers investigate in their data the purchases of each person in the last 12 months and imagine that there are seven transactions with coffee for a certain shopper. If six out of seven times the brand is the same, but the type of bean is different each time, shoppers are more loyal to the brand than to the type of bean. Cookies and user logins allow the same principle to be followed online.
- Knowing if transactions over time belong to the same shopper is not a prerequisite. Scanning data could do the job when retailers measure cross-price elasticities. For example, if a price increase of product A makes demand of product B go up while sales of product C remain more or less stable, product A and B apparently serve the same shopping need and are substitutes. Product C is considered complimentary. Working with cross-price elasticities is possible when there is sufficient variation in prices and it helps if the composition of assortment changes over time or is different by outlet.

- If loyalty card data are absent and shoppers buy several products from the same category on the same shopping trip, the level of complementarity could be distilled as well. A shopper that buys both Doritos Nacho Cheese and Lays Salted on the same trip apparently perceives these as complimentary. Investigating a large number of all sorts of combinations could give retailers a hint on product groupings from a shopper perspective.
- A commonly used method for categories with low purchase frequency such as consumer electronics and home décor is to organise accompanied shopping trips with some 20 shoppers. Interviewers walk along with shoppers, observe their behaviour, probe and ask questions for clarification. Many non-food retailers rely on this method.
- Instead of surveying shoppers, store staff could also be interviewed about the information that shoppers seek and which attribute they ask for first.
- Online retailers can measure on which filters shoppers click, and in which order. This helps them to figure out the importance of elements such as brand and price, possibly split by shopper type and shopping trip.

Comparison of Methods

Most importantly, the shopping decision tree should be derived from the moments when the transactions actually occur. This makes the conjoint method and to a lesser extent the MaxDiff method less suitable. A conjoint questioning could easily take 15 minutes and it is difficult to find shoppers prepared to spend this time right after the moment they made their purchases. The disadvantage of the survey method is that it assumes that shoppers know the attributes that are important to them and that all relevant attributes are known in advance. Therefore, purchase data-related methods generate a sounder basis for conclusions. However, the disadvantage of such data methods is that the decision factors are derived and therefore more open to more subjective interpretation.

In-the-moment methodology is crucial because shoppers easily forget, and a change of context may induce new thoughts. Though online surveys offer speed and cost efficiency, it is doubtful if they are suitable for the identification of shopper decision trees. Respondents are sometimes asked weeks or months after their actual purchase to remember how they behaved or asked to imagine how they would behave. The survey context, at home, on the go in the train and so on provides a very different context than the place the decision was made. This brings me to something else. Practitioners may speak of consumer decision trees; however, this concept refers to the categorisation of consumption needs and how products fit in, and this is different from shopper decision trees. And to make things more complex, retailers may mistake their product hierarchy in their data systems for shopper decision trees. However, these product hierarchies are very often a reflection of how the category managers are organised in functions and how the retailer did things in the past. For example, for purchasing and negotiation purposes it may make sense for a home décor retailer to group all wooden products such as tables, baskets and cooking utensils into one buying group, though this probably does not relate to shopper decision-making. A shopper decision tree informs the retailer what is important to the shopper in a particular shopping context. Retailers should assume a priori that shopping decision trees are different for each category, country, type of channel and retail format. In my personal experience, the shopping decision trees are similar for different retailers operating in the same type of store, so homogenous results for high-street convenience stores but a priori assumed to be different for other types like medium-sized grocery stores.

Visual Search Tree

After identification of the shopper decision tree, retailers are recommended to check on what I call a visual search tree. Let me explain this with a case study when I learnt on this by making some mistakes. Some 20 years ago, I constructed a shopper decision tree for the chocolate category in the Netherlands. The analysis showed crystal clear chocolate tablets and bars were subdivided by flavour. So, shoppers of milk chocolate stayed away from dark and white chocolate and each segment had its own distinctive user group. To the horror of the marketing department, I then experimented with planograms grouping tablets and bars by flavour. To their relief I compared these with pilot stores with brand blocking and benchmark stores without amendments. Well, the marketing team was right: Though the shoppers decided by flavour, they searched differently. Chocolate brands like Côte d'Or, Toblerone and Milka have such distinctive packaging and colour coding that mixing the brands over flavours created discomfort in the search. Similarly, it may make sense to divide diapers by age group as parents are not going to buy diapers that are too small or too large. Still, research could provide evidence that shoppers are very loyal to a certain brand and prefer to buy diapers and perhaps other baby necessities only of one brand. The lesson that I learnt is that building a planogram starts with the construction of a shopping decision tree but requires a test market to validate that certain search cues are not distorted.

During the product search phase, most of the attention of the shopper is focused on the products themselves, as that is what they came for. Therefore, the concept of decision trees is important. Retailers could support or even try to steer decision-making with the help of visual merchandising materials such as banners, coloured or branded shelf strips, shelf dividers, text balloons or shelf talkers. As shoppers focus on the products themselves, any communication placed adjacent to the product has better chances of being noticed. Therefore, ceiling hangers and narrow casting TVs are often less effective in attracting the shoppers' eyes.

Learnings on Search Behaviour from Eye-Tracking Studies

A great way to discover how shoppers search in a shopping environment is to invite shoppers to wear eye-tracking glasses. This research method provides great insights on what shoppers actually see. Much of the way shoppers perceive the retail context is the same; however, practitioners should carefully watch for differences in their target groups. For example, the outcomes often greatly depend on the experience of the shopper with the category and the context provided in online versus brick-and-mortar stores. For example, shoppers who are familiar with the planogram point their attention immediately to their reference product. If the purchase frequency is very low, shoppers may adopt a more systematic method such as browsing the product offer from left to right.

In an article by Chandon and colleagues (2009), a useful overview is given of how the eyes of shoppers move around the product assortment. It seems people's eyes make smooth and conscious movements; however, eye-tracking studies show that our eyes make rapid jumps, called saccades, from one point to another. On these points, the eye rests for a moment; in fact it is a small rest of 0.2–0.5 seconds per fixation. The saccade takes even less time, 0.02–0.04 seconds, and moves away 3–5 degrees in distance. During saccades no relevant information from the retail context is absorbed. This is different for the fixations. Fixations are a requirement for the identification of objects and therefore an analysis of fixations tells retailers what shoppers have seen. The visual area of a fixation is really small, about twice the width of the thumb if the arm is stretched out. It is a superior view on a small area. Eye fixations help memorise the object, while objects perceived only in periphery are not stored. The first eye fixation delivers a lot of information to the shopper. In combination with a less detailed view on the periphery the first fixation identifies the meaning of the context ('this is the coffee category in a supermarket aisle'), the spatial construction ('there are seven shelves') and the level of complexity and disorder. Shoppers need more fixations to get to know brands and identify which particular products are available. In eye-tracking studies, the first fixation on an object is known as noting. The information comprised in half a second gives shoppers a hint if this is what they searched for. If the object is noted depends on characteristics of the object, previous fixations on other objects in the retail context and a priori knowledge and experience. The second fixation on the same object is re-examination. For this to happen, the object is required to have a relationship with the particular shopping task.

> ### Deeper Insight: A Practical Example of Eye-Tracking
>
> In a study on laundry detergents, Van der Lans et al. (2008) illustrate the type of information that retailers obtain from eye-tracking:
> - Shoppers needed 3.82 seconds to identify the location of a particular laundry detergent. Thirty-two per cent of these few seconds were spent searching the shelf with in total 6 brands and 16 products. The remainder was spent on product identification. Nine out of ten times they identified the product correctly. The most occurring movement across the shelf was a zigzag starting at the left, moving the eyes horizontally, next diagonally to the left and finally horizontally towards the right again. This zigzag movement from the left happened more often than the zigzag movement starting at the right. On average 64 per cent of the brand salience depended on the visual characteristics of the packaging (bottom-up factors) such as packaging colour and luminance. Thirty-six per cent of the brand salience was influenced by the task at hand, which was localising a certain brand (top-down). Advertising played a role in this and therefore whether fixations landed on the products was different by brand. Brand search is faster when the brand is different on one characteristic (mostly colour in this research) and the others are different from this but similar among them.

Making Products Salient Versus the Rest of the Assortment

People have this fantastic gift to quickly extract information relevant for them. This capability helps shoppers to process information quickly and to let themselves feel entertained in a highly complex retail context that sends out a multitude of messages. It's not sufficient to know how fixations move around and are processed, and both retailers and suppliers need to know why people choose to fixate on certain areas. Retailers want to make sure their destination categories are observed, because that is what they want to be famous for. Brand owners of a national or private label brand want their concepts to be noticed and picked up. What can they do in order to make sure the category and products are more salient in a retail context?

Over the years, I have constructed my own view on how to make products salient based on my own studies and interpreting those of others. The rule of thumb that I apply to retail design is to first attract attention through movement, next shape, colour, images and finally text. The way to explain this order of importance is by imagining that our brains have evolved from prehistoric times and that humans were first of all attentive to any object coming towards them. If a human is attacked it does not matter that much what it is, but in the mere mini-seconds that follow people try to identify what it is by its shape: Is it more likely to be a tree falling or lion jumping? Finally, colour is important. Translating this into a retail context, a distinctive proposition is made by designing interactive elements (inviting people to trial a cream, self-starting movies online, swinging shelf talkers), distinctive shapes (ambitioning the iconic dimensions of a Coke bottle) and contrasting, alarming colours (using red and orange for promotions).

Aspects That Make a Salient Image

By presenting hundreds of images and coding objects displayed on each of these images, Xu and other researchers (2014) could predict where people look. Their first contribution is a great categorisation of product attributes that help in designing products and retail contexts that are more salient. Before going into the role and effectiveness of these attributes please find a convenient list divided into pixel-, object- and semantics-related attributes:

1. Pixel-level attributes describe the image of products or retail environments in the most objective manner. Think of colour, contrast, edges, intensity and orientation.
2. Object-level attributes are those characteristics that apply to all objects and are independent of the interpretation by shoppers. The reason to talk about objects is that people have the tendency to cast their gaze on interesting objects and look near the objects rather than at the background scenery. The researchers used a number of ways to describe objects:

   (a) Size;
   (b) Complexity: This determined by the length of the contour line, so circles have minimum complexity;
   (c) Convexity: This term describes how round the edges are.
   (d) Solidity: This measures both convexity and whether there are holes in the object; high solidity means the object is convex without holes.

(e) Eccentricity: This describes the surface when an ellipse is drawn around an object; the more the ellipse becomes a line rather than a circle, the higher the eccentricity.

3. Semantic-level attributes focus on the meaning that people derive from the object. As a rule of thumb on the type of objects that generate high saliency with people, one can think of faces and concepts related to humans' survival as a species (food, sex, danger, pleasure, pain). The researchers suggest four groups of semantic attributes:

(a) Attributes related to people: Think of front and profile of faces, faces with obvious emotions, objects touched by a human or an animal, and objects gazed upon by a human or an animal
(b) Flying and moving objects or implied movement in the image
(c) Objects that are related to other, non-visual senses: They produce a sound (talking person, musical instrument), come with a scent (a flower, a fish), can be tasted (food, drinks) or generate a strong tactile feeling (a sharp knife, a cold drink);
(d) Objects that are designed to attract attention or for interaction with people. Think of text (digits, letters, words and sentences), watchability (man-made objects such as paintings that are designed to be watched) and operability (tools that are touched or held by hands).

The question arises which factor will drive more attention than others. A large eye-tracking study by Xu and his colleagues provided clear evidence on what worked and what did not. They labelled all objects on hundreds of images on pixel, object and semantic values and asked participants to look at them for 3 seconds. To avoid any a priori bias, it was a natural exercise without any specific task. The images represented daily sceneries, sometimes with several dominant objects. Each fixation of participants was linked to an object or to the background. The study showed that 68 per cent of salience was driven by semantic-level attributes, 21 per cent was the result of the object and only 11 per cent was driven by pixel-level attributes. Attributes that were large contributors to the attention that people allocate were:

- Faces: As human beings we have learnt to make a quick assessment of someone's intentions and mood by looking at the face.
- Text: Perhaps a bit of a surprise that words score highly; however, also think of traffic signs where people have learnt to look out for words like 'Stop' and 'Danger'.

- Gazing: People detect the focus of attention of other people by looking into the same direction. Advertising can be made more effective if the first three attribute guidelines are combined by displaying a face that is directed towards a word or line of text.
- Solidity: Convex objects without holes attracted more attention.
- Taste: Images where people see food and drinks do well.

On object level, the researchers concluded that smaller, convex objects appear well in the foreground. Large objects could have a more attractive design; however, they have chances of being ignored as background. Highly complex shapes contain more information and are therefore more salient. Less eccentric shapes, so round and bubbly rather than long ellipses, are better for attention. Like other eye-tracking studies would predict, most fixations fell in the centre of the image, as that is where people start. This is called centre bias or central fixation bias. In addition, the participants also looked at the middle of any object, the so-called object centre bias. Interestingly, the researchers investigated how the importance of attributes changed during the viewing time, which helps retailers to predict the sequence of fixations. They concluded that all pixel attributes, two object attributes (size and eccentricity) and three semantic attributes (face, eye, emotion) decrease in importance over time. Especially face and emotion draw attention very quickly. On the other hand, the importance of the attributes text, sound, touch and gazing increases. For me, this research meant a real mind-shift in the manner in which I judge the effectiveness of product packaging, retail in-store communication and website images. It sometimes feels that in the online retail world, professionals have too much of a pixel focus whereby they try to get the colour and cropping of the image right rather than spending time on the semantic values that make shoppers pay more attention to a website.

Product Selection

Actual product selection is a click, a swipe or an arm movement. Rather than the actual number of seconds that a selection takes for most regularly purchased products like grocery items, I learnt more from the comparison among categories. In an assignment for a grocery retailer I have once been able to follow product selection behaviour in great detail with the help of video cameras: The conversion from visit to purchase, selection of product and return of the product to the shelf. This allowed the grocery retailer to identify on which activities shoppers spent time, for example, if shoppers were looking up information or feeling pleasantly entertained. In some instances, shoppers spent more time than they actually liked. Next the retailer attempted to facilitate decision-making with a different planogram, product composition or merchandising materials. The video research also helped in streamlining the communication. As a general principle, getting the location of products right is more effective than communication through product ads on the entire website or attaching shelf talkers throughout the store. Of course, some categories do need more information and such video research points to where those categories are.

Creating Shopping Momentum

Retailers can promote selection of a particular product through a myriad of marketing instruments ranging from promotion to sampling to the application of scents such as from the bakery department. Creating the right ambiance for the first purchase leads to the so-called shopping momentum and promotes the selection of yet another product. IKEA is a master in this area: They apply a type of landing zone that converts the visitor immediately into a buyer. Shoppers at IKEA may have noticed that after coming up the escalator and trying to find out where to go, they bump into a display in the middle of the shopping path promoting low-priced items like scented candles or reindeer slippers. Shoppers tend to think: 'I don't need them, but hey, they are cute'! This type of display is called a wallet-opener and apart from adding a new piece of Swedish design to the shopper's home, it is meant to generate profit. Perhaps the cash margin on the reindeer slippers is low, but the reindeer slippers need to make shoppers ready for the purchase of a Billy closet or any other product. This is called shopping momentum, and this occurs when the first purchase of a product increases the likelihood of purchasing a second item. The shopping momentum is a mindset: It refers to the moments when shoppers move from a deliberative to an implemental mindset that drives further purchases. The potential gain from shopping momentum is huge for retailers: The most typical shopping trip for most retailers is the single-item trip.

Deeper Insight: Retailers Need to Create an Implemental Mindset with Shoppers

- A series of experiments by Dhar and his research team (2007) explain how shopping momentum works. First, they show that shoppers purchasing one product move into an action mode that triggers more purchases. Participants received a reward for completing an unrelated questionnaire. The first group received some money and was then offered the opportunity to buy a key chain at a low price. After receiving the reward, a second group was first offered an educational CD and next the opportunity to buy the key chain. The second group that had already made a purchase was likely to buy the key chain as well (65 per cent versus 47 per cent).
- In a slightly altered version of this experiment, the researchers first offered a group a pen as a gift and next the opportunity to buy the key chain. The remaining group had to buy both. The outcome tells us that the purchase act is a condition for shopping momentum. Only 53 per cent bought the key chain after receiving the pen as a gift, whereas 78 per cent bought the key chain after being offered to buy a pen.
- A third experiment offers more insight about the thinking process that leads people into action modus. The research team collected a number of thoughts that shoppers have when buying a car. These were divided into deliberative thoughts such as listing the pros and cons of buying a car, and implemental thoughts of things that needed to be done when purchasing a car. All participants received $1 at the beginning of the test but only half of the group was offered the opportunity to buy a snack of $0.25. All participants read a paper with 12 thoughts that a hypothetical person might have when deciding on and buying a car. After some time, there was a recall task. What happened? Shoppers who were offered to purchase a snack had significantly better recall of implemental thoughts regarding the car purchase. The purchase of the snack had taken shoppers into the mood to buy a car.
- And it appears that people do not have to actually buy something as a condition of being in an implemental mindset. Thought cues are sufficient as a fourth experiment showed. Participants were led into either a deliberative mindset or implemental mindset by asking them to list pros and cons of buying a car or steps needed to buy a car respectively. After listing their thoughts, they were offered to buy a key chain. A group in the implemental condition bought the key chain more often: 66 per cent versus 41 per cent.
- A final experiment showed that there could be all kinds of distractions stopping shoppers from buying a second product. There are all kinds of distractions thinkable in a real-life retail environment like behaviour of other shoppers or displaced products. Dhar and the research team applied a type of behavioural bias as disruption. This entails that partitioning a pool of resources into several smaller chunks decreases spending and consumption. In this experiment, some participants got 30 rupees after completing a questionnaire. A second group received 20 rupees for a first questionnaire and after some time 10 rupees for a second questionnaire. From a rational perspective, it should not make a difference, because in both cases the total amounts to 30 rupees, but it did. In a next phase, participants were offered to buy a floppy disk for 18 rupees and also a key chain for 7 rupees. A comparable

number of people bought the floppy disk, the first product, in both conditions. However, shoppers who had received the money in two instances were much less likely (43 per cent) to buy the second product (a key chain) than shoppers who received their budget in one envelop (70 per cent). Partitioning of the monetary reward had created two mental accounts that the participants came to see as different sorts of budgets.

From a traditional economics perspective, the shopping momentum is difficult to understand. Dhar speaks of the difference between deliberative and implemental mindsets. Rationally speaking, shoppers are expected to assess the value of each item separately. However, it seems that if one purchase has happened, the second purchase becomes easier and an automatic response system triggering impulse purchases is switched on. The part of the human brain involved in deliberate thoughts that handles more topics at the same time and is capable of stopping the automatic response is smaller than the human automatic response system. Emotions like worry and choice stress may clog System 1, as Kahneman (2011) calls this automatic system, and hinder well-considered decisions. And perhaps the shopping momentum makes sense from a physics perspective. According to Newton's first of three laws of motion, an object continues to do whatever it happens to be doing unless a force is exerted upon it. Or stated in retail terms: A shopper continues to buy unless store and other factors disrupt the shopping process. A fresh physics perspective to look at shopping!

Maximising Versus Satisficing

From a rational perspective, shoppers are expected to enjoy searching for more options as long as the benefits are larger than the costs. Traditional economic theory states that selection from a range of options is carefully evaluated. All information is at hand so that the shopper can maximise the total, personal utility. This belief is difficult to defend in crowded retail environments, for large assortments without any organisation and in moments shoppers are stressed and in a hurry. So, shoppers are more emotional and rely more on heuristics than previously thought. Still, there are situations when the same shopper is more rational than in other ones or for the same situation where one shopper responds more rationally than someone else. To examine the differences between shoppers, Schwartz and a team of colleagues (2002) applied the concept of maximising versus satisficing developed by Simon (1955) in the 1950s. According to this theory, a maximiser searches through all available products in order to find the best. The term satisfice is a combination of the words 'satisfy' and 'suffice'. A satisficer evaluates products and settles for the first option that exceeds a predefined level. When satisficers walk into another product accidentally, they may replace this option if it is better. The question that the researchers asked themselves was which of the two groups of shoppers ended up being happier.

Deeper Insight: Maximising Does Not Make Shoppers Feel Happier

- In a first step, the team developed a questionnaire that measured the extent of regret (think of survey questions such as 'Once I make a decision, I don't look back') and maximisation ('I never settle for second best'). Next, they described the personality traits of the two groups with the help of a large survey. Compared to satisficers they concluded that maximisers experience more regret and depression, are less optimistic and happy, say they are less satisfied in life, have lower self-esteem and show perfectionism. It seems that maximisers struggle running through all available options and comparing them carefully. And assuming they had the time, they may doubt after their choice if they should not have worked slightly more. Finally, maximisers are more often men. An important remark is that the study shows correlations, not causalities. Does happiness make shoppers satisficers or is the reverse true? One could also argue that objectively maximisers make the best decision but that unfortunately it did not feel that way.

- This brings me to another question raised by Schwartz and his colleagues: How do maximisers know the outcome is the best possible one? How can shoppers judge that their refrigerator, salami or pair of shoes they just purchased is the best there is? There could be several bases for comparison, such as the shopper's previous purchase or options that the shopper constructed in their imagination. Another way is comparing themselves with others. Maximisers seem to be people who compare themselves with both people who do better (upward social comparison) and people who do worse (downward social comparison). To see how social comparison worked, the researchers set up an experiment to measure the mood changes of maximisers and satisficers as a result of social comparison. An experimenter handed out puzzles for 15 minutes and once completed participants returned them in exchange for a new one. They did not know that the person sitting next to the participant was hired by the experimenter and asked to 'solve' the puzzles either slower or faster. Though participants were not explicitly told about their relative performance, the back-and-forth handing of puzzles made this salient. The outcomes showed that 'slower' or 'faster' participants or maximisers and satisficers did not differ in number of puzzles that they actually completed, but they experienced the task differently. The maximisers who worked alongside a 'faster' peer showed a greater increase of negative mood and assessed their puzzle abilities significantly lower after the task. In contrast, satisficers responded more or less the same to seemingly better or worse performing peers. While feeling regret and less happy when comparing themselves upward, maximisers somehow do not experience positive feelings when comparing themselves downward.

An important learning from the studies is that personality traits influence the way shoppers make decisions. Satisficers seem to be people who are more easily pleased, and retailers are encouraged to find out how they could make maximisers happy with their purchase as well. There are several approaches I would like to offer. Maximisers do such a great job in finding options that the second-best option is excellent as well. Knowing that maximisers always want the best option and are prepared to go through extensive search to find options, to compare these, to check the facts and to compare how they performed versus others, retailers could offer tools to facilitate this search. They could also make the search cost transparent and provide feedback to maximisers who did a great job in their acquisition of information compared to others. I think that online retail offers great opportunities to provide maximisers with personalised feedback, to encourage them and give compliments. Another trait of maximisers is that they are inclined to have regret. Therefore, maximisers will obtain higher levels of satisfaction knowing that their choice is final and that return of the product to the store is not possible. The irreversibility of their choice encourages them to post-rationalise they did a great shopping job. Retailers could also try to take away any doubts with maximisers by staying in contact after the purchase and congratulating them with the 'best' choice they could make. A third characteristic of maximisers is their setting of high standards. This is a huge challenge for service-oriented retailers compared to price-oriented retailers. The former requires high-quality requirements for products and training for staff, while in discount-shopping environments retailers are more easily forgiven. Finally, maximisers are not the type of people who forgive themselves easily. They want to shop in environments with many options, but this may also create more stress. When the retail environment has a few options, they might be less satisfied than satisficers, but they can blame others. In a retail environment with a large number of options search efforts go up, chances of regret increase and maximisers feel only they can be blamed. The negative effects of over-choice are more likely to occur with maximisers. Perhaps personal assistants, either in person or computer-aided, could improve the experience because in such a case still the world around the maximisers could be blamed for a bad choice. It seems people are worse off being maximisers; however, this may depend on the field of decision-making. For example, maximising shoppers find new holiday locations because they are more ambitious or find a medicine without side effects because they did more research. I do not expect that people are maximisers in all decisions they make, from choosing a life partner to buying a jar of peanut butter. It is up to retailers to identify what type of shoppers they attract for their categories, and which type they would like to have in order to steer their shopping environment accordingly.

Ideal Point Availability

If the shopper knows exactly which product they want, the shopping process is easy, provided this option is indeed available within the retail assortment. Shoppers retrieve the evaluation of the product option from memory without actively thinking about which attributes are relevant and which levels of the attributes will best match the shopper needs. In this case, an ideal point is said to be available. However, shoppers may approach the decision without predefined preferences. They may be aware of relevant attributes such as jar size and percentage fruit content for their jam and may even have placed these attributes in a certain order but may not have yet defined which product option they would like to buy. Others may come up with relevant attributes in advance but have not attached importance to these before buying. The task of both formulating the best combination of attributes and the search within the available range is likely to be more difficult when the assortment grows with unique products. On the other hand, having an ideal point available might make things more difficult in case of small assortments, because there is less chance it is available. If shoppers have an ideal point in mind, the selection from a large assortment becomes easier.

> **Deeper Insight: Good to Have a Safe Option for Shoppers Without Ideal Point**
>
> - The relationship between ideal point availability and assortment size was studied by Chernev (2003). He made the ideal point salient with a group of Godiva chocolate shoppers by asking them to select the most attractive value (e.g. dark or white chocolate) for each attribute (e.g. cacao content, nut content) and rank these outcomes. Another group of shoppers could make their selection right away. Shoppers chose either from a small assortment of 4 Godiva chocolates or a large assortment of 16 chocolates. He challenged their confidence in the selected chocolates by asking if they would rather take home two samples of the Godiva chocolates they just chose, or if they preferred two chocolates of what were described as two of the most popular Godiva chocolates. When comparing shopper groups with and without an ideal point in case of a large assortment, the level of switching to the 'safe' option of the popular chocolates was highest among shoppers without an ideal point. Only 13 per cent of the shoppers, who had defined an ideal point and selected their favourite chocolate in advance, switched to the popular chocolates, whereas many more (38 per cent) shoppers without articulated preferences

changed their preference. Shoppers without an ideal point available found it much easier to select from a small assortment, as was evidenced by the fact that only 9 per cent switched to popular chocolates (compared to 38 per cent when the same group shopped in a large assortment).

- There are several possible variations of the formulated ideal points possible. Therefore, Chernev also tested two situations in which ideal points were not exactly articulated but in several levels of strength of preference. Again, shoppers could select from a small and a large range of chocolates. The first group was instructed to trade off the attributes such as flavour and solid versus filled chocolate. The other group rated the attributes in terms of importance but did not compare the attributes with each other and formulated the ideal point to a lesser degree. When comparing these two groups in case of a large assortment, 45 per cent of the shoppers without a strongly articulated ideal point switched to the safe choice of assumedly popular chocolates compared to only 17 per cent of the shoppers switching who had a more articulated preference.

- It is also possible that shoppers attach a dominant importance to one attribute which drives the selection of the product, whereas others compare several attributes without a large difference between the most important attribute and the second most important. The first are believed to have a more spontaneously shaped ideal point. Chernev compared shopping decisions between assortments of 6 or 24 options for vacations, sofas, refrigerators and computer-carrying cases. Shoppers with a strong ideal point were less likely to switch in case of large assortments (11 per cent versus 35 per cent) to an option that was described as the recommendation by store staff.

- The studies by Chernev demonstrate that large assortments make shoppers with a strong ideal point happier whereas they may become frustrated with small assortments. For shoppers without a strong preference the reverse is true. The more that retailers inform about relevant attributes and attribute levels in a category and let shoppers think about the match to their personal needs prior to the purchase decision, the more shoppers perceive confidence they can handle large assortment variety.

Shopper Beliefs and Congruency

Not all shoppers are the same and very often groups of shoppers expect different assortments and merchandising. Should the retailer have the profound knowledge, preferably on shopper level, what the expectations are, they could adapt their online store. Brick-and-mortar stores do not have that choice. The assortment and planograms correspond with what most people want most of the time. The question arises what happens if shoppers visit a category that is organised differently from what they had expected to see. This is bound to happen as shoppers enter the store environment with different levels of experience, knowledge and familiarity with the category. This is called incongruency and refers to the difference between the internal scheme (the criteria and beliefs that shoppers have created inside their brains) and the external organisation of the assortment.

Morales and a group of researchers (2005) investigated how shoppers buy microwave popcorn in store environments that are either congruent or incongruent with their beliefs. To differentiate the original beliefs and final choice they set a series of tests for shoppers over time. First, they determined the decision structure of each shopper by measuring the importance of four attributes (brand, flavour, size and price) when buying microwave popcorn. This test delivered the internal decision schemes for each shopper. After a month, the shoppers were asked to select 1 popcorn product from an assortment of 25. The assortments were either merchandised in a congruent manner whereby the grouping followed the importance that the shopper attached to brand, flavour, size and price or in an incongruent presentation whereby the researchers changed the preferred order in the grouping of products. The researchers found that, if shoppers were irregular users and largely unfamiliar with the category, satisfaction of shoppers and their perceived level of variety were the same in both the congruent and incongruent planogram. So, shoppers need to be familiar with the category to let the external situation confuse them! When the presentation was congruent with the internal scheme, they found it much easier to use. Shoppers who were familiar with the microwave popcorn category reported higher level of variety if they shopped in a congruent assortment compared to an incongruent one. These shoppers scan the assortment at ease, take the time to process information, locate the subsegment they are interested in and in the meantime perceive more variety. When the presentation was incongruent, shoppers familiar with the category found it hard to decode all information. Although this fact in itself increased the recall, there was no effect on perceived variety.

In conclusion, the level of experience and familiarity with the category is an important driver of differences in shopper behaviour. Shoppers who visit the category frequently become experts in their own field. They have defined their preferences well and armed with this knowledge they are able to face a much larger assortment without facing choice stress, provided of course their favourite option is available. The unfamiliarity with the category might be due to infrequency of purchase of a given category. For example, washing machines are re-purchased every 15 years or so. The expenditure will make shoppers do proper research, but as the laundry cannot wait, the often sudden failure of the machine requires them to do a fast and deep information search. At such moments, the type and significance of the functional elements are just dazzling. Will 5.2 cubic feet deliver really more for the shopper than 4.8? Is a separate washing program for jeans a necessity? Retailers may rely on techniques such as filtering and reviews to guide the shopper. Online retailer Coolblue (2018) in the Netherlands added descriptions to washing machines telling who would be the most likely target groups of specific machines. For example, a Zanussi with loading capacity of 7 kg and programmable starting time is described as 'our choice for a washing machine for a single or couple' and an energy efficient AEG of 8 kg loading capacity is presented as 'our choice for a washing machine for a family with 1 or 2 children'. The descriptors reassure shoppers the machine will fit their family setting, mostly likely forgetting that in a few years they transition to a different phase of the family cycle and most likely still do their laundry with the same machine. Retailers could also guide inexperienced shoppers in a category by applying one overlaying merchandising principle. Consumer electronics retailer MediaMarkt is an example that ranks their products in brick-and-mortar stores by price, so that once shoppers have visited MediaMarkt a couple of times regardless of the category, they have come to expect and appreciate the familiar presentation mode. At other times, purchase frequencies in a category fluctuate among shoppers and it becomes more challenging for the retailer to align their merchandising: Some people love to bake cakes and visit the baking ingredients category on a weekly basis, while others find themselves in this section once a year. On product level the differences could be even more extreme. Take parsnip, one of the oldest cultivated vegetables, where some feel comfortable how and when to cook and others don't. Giving detailed product information to each alternative will make the website category landing page or brick-and-mortar store feel cluttered, so the fit to the retailer target group, the category's importance to retail strategy and the return on investment should determine the placement of category information.

Influence of Shopper Characteristics with Regard to Previous Chapters

The diversity in shopper target groups in relation to the breadth of categories and retail contexts makes the number of possible interactions infinite. In Chaps. 2, 3 and 4, I discussed generic principles on the size, composition and way of organising products. The results of the studies that I discussed could be further refined when making a distinction among types of shoppers.

Deeper Insight: All Findings with Regard to Assortment Size and Composition May Be Different by Shopper

- Earlier, I discussed the relationships between shopper experience and the effectiveness of applying labels for the category. Shoppers who were familiar with their decision process for the category, the so-called preference matchers, were happy with their shopping independently of category labels. This was different for the preference constructors who have less experience with the category. Their perception of variety and satisfaction was significantly higher in case of 18 more specific labels compared to 3 generic labels to segment the category of magazines. Shoppers who are unfamiliar with the category rely much more on external cues such as labels for segments and product information.
- Being in a good mood and feeling better allows shoppers to recall experiences better. Retailers could try to entice this positive feeling, but stores may find it difficult to convert shoppers from a bad mood into a shining shopper.
- In Chap. 2, I discussed that the importance of assortment for selecting a store varied widely among shoppers, whereas response to price and location was more uniform. Some shoppers weigh the number of brands over variety within a brand, while others don't and can do with fewer brands.
- Another example of a shopper characteristic that influences shopping behaviour is the mindset of the shopper. Chapter 4 showed that shoppers in a concrete mindset are looking for specific attributes like flavour rather than for benefits like energy boost. When confronted with a benefit-based planogram they become less satisfied. Shoppers looking for a certain benefit saw no difference in variety because their abstract mindset made them see the relationship between products in the same manner. The level of abstract thinking differs per person but will also vary over time for one individual and might therefore be difficult to determine for retailers.

Starting with the research findings and general principles on shopper behaviour, retailers are encouraged to conduct their own market research. Previously it was discussed that shoppers are likely not to observe any assortment reduction as long as their favourite product is still present. This is a helpful starting point but still requires retailers to do their homework: Who is my target group and how can I best meet their needs?

Finally, retailers are encouraged to discover how social media and Internet influence the information search, product comparison and purchase by shoppers. Most likely there are generational differences. However, what I found helpful is to start the search considering all similarities. No shopper is immune to a discount. Human vision and information-processing capabilities will lead to broadly defined conclusions on shopping behaviour. Next, retailers could start testing hypotheses, for example, if their millennial target group strictly rejects brand choices their parents made, or if they make an exception for Old Spice aftershave. Seniors might find online product reviews as useful as younger generations but as they have arrived at an age that they need less stuff and have more time for a chat, they may choose to use fewer of them. This is not to wave away all differences, and there certainly will be more teens on Snapchat or Instagram than seniors, but this is a reminder that evolution has provided human beings with the same base, that most retailers attempt to appeal to a broad spectrum of shoppers and in-depth research is required for the discovery of in-the-moment shopping needs.

Important Learnings from This Chapter

- Most stimuli from products, merchandising, communication and other people around the shopper are deselected. Shoppers sort, name and remember the stimuli in seven chunks.
- Navigation should feel as natural as possible to the shopper.
- Product selection is made with the help of a shopper decision tree: A schematic representation of the choices that people make in a buying mode and showing the order of importance of category attributes. This should be aligned with the visual search tree.
- Eye-tracking studies provide great insight into what shoppers actually see. The visual area of a fixation is very small, and fixations take some 0.5 seconds. If the object is noted depends on characteristics of the object, previous fixations on other objects in the retail context and a priori knowledge and experience. The second fixation on the same object is re-examination. For this to happen, the object is required to have a relationship with the particular shopping task.
- The rule of thumb for retail design is to first attract attention through movement, next shape and finally colour.
- Attention in retail design is driven mostly by the semantic value that shoppers perceive (faces or alerting text messages like 'stop') and are to a lesser extent the result of the shape of the object or pixel qualities such as colour.
- The most typical shopping trip contains one product and retailers can use the shopping momentum to trigger new purchases.
- Being a maximiser or satisficer determines how thoroughly shoppers evaluate the assortment: The maximiser searches through all available products in order to find the best and a satisficer settles for the first option that exceeds a predefined level.

- If shoppers have an ideal point in mind, the selection from a large assortment becomes easier. Shoppers with a strong ideal point may become frustrated with small assortments.
- If the store assortment is congruent with internal beliefs, the shopper scans the assortment at ease and perceives more variety.

References

Chandon, P., Hutchinson, J. W., Bradlow, E. T., & Young, S. H. (2009). Does In-Store Marketing Work? Effects of the Number and Position of Shelf Facings on Brand Attention and Evaluation at the Point of Purchase. *Journal of Marketing, 73*, 1–17.

Chernev, A. (2003). When More Is Less and Less Is More: The Role of Ideal Point Availability and Assortment in Consumer Choice. *Journal of Consumer Research, 30*, 170–183.

Coolblue. (2018). [Online]. Retrieved May 19, 2018, from https://www.coolblue.nl/zoeken/producttype:wasmachines?query=wasmachine.

Dhar, R., Huber, J., & Khan, U. (2007). The Shopping Momentum Effect. *Journal of Marketing Research, 44*(3), 370–378.

Kahneman, D. (2011). *Thinking, Fast and Slow*. London: Penguin.

Miller, G. A. (1955). The Magical Number Seven, Plus or Minus Two Some Limits on Our Capacity for Processing Information. *Psychological Review, 101*(2), 343–352.

Morales, A., Kahn, B. E., McAlister, L., & Broniarczyk, S. M. (2005). Perceptions of Assortment Variety: The Effects of Congruency between Consumers' Internal and Retailers' External Organization. *Journal of Retailing, 81*(2), 159–169.

Schwartz, B., Ward, A., Monterosso, J., Lyubomirsky, S., White, K., & Lehman, D. R. (2002). Maximizing Versus Satisficing: Happiness Is a Matter of Choice. *Journal of Personality and Social Psychology, 83*(5), 1178–1197.

Simon, H. A. (1955). A Behavioural Model of Rational Choice. *Quarterly Journal of Economics, 69*(1), 99–118.

Storm, M. (2018). *Presentation "An Introduction to the Shopper's Brain"*. Shopper Brain Conference, Amsterdam, 8 November 2018.

Van der Lans, R., Pieters, R., & Wedel, M. (2008). Competitive Brand Salience. *Marketing Science, 27*(5), 922–931.

Xu, J., Jiang, M., Wang, S., Kankanhalli, M. S., & Zhao, Q. (2014). Predicting Human Gaze Beyond Pixels. *Journal of Vision, 14*(1), 1–20.

6

Shopping Missions

Image 6.1 Integrated assortment and merchandising model

Learning Objectives

- Understand how different modes of shopping, such as browsing versus action-oriented, influence the perceived variety of assortment.
- Describe shopping missions in terms of browsing, level of decision focus, congruency between shopper belief and retail context, public accountability and public justification.
- Learn that the type of shopping mission has a large impact on the shopping decision.

© The Author(s) 2019
C. Berkhout, *Assortment and Merchandising Strategy*,
https://doi.org/10.1007/978-3-030-11163-2_6

Definition of Shopping Mission

This chapter investigates how shopping missions impact the assortment perceptions and behaviour of shoppers. Shopping missions are the combination of needs and reasons to visit stores. They form both the emotional needs and objectives at the consumption moment ('I feel better when the children eat healthy') and the often more practical and concrete needs and expectations as a shopper ('I have 15 minutes to prepare food for the kids' or 'this should not cost me more than 10 euros'). If defined in a narrow manner a shopping mission always concerns the planned goal to purchase a product. In case of categories like groceries the shopper is mostly successful at once, so that the shopping mission refers to one shopping trip. The purchase of non-food categories such as fashion and consumer electronics often involves more than one shopping trip all belonging to the same shopping mission. A shopping mission could be spread over time, for example, when the shopper first takes the time to read product reviews, visits a price comparison website and finally visits a store. When shopping missions are defined in a broad sense all sorts of non-product related objectives are included as well. Examples are the visit to a flagship store offering great experiences, a workshop at the DIY store preparing the shopper for the next job and a visit to the local grocery in order to meet acquaintances from their neighbourhood. A broad definition of shopping missions is useful because the contacts between the shopper and retail environment may lead to conversion from visitor to customer on the next occasion. In addition, the shopper gains impressions in a conscious or unconscious manner during each contact that may play a role in a more purchase-driven part of the shopping mission. The benefit of working with shopping missions is that retailers consider the needs of shoppers at a specific moment in time. This is a difference with a (traditional) category management approach that puts products and their characteristics first. Application of shopping missions is rising because the number and diversity of stores are increasing and because shoppers have become less loyal to a specific format or store.

While retailers make their own decisions on assortment size, composition and organisational form, the level of perceived variety also depends on aspects that are not directly in their circle of influence: The shopper and on the type of mission they are on that moment. Shopping missions drive the way shoppers search and select. Based on shopper research, practitioners may expect certain behaviour from their target group but nothing is more unpredictable than shopper behaviour. Kahneman and other behavioural economists taught us that shoppers are greatly influenced by their environment in choosing their products. And shoppers visit an increasing variety of retail contexts. They may transfer from a more utilitarian goal for cereals that are needed for breakfast next morning or finding the best cereals deal towards more hedonistic or fun shopping: Escaping reality and hoping to be entertained, picking up ideas, socialising or buying presents for someone else or oneself. On top of the retail context the shopper interchanges the goals for which they buy the product. Or explained alternatively, the shopping missions of a shopper vary over time. The same shopper and the same product, let's say a chocolate bar, could play a part in an urgently needed snacking trip or in a well-planned weekly shopping mission. In the first case, the shopper will not pay much attention to variety but will rely on the brand name for quality. In the latter case, more time is available for sorting out the best promotion and making sure everyone in the family is made happy with the weekly catch from the supermarket. Considering the shopping mission is important because the goal set by shoppers will make them focus their attention on information related to that goal. Shoppers ignore large sections of the store and retailers find that some of their finest assortment completely escaped the attention of their shoppers. Retailers may try to change or amend the shopping goal. They could do so by tapping into the human nature of paying attention to anything novel, unexpected, moving or perhaps dangerous.

Each retail sector has popular approaches to describe shopping missions. For example, in grocery it is common to speak of weekly routine trips, urgent top-up trips and fresh top-up trips. Fashion, DIY and other retail sectors describe shopping missions in other ways. All these approaches can be described with the help of five factors:

1. Level of browsing
2. Decision focus
3. Congruency with shopping goal
4. Public accountability
5. Public justification

Browsing

On some occasions shoppers take an open approach whereby they let themselves be guided by their curiosity and by whatever they find. They seem more relaxed and talkative and they learn both about the options available in the store and about their own preferences. At other times, shoppers seem to already know what they want, walk faster and approach the assortment in a more results-driven manner. The first mentioned is called browsing and is often found in categories like consumer electronics and home décor. In the latter situation, shoppers are more in a buying mood and this is a common focus in drugstores and groceries. So, some types of retail attract more of one kind of shopping than the other. One category or retail format is bending more towards browsing than the other. In addition, the way the store is merchandised and decorated invites more to the one or the other. A free format grid layout attracts more browsing than long aisles; different floor colours for store sections and store transit routes make it comfortable for both browsers and shoppers to navigate and walk through the store. Setting up stores for browsing versus buying has a significant impact on shopping behaviour. For example, groceries succeed in converting the vast majority of visitors to buyers whereas I worked with non-food brick-and-mortar stores that were satisfied with some 35 per cent conversion rate. Both types of shopping modes could occur in the same store.

A way to investigate the effect of browsing on assortment choices is by splitting the buying decision into two partial decisions: Deciding on the best option and deciding whether to buy. This is the approach that Gao and Simonson (2015) took. They wondered what happened if the order of these partial decisions changed. They distinguished two types of decision-making. In the 'select-first' mode, shoppers ask themselves if they want to buy from the available options first and then buy. This feels like browsing the options. In the 'buy-first' mode, shoppers decide to take on the task to make a purchase decision, and then look around to do so. In this mode, shoppers are more action-oriented and prefer a large assortment. This conclusion is slightly counter-intuitive to me: Action-oriented buying is a means to achieve a given goal, while browsing feels for shoppers like the goal itself. Therefore, the effort of browsing is more enjoyable than the effort of goal-oriented purchasing. My conclusion is that shoppers evaluate browsing store environments with large assortments as pleasurable but when the browsing leads to the desire to select an item, the high variety deters them. Browsing large assortments is pleasurable until the moment the shopper has to make a choice. A similarly large assortment delivers more complexity and choice stress for action-oriented buyers, but the effort is worth it because they have a buying objective in mind. Shoppers who have to make an additional effort are in the end more satisfied with their decision-making.

> **Deeper Insight: Browsing Is More About Looking Around Than Buying**
>
> - In order to find out about the different effects on shopping behaviour, Gao and Simonson set up two experiments. In the first study, they asked people to buy jelly beans from an assortment of either 10 or 30 flavours of jelly beans. They simulated the select-first mode by asking shoppers for their favourite flavour. Next, they had to make a choice between actually receiving a bag of jelly beans and receiving an equivalent value in cash. The preference for jelly beans was seen as an indicator of purchase likelihood. In the buy-first mode, the shoppers first had to decide between jelly beans and cash, and next they could choose their favourite flavour of jelly bean. When the selection of flavours was limited to 10, 47 per cent of the shoppers in the select-first or browsing mode bought jelly beans, while only 26 per cent did so in the buy-first mode. In case of a three times larger assortment, the purchase intent in the browsing mode went down indicatively. However, the purchase intent increased significantly to 49 per cent in the buy-first mode. So, when shoppers had decided to buy, the larger assortment only made it more interesting for them. They reviewed all options and enjoyed the variety. Shoppers in the select-first mode had an initial task to make a choice from the available options, which might have been overwhelming in case of a large assortment.
> - In a second experiment, Gao and Simonson confirmed the finding that a larger assortment works better for shoppers in the buy-first mode. This time shoppers were tasked to browse online in a webstore of chocolate specialties. In the select-first condition, shoppers first chose their favourite chocolate from the available options and next could choose between a monetary reward and chocolate. In the buy-first condition, shoppers reviewed the options, were asked to choose between chocolate and cash as a reward for participating in the study and next were asked to share their favourite chocolate. When shoppers could select from six chocolates in the buy-first condition, 40 per cent preferred to receive the chocolate. This more than doubled in case of a large variety of 30 chocolates. They experienced more difficulty but also more variety.

Decision Focus

The degree to which shoppers appreciate variety of the assortment depends on whether they select among assortments or whether their focus is on product level. This is called decision focus. Making a choice between an assortment of skirts and an assortment of jeans is experienced differently from selecting an alternative from an assortment of pants. When the focus of the shopper is on assortment level rather than on product level when selecting from a given assortment, shoppers can better process large assortments. A shopper on a mission for dessert may search among 'yoghurt', 'fruit' and 'ice cream' or they may look among the peach flavours in the yoghurt chiller.

Deeper Insight: It Is Easier to Appreciate the Variety If the Shopper Makes the Decision on a Higher Product Level

- Chernev (2006) showed shoppers deal with more complexities searching on product level. He created a store environment with two vending machines. One vending machine offered 36 snacks, 6 varieties from the 6 subcategories. The other vending machine offered only six varieties, the most popular snack from each of the six subcategories. Shoppers were led to the two vending machines and given either of the two following shopping instructions: The first group was to choose a vending machine, while another group had to pick a product. The results were very clear: Only 2 per cent of the shoppers with an assortment focus chose the vending machine with the low variety while 35 per cent of the shoppers did so when they focused on a certain product. This is explained by the fact that the choice is composed of two phases. If the shoppers perceive the selection of the assortment and the subsequent individual product as two independent decisions, they prefer the larger assortment. However, in the case of the product focus the two phases are considered at the same time. As a result, shoppers are expecting more difficulties in having to make a choice and therefore they rely on the pre-selected, smaller assortment. Shoppers in the product-focus condition indicated significantly more than the other group they had done so for the reason of easy decision-making. In contrast, 95 per cent of the assortment-focus group indicated variety as their most important reason for their behaviour compared to 55 per cent for the product-focus group.
- Through a second experiment, Chernev found out that previous experience with the assortment makes a difference. Having been through the complexities of selecting from a large assortment makes shoppers hesitant to opt for large assortments again. Chernev divided his study into two phases. In the first phase, he manipulated the shopping experience by giving part of the shopper group the instruction to make a choice from an assortment of 80 different types of Godiva chocolates, and he asked a second group to simply evaluate the assortment without making a choice. The assortments were offered online with each of the chocolates displayed with an image and a description. After the initial task the two groups were asked to redeem a gift certificate in either a chocolate store with 24 chocolates or a chocolate store that offered a total of 88 chocolate varieties. Shoppers who were given the instruction to pick a certain product were more likely to avoid the large assortment because they associated the store with many varieties with high complexity and more choice stress. Sixteen per cent of the shoppers who had chosen a specific product before preferred the store with the smaller assortment, while only 2 per cent of the shoppers did so when they had been asked to (only) examine the assortment in the previous task.
- The more shoppers are aware they need to select a given product and the complexity becomes salient, the more likely the shopper is inclined to prefer a smaller assortment. This also holds true when the choice for an assortment and for a product from this assortment are separated in time. This temporal effect is tested in Chernev's third experiment. Shoppers were asked to select a store with 12 Waterman pens or a store with 60 Waterman pens. The shoppers were randomly assigned to one of the two following shopping contexts: After the store selection, they had to immediately purchase the pen, or they

were requested to pick their store now and were told they would select the pen next month. Nineteen per cent of the shoppers, who had to make an instant decision, chose the store with smaller assortment whereas only 3 per cent of shoppers did so who could delay their product decision. Shoppers who made an immediate decision were more satisfied with the small assortment than those who delayed the decision.

- When retailers carry a large assortment, they can help shoppers overcome the perceived complexities in relationship with the decision focus. In a fourth and final experiment, Chernev asked shoppers to choose between two travel agencies for a trip to Bermuda. Both were highly recommended and indeed there was only one difference: One offered 24 five-star hotel resorts while the other listed 6, a subset of the first. Shoppers were either asked to select a travel agency (assortment-focus) or a resort (product-focus). This time there was some help to make the decision easier for shoppers. They were given so-called dominant options. For some the familiar Ritz-Carlton hotel brand was part of the selection, while the other resort brands were relatively unknown. Other shoppers were told that one hotel performed much better on an important attribute because it was at the beach rather than near the beach. And it worked. In the absence of a dominant option, 34 per cent of shoppers preferred the smaller assortment when selecting a specific resort, while only 2 per cent did that when they had to choose an agency. When Ritz-Carlton was included in the list of hotels, 0 per cent preferred the small assortment when having to choose a resort compared to 4 per cent of shoppers who were assigned the assortment-focus of selecting a travel agency.

Congruency with Shopping Goal

Is it wise to organise the retail shelf or website according to the shopping goal? Well, it sounds like an obvious approach to please shoppers. However, if retailers wish to be known for the breadth and width of their assortment, there might be better ways.

Morales and a group of researchers (2005) investigated the congruency between the shopping goal and the external assortment. They came up with a fictional category called 'trinkets' to make sure that all participants of the study were unfamiliar with the category. Some participants were trained to learn the three attributes (brand, scent and size) and adopt a certain weighing of attributes. Others received no training to represent shoppers without an internal scheme. Part of the participants was given no shopping goal at all, others were asked to buy a certain brand of trinket or a freshly scenting trinket. If shoppers were familiar with the category, congruency between their internal schemes and the external assortment resulted in higher perceived variety and higher satisfaction. If shoppers were unfamiliar, they had a shopping goal and the external assortment was organised in a congruent manner, they perceived a lower overall variety, though they saw more of the product they had bought. Having a shopping goal makes shoppers check if each product meets the requirements. If the shopping goal and external assortment are congruent, the search takes place faster. However, if shopping goal and external assortment are incongruent, the shopper needs to search more and consider more products and as a result the perception of variety increases. Very importantly, the study concluded that shopping goals had a larger impact on influencing variety in the external environment than internal schemes held by shoppers.

While the perception of variety in the complete category may decrease if the shopping goal relates to a given product, this works differently on subcategory level. Shoppers who are goal-driven and seek a certain assortment spend more time to inspect and choose among the alternatives that are consistent with the goal. If the retailer organises accordingly, shoppers process the products more one-by-one in the subcategory and tend to buy relatively more from the segment consistent with their goal. So, on segment or subcategory level the perceived variety could increase when the retail context and shopping goal are congruent. The researchers Van Herpen and Bosmans (2017) generated new insights on the perception of variety when they investigated whether organic food should be placed in a separate group (aisle/website page) or if the organic products should be placed with functionally related products.

Deeper Insight: Only If the Subcategory (e.g. Organic Tea) Is the Target of the Mission and Large, Shoppers Perceive More Variety in a Separate Presentation Versus a Mixed (Organic and Non-organic Tea) Presentation

- This is still a current topic on many grocers' minds. They wonder if shoppers undertake specific organic foods shopping trips. And whether they could please shoppers by grouping all organic alternatives in one department for organic foods or if they should place the organic tea alternative with the remainder of the tea category. For this question on placement, Van Herpen and Bosmans asked participants to shop online for a red wine. Part of them selected from 16 wines presented on one page, and the remainder chose from two pages whereby the wines were split into organic and non-organic types. In both scenarios each wine was matched with an alternative that was similar in dimensions such as price, region and type of grape. Separating organic from non-organic wines generated a larger perceived variety of organic wines than that of non-organic wines. In contrast, in the mixed presentation the variety of organic wines was perceived lower than the variety of non-organic wines, though in both scenarios the number of organic wines and online descriptions were the same. If shoppers already had an interest in organic wines, the assortment variety of organic wines in the separated presentation was even higher. The researchers also concluded that the way of organising did not alter the intrinsic interest in organic wines. Creating a different product block for organic wine allows shoppers that already have an interest in such products to focus more and perceive more variety within the segment (organic wine) and lower variety of alternatives. Similar outcomes were obtained when shoppers were tasked to buy tea online. They had to specifically buy tea without caffeine from three types of online presentations: Separation of caffeine and non-caffeinated teas; separation by a non-related shopping mission characteristic, here fair trade; or a mixed display of caffeine and non-caffeinated teas. Similar to the wine experiment, shoppers perceived a larger variety of non-caffeinated teas when the display of caffeine teas was separate.

- Next, Van Herpen and Bosmans researched what happened with variety perceptions if the retail context was not aligned with their expectations. For this they played with three variables at the same time:

  - The type of shopping mission: They offered tea with caffeine or tea without caffeine.
  - The number of alternatives: This was either small (4) or large (16) within the specific tea segment, while overall assortment size was kept at 20 tea options.
  - The way of merchandising: Teas were merchandised based on presence of caffeine or were presented in a mixed display.

- When 16 out of 20 products belong to one segment and are presented in a separate block the dominance of this segment becomes very clear. From a rational perspective it is expected that shoppers will always find that assortment variety is higher in the separate, large segment versus a mixed display. However, shopping behaviour will also depend on the goal. I illustrate the outcomes of the study with the example of a shopper that has in mind to buy tea with caffeine. Only shoppers that were searching for tea with caffeine perceived a larger variety in the separate display than in the mixed presentation. If the segment that was related to their shopping mission was large (tea with caffeine), the shoppers perceived a higher variety of their shopping mission related tea (with caffeine) in a separate display than they perceived in a mixed display. They assessed the variety of the non-caffeinated tea (that is not related to their shopping mission) to be lower in the separate display than in the mixed display. When shoppers had the goal to buy tea with caffeine, and the actual segment was small, there was no difference in perceived variety between a separate and mixed display. So, when shoppers set themselves the goal to search a certain segment (tea with caffeine) making a separate block of tea with caffeine has no impact if this segment is small: Shoppers see no difference in variety of caffeinated tea between a small block of 4 caffeinated tea products and 4 caffeinated teas immersed in presentation of in total 20 tea products.

Organising products into a separate block will stimulate shoppers to think these products are similar. If the shopper is on a certain mission, they search and absorb information according to that mission. The studies by Van Herpen and Bosmans show that shoppers perceive a larger variety when the assortment is organised based on their shopping mission. Only shoppers on that mission see a difference. They buy more often from the segment that corresponds with their mission and perceive lower variety in the other segments. While previously total size of the assortment was discussed, it becomes clear that the size of segments in relation to the shopping goal also has an impact. Only when the goal-related segment is sufficiently large a separate display leads to higher perceived variety than a mixed display. Returning to the challenge for groceries of promoting organic foods I conclude that if shoppers visit the store on an organic mission and the store assortment is large, the organic foods are better placed as a separate block as part of the category. The consideration of separate versus mixed blocks addressing certain shopping goals seems less of a challenge in online environments: Stores can apply filters so that after one or two clicks the shopper is led to the desired assortment that meets the goal. In addition to the question of mixing versus separating organic foods, retailers may consider placing all organic foods together within one department of the store. This is the approach that Carrefour took in their Planet hypermarket format. For shoppers who exclusively buy organic foods, this allows them to shop fast and conveniently. To identify if their shopping trips focus primarily on organic products, Carrefour could analyse transaction-level basket data. In my experience, in Western markets the majority of organic foods shoppers also buy non-organic products and placement within the regular aisle better answers their shopping needs.

Public Accountability

Shopping at a tablet or PC from home offers many conveniences such as 24/7 access, no car parking, relaxed couch and, not least, privacy; there are no other shoppers or staff that walk around, look over one's shoulder or even have a strong opinion of what shoppers buy. When on a shopping mission shoppers act differently when feeling observed. The concept of accountability describes situations in which shoppers know that their purchases are observed and they want to convey the right signal to others even when it comes to the purchase of everyday products. The researchers Ratner and Kahn (2002) asked themselves whether shoppers who perceive to be held accountable for their choices anticipate the opinion of others by choosing a different level of variety. And they do: Shoppers opt for more variety when they are observed.

Deeper Insight: Shoppers Choose Higher Variety Because They Wish to Be Perceived as More Rational or Inspirational

- To see how public accountability works Ratner and Kahn offered students a bag of five candies in the classroom, whereby a student could choose any combination so also five candies of the same type. Candies are a hedonistic type of product rather than utilitarian where rational evaluation would perhaps lead to one best option. Instead of asking everyone to come up to the front of the classroom they distributed pink and green papers on which students could write their choice. Students with the pink paper were asked to hand over their sheet to their neighbour with the green sheet who would then collect the bags of candies on their behalf. Ratner and Kahn found that students making their selection in public rather than in privacy chose significantly more types of candy (3.3 versus 2.7). One reason could be the belief that shoppers who enjoy a wide spectrum of products are perceived to be more interesting and creative people. Even though candy is a simple product and students did not even know what choice their neighbour made, they still felt the pressure to be perceived more positively by selecting a high variety. Students were also asked to rate their satisfaction with each candy. Students who made public selections switched away from their favourites and ended up choosing candies they preferred less.

- The reasons for opting for variety depend among others on personality traits. The aspect of personality that the researchers looked into was self-monitoring. If someone scores high on self-monitoring, they want to understand how others perceive their behaviour and next they try to consciously control and adapt. The researchers designed three kinds of scenarios with different levels of privacy: A private choice, a situation in which they were asked how their neighbour would perceive how interesting their choice was and finally they were asked to evaluate how rational was their choice.

  - The results showed that high self-monitors chose a significantly higher number of types of candy (2.9 versus 2.2) when they were told that others would rate them on how interesting their selection was compared to a private choice. If high self-monitors were told they would be rated on the degree of rationality of their choice, there was no difference.
  - In contrast, there was no difference for low self-monitors between a private choice and a public choice that would be rated on how interesting it was. However, low self-monitors chose a significantly higher number of varieties (3.2 versus 2.6) when they were asked how rational their choice was. Low self-monitors are concerned about how others perceive them as making consistent, principled choices and they think choosing a high variety is more rational.
  - All shoppers were also asked to assess how others perceived their choice on a range of descriptions. This showed that if they select a number of different types of candy, people expect their choices to be seen as more innovative, risk-seeking, favourable, interesting and creative. So, when choosing high variety, shoppers portray themselves as more open-minded people and they are inclined to increase the variety in public. Highly self-monitoring people who constantly adapt their behaviour choose a higher variety in public in order to be perceived as interesting and open-minded. On the other hand, low self-monitors choose higher varieties in public because they want to be perceived as rational decision-makers.

Public Justification

When shoppers know their choices are not only observed by others but they also need to explain their choices to them, the accountability becomes explicit justification. And a larger assortment makes justification more difficult. Let's say the shopper buys a new coffee machine, others in the household will certainly probe for explanation of the style and brand of the machine, let alone the type of coffee making such as filter or espresso. The shopper is most likely to do more research in advance, find expert advice from store staff or website and identify reasonably sound features that make it sound like a perfectly rational choice. The effect of justification depends on the retail context as Scheibehenne and his colleagues (2009) proved. Following an unrelated experiment, they offered participants the opportunity to give a donation of €1 that they had just earned to a certain charity. The researchers wanted to know if the effect of justification would change when participants experienced different levels of choice stress. They could choose a charity from a list of small, presumably less well-known German charities that listed 5, 40 or 80 names of charities together with a description of one sentence on their respective missions. If they wanted to donate a euro, they were asked to write down why they had chosen a certain charity. Scheibehenne and his colleagues found that the percentage of participants who donated decreased when the list of available charities became larger, respectively 88 per cent compared to 72 per cent and 74 per cent. Justification of a certain option is more difficult for shoppers in a large set than in a small set. This also becomes clear in the number of words that shoppers required to come up with their justification. The participants needed some 30 per cent more words to justify their choice from 40 or 80 charities compared to making their choice from 5 charities. Apparently, participants found it more difficult to describe their choices when the number of options increased.

In-Store Versus Out-of-Store Influence

Shoppers visit a store with given personalities, mood, aspirations and expertise. These characteristics are a given in advance of the shopping trip mix and they are mixed with the shopping trip in the retail context. Even if the retailer knows who is shopping, the next challenge for the retailer is to identify on what mission they are today: Do they use the retail touchpoint to buy or browse and what type of information do they need? The relationship of these variables before and during the shopping trip is described well in a model by Chandon and a group of researchers (2009) and shown in Image 6.2. This was

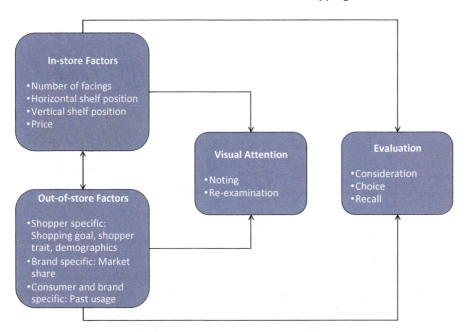

Image 6.2 Drivers of attention and evaluation at the point of purchase. Source: Chandon et al. (2009)

originally designed to understand if and how in-store marketing works, and it includes aspects like pricing. Though their starting point was not so much assortment management, they define in-store marketing with dimensions closely related to the management of assortment and merchandising, and therefore the model is interesting here as well. Their framework of attention and evaluation provides insights into the interrelations between what happens in-store and out-of-store. This sounds 'brick-and-mortarish' but the underlying factors resonate with the online world as well. They made a distinction between in-store factors such as number of facings and type of horizontal shelf position and out-of-store factors such as brand market share. They concluded that out-of-store factors have more impact on the consideration of certain products than on the attention of these products in the store.

The researchers collected the data on all these variables with the help of an eye-tracking study in the US. Shoppers made a choice from 12 brands of soap bars and 12 pain relievers. These products lent themselves well for the purposes of the eye-tracking study because they have a brick-shaped packaging that excludes effects of shape and size. As a result, participants focused on reading the brand name on the packaging. The research team alternated the level of the variables. The number of facings varied among 4, 8 and 12. In terms of shopping goal, the shoppers were given either a brand choice or a consideration goal.

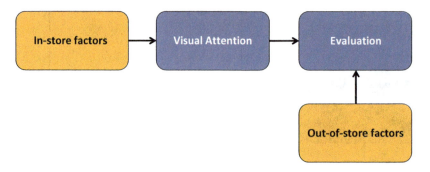

Image 6.3   Direct impact from out-of-store factors on evaluation. Based on Chandon et al. (2009)

In case of a brand choice, they were asked to tell the name of the brand they would buy. And when the planogram was off the screen, they also stated the brands they had considered. When given the consideration goal shoppers told first the names of the brands they would consider, and after browsing the planogram they stated the brand they would select. Products had either a regular price or a discounted price. The researchers were interested to know how all of these variables influenced both attention and evaluation. Visual attention was measured by taking the eye-tracking outcomes on noting (at least one fixation on the brand) and re-examination (the brand received at least two fixations). Evaluation was a combination of questions on recall, consideration and choice. The overall conclusion was that in-store factors first have to grab the shopper's attention and only indirectly influence evaluation. This is visualised in Image 6.3. So, merchandising and assortment changes first need to grab the shopper's attention before they are processed and lead to market share changes. Out-of-store factors like brand choice and market share impacted evaluation most.

Their study confirms many findings on assortment and merchandising discussed earlier but the beauty of this study is in the holistic framework and in the opportunity to identify the interrelationships and strength of individual components:

Out-of-Store Factors

- From all individual components there were two that had the most positive impact by far, both of which were out-of-store factors: Higher purchase frequency and higher brand market share.
- As expected, a regular user of the brand noticed and re-examined the brand more often than non-users.

- An increase of the number of facings had a larger impact on users of the brand than it had on non-users. The number of facings raised both consideration and choice of low market share brands.
- When the shopping goal was open in terms of brands shoppers ended up with larger evoked sets of brands than when the shopping goal was focused on a particular brand.
- Shoppers who searched value and made a trade-off between price and brand considered more brands and the number of facings had a more significant influence on them than it did on price- or brand-focused shoppers.
- Shoppers with a high education paid attention to fewer brands, but they remembered more brands. A higher number of facings influenced shoppers with higher education more. Apparently, they were more open to impulse decisions.
- Age of shoppers had no effect on noting; however, older shoppers considered fewer brands and responded less to changes in the number of facings.

In-Store Factors

- More facings for a brand generated higher attention and as a result higher evaluation. The impact on attention had a diminishing marginal return, whereas the number of facings influenced the evaluation dimensions in a linear way.
- There is no difference in outcomes between brands on the left or right side of the planogram. Being in the horizontal centre is much better for attention and evaluation than a location at the extremes of the shelf.
- Different pricing levels did not affect attention, though premium priced brands were recalled better and considered more often.

Factors Driving Choice Overload

After reading the detailed list of factors that play a role in the final shopping decisions the question comes up which factor has the most significant impact. Each single study that I discussed generates a piece of the puzzle. Chernev and a group of colleagues (2014) collected 51 studies representing more than 7200 participants that cast a clear view on what the image of the puzzle looks like. The researchers bundled the complex myriad of individual factors together into a framework with four explanatory factors (see Image 6.4). The factor with regard to the shopping mission was identified as most impactful.

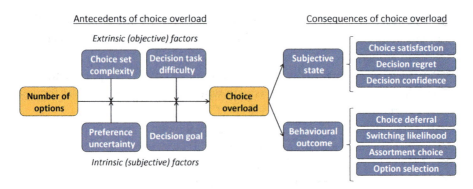

Image 6.4 Factors of choice overload. Source: Chernev et al. (2014)

Though their objective was to better understand drivers of choice overload, this relates to the balancing act that retailers perform when taking decisions on assortment and merchandising: Shoppers love variety and can assess the level of variety often by casting a quick glance but at times the complexity of the retail context and shopping moment exceeds the cognitive resources of the shopper. As a result, the shopper's emotions are affected (less choice satisfaction, decision regret, lower decision confidence) and/or they behave less favourably towards the decision at hand (choice deferral, more likely to switch to other stores/brands, select product less often). If shoppers were perfectly rational, a larger assortment would always make them more delighted; however, it does not.

Decision Task Difficulty

This is the first of two extrinsic factors that represent the products dimension and the retail environment. Decision task difficulty refers to the general, structural characteristics of the decision the shopper makes such as any limitation on available time, accountability towards others, the number of attributes per product, the way information is presented (text versus visuals) and the number of alternatives. The first two dimensions may need further explanation: Time constraints force shoppers to a less systematic, faster evaluation of options. And more severe time pressure makes shoppers rely on simple heuristics. Chernev and his colleagues look at time constraints as part of a structural characteristic of the decision problem. In working with retailers, I have personally associated this with the shopping goal to emphasise that the same product might be purchased on different trips. Finally, when shoppers are accountable for their choice, they generally prefer a larger assortment to make sure they get it right.

Choice Set Complexity

These are extrinsic aspects associated with the choice alternatives such as the presence of a dominant option, the overall attractiveness of alternatives, alignability of the options and complementarity. When there is an alternative available that is superior to all other options, shoppers are more inclined to make a choice. In a similar manner, the addition of an inferior option makes the dominant option shine even more. Adding complementary options makes it more difficult to choose.

Preference Uncertainty

Intrinsic factors relate to shopper dimensions. This intrinsic factor describes the extent to which shoppers have certain preferences before they decide and the level of understanding that allows them to prioritise the benefits of the options they compare such as product expertise and if they have an ideal optimum attribute level. Should shoppers have less knowledge on the attributes and the spectrum of levels, they defer making choices in large assortments, whereas shoppers with much expertise on the decision at hand defer their choice in small assortments.

Decision Goal

This intrinsic factor refers to the cognitive effort that shoppers make and try to minimise such as decision intent (buying versus browsing) and decision focus (choosing among types of assortments versus selecting one specific option from an assortment). Shoppers obtain fun from browsing but if it leads to actual purchases, large assortments may not be preferred. Shoppers approach the assortment without the goal to learn more about the available options and/or about their own beliefs, and experience larger assortments quicker as stressful. If shoppers focus on the choice among assortments, they do not need to evaluate each alternative and weigh the benefits against each other, which makes the cognitive load smaller.

Chernev and his colleagues concluded that all four factors contribute significantly to explaining choice overload. The decision goal which describes the cognitive effort for their product selection process is the most important explanation, closely followed by the extrinsic choice set complexity that refers to the difficulty that the aspects of alternatives give to the shopper. Decision task difficulty and preference uncertainty are equally less decisive factors on choice overload. In short, it means that if the task and structure of the assortment given the time are difficult, if the alternatives are complex and if shoppers are uncertain about their preferences, they experience more stress and choice overload. Furthermore, the researchers concluded that the outcome variables satisfaction, decision confidence, choice deferral, regret and switching likelihood are mutually exchangeable to measure choice overload. Assortment size proved to be not a reliable measure of choice overload. Assortment size had a significant effect on choices that shoppers made; however, the size of the effect is subject to many context factors in the retail environment. This is aligned with the other evidence that emphasises that not the actual number of products but the perceived variety influences product and store choice decisions.

Important Learnings from This Chapter

- Shoppers who are in browsing mode feel better when the assortment is perceived to be small. If shoppers are more in action mode, they enjoy increased variety.
- Deciding among product options is experienced as more complex than deciding among (sub)categories, and therefore large assortments are less favourable to product-level shopping modes. Inserting a dominant, well-known option helps solve this.
- If the shopping goal and the external assortment are congruent, shoppers perceive a lower overall variety of the complete category assortment, though they see more of the product they buy and perceive a higher variety in the subcategory.
- Shopping goal is more impactful on perception of variety than internally held beliefs.
- Shoppers who select in public rather than in privacy are inclined to increase the variety. Highly self-monitoring people who constantly adapt their behaviour choose a higher variety in public in order to be perceived as interesting and open-minded. On the other hand, low self-monitors choose higher varieties in public because they want to be perceived as rational decision-makers.
- If shoppers need to justify their decisions to others they prefer to select from a smaller assortment.
- Out-of-store factors such as brand and shopper aspects impact recall, consideration and choice of products most.
- The shopping goal is probably the most decisive factor in explaining shopping decisions.

References

Chandon, P., Hutchinson, J. W., Bradlow, E. T., & Young, S. H. (2009). Does In-Store Marketing Work? Effects of the Number and Position of Shelf Facings and Brand Attention and Evaluation at the Point of Purchase. *Journal of Marketing, 73*(6), 1–17.

Chernev, A. (2006). Decision Focus and Consumer Choice Among Assortments. *Journal of Consumer Research, 33,* 50–59.

Chernev, A., Böckenholt, U., & Goodman, J. (2014). Choice Overload: A Conceptual Review and Meta-Analysis. *Journal of Consumer Psychology, 25*(2), 333–358.

Gao, L., & Simonson, I. (2015). The Positive Effect of Assortment Size on Purchase Likelihood: The Moderating Influence on Decision Order. *Journal of Consumer Psychology, 26*(4), 542–549.

Morales, A., Kahn, B. E., McAlister, L., & Broniarczyk, S. M. (2005). Perceptions of Assortment Variety: The Effects of Congruency Between Consumers' Internal and Retailers' External Organization. *Journal of Retailing, 81*(2), 159–169.

Ratner, R. K., & Kahn, B. E. (2002). The Impact of Private Versus Public Consumption on Variety-Seeking Behaviour. *Journal of Consumer Research, 29*(2), 246–257.

Scheibehenne, B., Greifeneder, R., & Todd, P. M. (2009). What Moderates the Too-Much-Choice Effect? *Psychology & Marketing, 26*(3), 229–253.

Van Herpen, E., & Bosmans, A. (2017). Arranging the Assortment to Arouse Choice: Effects of Goal Relevant Assortment Organization on Food Choice and Variety Perceptions. *Food Quality and Preference, 64,* 192–204.

7

Retailer Assortment and Merchandising Plan

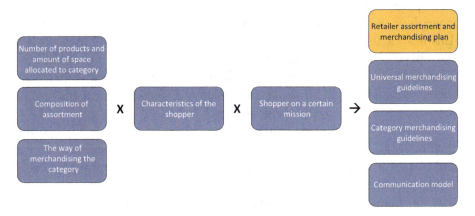

Image 7.1 Integrated assortment and merchandising model

Learning Objectives

- Ensure that the desired retail brand image, the target group and overall retail objectives are available ingredients for giving the retail assortments their own signature.
- Derive perspectives for assortment and merchandising objectives from various functional areas in the organisation.
- Create a phased approach for building assortments that combines online and brick-and-mortar shopping decisions.

© The Author(s) 2019
C. Berkhout, *Assortment and Merchandising Strategy*,
https://doi.org/10.1007/978-3-030-11163-2_7

- Apply the assortment role framework to drive decisions on number of products, number of brands and type of brands.

The previous chapters laid a foundation of knowledge on types of responses from shoppers on size and composition of assortment, the way of organising products and how shoppers have different needs depending on their shopping goals. Retailers need to make trade-offs as to how shoppers perceive them. For example, an apple from a local farm may have less taste but also result in less environmental impact compared to an imported apple. A retailer needs to decide if both types of apples are listed or only one is permitted. This means the retailer needs to decide what they think is more important for their brand name, taste or environment. Even if there is sufficient space to list both apple varieties there might be a minimum required level of taste and a maximum to the accepted environmental impact for the retailer. As a consequence, retailers are required to define and measure these aspects. Each time retailers need to make their own decisions and, in this way, shape the assortment proposition. This is what this chapter is about. An essential guide in these decisions is a description of the desired shopper target groups, their needs, moods, motivations and behaviour. This is easier said than done, not only because these take energy to measure well, but also because many retailers have the tendency not to exclude anyone from their target groups.

Sometimes I wonder how much choice retailers actually have in choosing their categories when they operate in a certain sector. A shoe store has brown and black leather shoes, low and high heels for women. An optical retailer is expected to carry eyewear for men, women and children. And then to think that the frames are often the same anyway, just merchandised twice as a response to shoppers who want to make sure they wear glasses of their own gender. Grocery stores are expected to offer milk, bread and meat. And in terms of assortment size brick-and-mortar retailers are at a depressive setback compared to online stores. And from an online perspective, why should a retailer spend much effort on assortment selection when there are no space restrictions in large, possibly even outsourced warehouses? Still, there is so much to win by being different. Large online retailers such as Amazon and large online groceries are successful mainly because of their guarantee that their product can be ordered rather than through their product expertise. Their positioning is often based on ordering convenience, delivery times and accessible customer service and they compete heavily on doing things each time a bit faster than the other. What delivery mode will follow after city-bikes, vans and drones? Rockets? They do not differentiate based on the type of categories they carry or the pre-selection of products they make. They just have it all, which is a true shopper benefit, let's be clear about that. However, this does leave the door open for small webstores and brick-and-mortar retailers to focus on specific categories (or customer groups). And as a matter of fact, the focus on a set of categories or within categories could be a winner from a shopper perspective because shoppers do not always appreciate large assortments: They are short of time and suffer choice stress. Therefore, brick-and-mortar discount groceries such as Lidl are successful with an assortment that is small but is also of high quality and heterogeneous and surprising in the seasonal offer. Do-it-yourself (DIY) retailer Hornbach offers an amazing 55,000 products, twice as large as other retailers in the Netherlands. Once you are in-store the basket is large, however, Dutch shoppers are not prepared to drive more than 20 minutes for their construction shopping trip, and certainly not when they lack just one more tin of paint to complete the job. This creates opportunities for smaller city stores for do-it-yourself that focus on instant servicing of the largest do-it-yourself shopping trips. At the same time, large ordering screens in the city stores enable shoppers to select the bags of mortar and wooden window frames online without having to carry them. City stores of DIY retailer Praxis offer free services such as transport bikes and tools to carry out the DIY job inside the store itself.

Introduce Rigour in Retail Process

The purpose of the assortment and merchandising plan is for retailers to shape their own signature. At the same time, best practices, academic studies and frameworks are instrumental in doing so in an efficient manner. Launching a new product should not be seen as a project but as a continuous process of eliminating outdated assortment, shopper research, testing, implementation and evaluations from shoppers. In addition, some shopper behaviour is automatic and universal and allows for generic principles to be applied to the assortment and merchandising process. The discussed academic findings and models may give the impression that creating an assortment offer is a very rational process. However, they provide a great starting point for the retailer's own journey and offer frameworks to structure and inspire their thoughts. More rigour and thought are welcome in retail. However, in the daily routine of retail practice, I see more emotion than ratio applied. The organisation culture of detail and focus on buying and negotiation, the daily stress of category managers having to meet promotion deadlines, the administrative burden and the communication challenges between siloed departments and the growing dependence on long supply chains all make the process more human and pragmatic in real life. I realise that in retail, practitioners need to be able to respond fast to shopper demands, which does not leave much time for rethinking of current ways of doing. In addition, margins are often so thin that they do not welcome too much experimentation for innovation. However, when practitioners feel they are in an organisation where they reinvent the wheel regularly, I think there is a strong call to restructure the assortment and merchandising process and challenge the current shopper wisdoms in the organisation with fresh practices and academic insights. I sometimes wonder for whom I would like to create my local grocery store offer, a chef or a rocket builder. The chef chooses the ingredients based on the season and depending on mood will add more or less (or none?) to the pie. The oven is a bit worn and the numbers have disappeared over the years, so temperature setting is an approximation. The quality of the end result is variable, and this romantic description tickles my taste buds. The good news is this kitchen will produce numerous innovations. On the other hand, the rocket builder will carefully measure and test each ingredient. Most likely there are two kitchens (and perhaps a secret testing facility underground?) available should one of them unexpectedly stop working. After a carefully thought-out process, there will be an official launch date to which organisation dignitaries are invited. There are no surprises and customers get a high-quality cake that can be reproduced at constant quality. Building assortments as a chef or rocket builder both have their benefits and probably somewhere in the middle is the best recipe. This chapter first addresses briefly the impact of the brand positioning on assortment and merchandising decisions. Next, we look separately into elements of assortment and merchandising that retailers include in their strategic and tactical plans. They are illustrated in a combined way in online and brick-and-mortar examples to make sure that visual merchandising concepts are applied to meet the ambitioned shopper perceptions.

Know the Desired Retail Brand Image

Before category managers start working out their assortment and merchandising plans, they should know the desired brand image. Indeed, this is the starting point for any retail activity, whether they are related to building the supply chain or creating marketing communication campaigns. The first step when transmitting the brand message is getting to know the retail target groups and obtaining profiles of each of these. The target groups are not necessarily described in socio-demographic terms, but it could be more abstract and need-based. While the target groups are considered a given input to the assortment and merchandising plan, I observe that it is not a given that retail management communicates to the category managers effectively who the target groups are, and to which extent deviations to the target group are permitted. The more management leaves the target shopper definition open, the more category managers give their own, personal interpretation to the assortment they purchase. I observed category managers at a Western European non-foods retailer travelling to Asia without any briefing apart from a maximum level of buying budget. Based on their intuition and local networks, they were able to spot fashionable products that became very successful. However, there were also dramatic failures. Some of these products had been stocked for many years. No alarm bells went off because the buyers were perceived 'kings' in the organisation and because it is not unusual for some non-foods retailers to have zero rotation for a product in a certain year. The scary observation I made was that each new category manager tried to address the issue with new products from Asia. For category managers this is often thought to be the most visible way to make impact. Part of the new purchases again contributed to the non-selling stock.

Other essential ingredients for the strategic assortment decisions are descriptions of the desired brand personality and the functional and emotional benefits that the retail brand offers to shoppers. Like any other marketing instrument, assortment needs to contribute to the retail brand positioning. This can be explained with the help of the example of Rituals, an international retail brand for luxurious home and personal care products operating hundreds of stores in some 30 countries. Based on my observations in-store and online, my guess is that one of the personality traits of the Rituals brand is 'calm & relaxed' and one of the benefits to the shopper is 'innovative aromas from the world'. When it comes to assortment, the personality trait of calmness could be actioned upon through a limited assortment in order not to overwhelm and by product packaging with much open space. The benefit of innovative aromas could be found in the promise to launch one new product line per quarter and to give name and labels to private label products that remind shoppers of the exotic heritage. These desired brand features should find their way to all elements of the assortment programme such as quality level and share of private label versus national brands. The best-case scenario is when all categories and products resonate 100 per cent with the complete list of brand features (both brand personality traits and brand benefits); however, in practice a product will score well on most but not all of the selected brand features.

Best practice of a retailer that carefully selects categories and products based on its brand positioning is US pharmacy retailer CVS Health (2018). Their purpose is 'helping people on their path to better health' and they operate based on the values of 'innovation, collaboration, caring, integrity and accountability'. The retailer adopted a new strategy appealing to more health-conscious shoppers

(Wall Street Journal 2017). They added 'Health' to the corporate name and revised assortment accordingly. The first step was to ban all tobacco from their stores in 2014, which cost them $2 billion in annual revenue. In 2017, CVS Health moved the main aisle for sweet and salty snacks from the front of the store to the centre of the store and replaced the open space with healthier snacks. Not all snacks disappeared to less attractive spots: Candy bars are still sold at the checkout. One year in advance of bans by the authorities (FDA) taking effect the company stopped selling foods with artificial trans-fats. Some soft drinks were rationalised from the cabinet and the remainder was given less preferential space in favour of beverages with natural ingredients. Personal care products with excessive chemicals were taken off shelf as were sunscreen products with a protection level below 15 that do not offer people sufficient protection from cancer. CVS Health provides an excellent example of how assortment and merchandising measures are fully consistent with (a courageous strategic shift in) retail brand positioning.

Formulate the Assortment and Merchandising Objectives

Retail brand image (here simplified to brand personality and benefits), the desired target groups and the overall retail objectives are all necessary inputs for category managers to construct their assortment and merchandising plans. The relationships among these aspects are visualised in Image 7.2. Management in retail should also give direction to assortment and merchandising objectives. The category-specific objectives will be an integral part of the assortment and merchandising plan; however, I found it helpful when management communicates clearly what their expectations are. For example, category managers like to

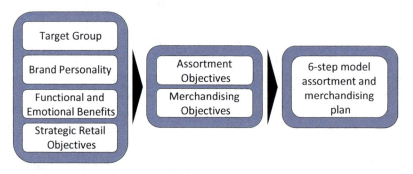

Image 7.2 Link between retail brand strategy and assortment and merchandising plan

know which specific competitor management perceives as most threatening and for which they wish to build an assortment that stops shoppers from switching away. Knowing those two or three key competitors enables category managers to deliver more focused outcomes. It is unavoidable that objectives change over time, but communication is crucial: Knowing whether management expects more revenue or gross margin has a serious impact on product selection. I would encourage retailers to formulate the assortment and merchandising objectives from different angles.

Assortment Objectives

- Competition: More or better than a certain evoked set of retailers, benchmarking of pricing
- Financial: Cost of goods, investment in stock, return on capital, return on sales, contribution level, revenue per metre
- Supply chain: Speed to market, flexibility
- Suppliers: Level of exclusivity, mutual dependence, local versus national versus international, long-term contracts or variance based on seasonality or auction prices
- Shopper: Perceived uniqueness, breadth and depth to which shopper needs are met, enjoyable shopping experience
- Retail brand: Quality level, sustainability requirements, share of private label, share of fresh versus packed products versus services

The assortment objectives should form a coherent part with the other elements of the retail marketing mix so that the shopper understands and appreciates the complete retail offer. Making sure the assortment is right across shopping goals and tailored to the context and positioning of the retail brand takes in-depth knowledge and experience with shopping behaviour and brand building.

Merchandising Objectives

Even when following principles derived from the assortment structure, shopper characteristics and type of shopping goal, the same products can be merchandised in innumerable ways according to the perspective of the retailer. Retail organisations make their own prioritisations as to which merchandising objectives are most important to them. Merchandising objectives can be formulated from five different perspectives:

- Supply chain

  - Availability (no or less chance of out-of-stock, always visually present)
  - Costs to transport and stock item throughout value chain

- Financial

  - Category revenue
  - Category profits (percentage or cash margin)
  - Category rotation
  - Return on capital
  - Increase category purchase, frequency, cross- and upsell

- Operations

  - Convenience to maintain (number of hours)
  - Fast to build and carry out changes
  - Degree to which merchandising tools are universal and easy to build

- Shopper

  - Overall satisfaction and pleasure
  - Choice efficiency for shopper (no complexity, limited time investment)
  - Ambition to increase perceived variety
  - Ambition to increase knowledge about category

- Retail brand

  - Enhance the retail brand/store image
  - Support private label development
  - Contribute to enjoyable shopping experience
  - Emphasis on price strategy

Some merchandising tactics tap into these objectives in a coherent manner and they cross-fertilise in different areas. For example, shelf-ready packaging for a new private label concept reduces cost of handling, improves category profits and supports the retail brand positioning. At times retailers need to make difficult trade-offs: The supply chain department may want to claim more shelf space in order to guarantee availability, which has adverse effects on available space for new, innovative varieties. For commercial reasons retailers may want to insert new private label launches next to the leading A-brand though this may confuse shoppers. Placing more expensive products on top of the screen view may impact profits positively but when shoppers do not take the effort to scroll down they may doubt about the overall price attractiveness of the online retailer in the category. Setting priorities in merchandising should not happen in isolation. The selected merchandising objectives and their relative importance should be aligned together with other elements of the retail marketing mix such as breadth and width of the assortment and pricing objectives into one coherent retail marketing programme.

Impact of Category Role

Based on the overall retail strategy and the selected target shoppers generic merchandising objectives are formulated which then need to be specified on category level in more detail. Knowing which categories need more merchandising investment is an essential follow-up of the assignment of category roles and is part of the retail strategy plan. The category roles define the playroom for each retail marketing mix element. On a directional basis, Table 7.1 shows what it could mean for destination, routine and convenience categories.

The shopper journey will have a diversity of online and offline touchpoints and the assortment and merchandising retail marketing mix needs to reflect this. In Tables 7.2 and 7.3 there are two examples that provide an illustration

Table 7.1 Category role drives assortment and merchandising

	Destination	Routine	Convenience
Assortment	• Wide and deep • Exclusive national brands and suppliers • All brands available • Multi-layered private label • High innovation, tapping into newest trends • High quality	• Wide but not deep in brick-and-mortar • Wide and deep online • Standard private label targeting the brand leader • Focus on some brands • Meet standard quality levels	• Not wide, not deep • Focus on one leading national brand • High quality
Merchandising	• High space versus sales share • Decorative design elements • Story-telling and images • Entertainment • Tables	• Space in accordance with sales • Highly structured • Volume and mass offer • Racks and shelves	• Low space share • Focus on visibility at service counter or basket filler before (online) checkout • Trust in appeal of product packaging itself • Little entertainment

Table 7.2 Fictitious example of category role differences for online retail store

	Destination	Routine	Convenience
Number of products	20 per cent more than brick-and-mortar	Same as key online competitor	10 per cent less than key online competitor
Supply	Mix of own stock, third party and market place	Focus on own stock	Only third party
Products per view	6	8	10
Landing page	Deals on landing page only from destination group	Scroll to offer at bottom of page	Not on landing page
Navigation	Mentioned first in navigation bar Each product group mentioned in detail	Mentioned after destination groups	Mentioned last
Filtering	Detailed filtering options	Limited filtering options	Limited filtering options
Content	Both inspiration and explanation: Always video, downloadable manuals, full product description in words, encouragement through shopper reviews	List of main specifications to allow easy comparison	Link to third-party website

of the type of assortment and merchandising criteria that retailers use to make a distinction by type of category role. For clarification purposes online and brick-and-mortar are presented here as two different stores.

Elements of Assortment Plan

A practical six-step model for assortment and merchandising management helps retailers to combine decisions on online and brick-and-mortar and to use a shopper perspective when making trade-offs between assortment size and perception of variety. In my vision, choices on assortment are inseparable from those on merchandising. This holistic approach drives decisions on:

1. Core and related categories
2. Amount of space and products
3. Online and brick-and-mortar
4. Star products: Icon, traffic builder, key value item (KVI)
5. Brand hierarchy
6. Service level

Table 7.3 Fictitious example of category role differences for brick-and-mortar store

	Destination	Routine	Convenience
Number of products	20 per cent more than main brick-and-mortar competitor	Same as key competitor	10 per cent less than key competitor
Location in-store	Accessible in main walking aisle Some placed at entrance of store	Visible from main walking aisle Often promoted from end-gondola	At checkout or from customer service counter
Communication	Large visual above shelf If applicable, through service counter Shelf hangers with product info	No additional visuals or product info allowed. Exception when in promo displays	No in-store communication
Private label	Always separate block for private label regardless of shopper decision tree Always on eye-level Always more space share than leading national brand	Private label placed right next to national brand	No private label, focus on one national brand per category
Merchandising material	Merchandising material placed on floor and against wall that together create a world Wood and metal Special materials and shapes allowed	Mostly found in floor merchandising material Metal	Integrated in design of checkout or service counter
Shelf type	Diversity of shapes and colours is allowed Shelves may hang flat or at gliding degree	Always contains basket with bulk presentation Only hanging flat Maximum height top shelf 170 cm	Limited depth of shelves to limit storage
Innovation	10 per cent of revenue originates from products launched this year. A-brands are removed in favour of innovative private labels	Private label alternatives available of all successful product launches by national brands within two months	Rely on national brands
Number of planogram amendments	Large changes allowed up to six times a year	One large planogram change per year plus two small ones	One small change per year

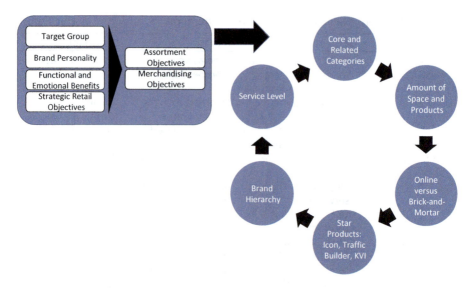

Image 7.3   Six-step model for assortment and merchandising management

Each of the steps is discussed in detail below. The assortment and merchandising plan is built on generic shopper truths and may be composed of the same ingredients for each retailer. However, organisational decision culture, the desired retail image, the selected target group and category specifics will make the plan different from others (Image 7.3).

Core and Related Categories

First retailers should define which categories and products belong to their core assortment and which categories or products are less relevant for the retail brand. Making this distinction helps ensure the communication to the shopper is focused and category managers know where to invest their budget and time. Although retailers may name them differently, retailers often use four types of category roles:

- Destination categories differentiate the retailer from others and are a primary reason why shoppers visit the store. These are the categories the retailer wants to be famous for and at the same time generate profits.
- Routine categories are frequently part of the shopper's basket and shoppers expect the retailer to sell them. They are very important for store traffic and cash flow.

- Convenience categories meet the shopper's need for one-stop shopping but shoppers do not have the retailer top of mind for these categories. These could also be services that the shopper may buy in addition to the core category offer.
- Seasonal categories reinforce the desired retail brand image and are important for the retailer profits. Seasonal categories could become so important for the retail brand that they become seasonal destination categories, whereas others remain more tactical seasonal categories.

In the last few decades, retailers have always been searching the boundaries with regard to what they 'ought' to sell according to the channel they operate in. I have seen DIY stores selling bikes and drugstores selling toys where categories have no consumption or shopping affinity to the core offering. When more channels act in the same way and towards each other, channel blurring is created. For example, a book store starts offering coffee and cake and a bar starts selling magazines. The reason might be excitement creation for shoppers or it might have been a desperate attempt to generate revenue. And other retail brands such as Action, Tchibo and Dollar General are positioned on this theme of making each store visit an entertaining surprise with products shoppers have not seen there before. Even in such cases retailers should realise that the brand stretch becomes wider and the brand becomes less famous for a certain core assortment. A fashion retailer may decide to leverage its trendy image among their shoppers to decorative products such as chill cushions and candles and funky gadgets. Space might be reserved for having a latte and checking mail on free Wi-Fi, all accessible without having to browse for the core category of fashion. Each of the product categories meets different need-states. Category managers need direction from management as to which need-states are the most important to be met. This could be symbolised with a pyramid where the target product category is at the bottom and represents

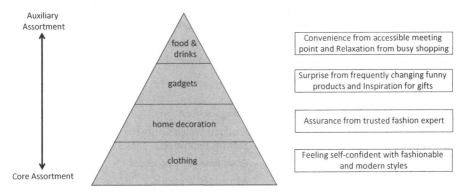

Image 7.4 Example core versus auxiliary assortment by benefit for fashion retailer

the core of the retailer proposition. Assortment size is likely to become smaller at each step to the top of the pyramid (Image 7.4 shows the relationship between type of assortment and shopper benefits in an example for a fashion retailer).

A final but often overlooked remark is that the definition of categories should be shopper based. This sounds more logical than seen in practice. I worked with a home décor retailer that grouped products by material so glass tableware with glass vases, and wicker chairs with wicker bins. In emerging countries where suppliers provide field merchandising support, the planograms are often divided by supplier so that each supplier can give its own, branded twist to the category definition. Another pitfall might be that the products are organised by responsibility of the category managers or by historic definitions of market research companies. Instead, I encourage retailers to think about the consumption context first. There are five steps in defining the category, as shown in Image 7.5 (ECR Europe, 1997).

When applying Image 7.5 for defining the category, the retailer starts at the centre and adds products step-by-step. I can illustrate this with an example. First, the retailer could define the need, for example, 'clean teeth'. Products that satisfy this need are toothpaste, tooth picks, tooth brushes. A substitute could be chewing gum or mint leaves that stimulate saliva production that cleans the teeth. A complimentary product could be a travel kit for the toothbrush. An associated product is dental health insurance. This way of thinking on category definition ensures that there is a focus on the real consumption need and that all sorts of competition are not overlooked. Once the category has been defined in the broadest perspective, the retailer can decide to meet all consumption needs through all their formats, or they can decide to leave part of the consumer demand to competition. After defining the category and products that fit the category need, the retailer may apply filters to reduce the scope of the category in a structured manner. There are several reasons for this simplification. First of all, the retailer may decide the principal need is satisfied in another category. Other considerations to remove products from the category definition are the complexity to manage the remaining products together, the lack of insight on category potential because of lack of market data and measurability and, finally, the assessment by retailers of their strengths compared to those of competitors.

Image 7.5   Defining the category. Based on ECR Europe (1997)

Amount of Space and Products

For all categories it should be clear how many products are available and how much space is allocated to both online and brick-and-mortar stores. For most retailers the total amount of physical space is a given in the mid-term and estimates for number of products per category are given within this scope. This may be amended in an iterative way when the type of merchandising and organisation mode is known. This is the moment that the retailer defines the breadth of the assortment (the number of categories each serving distinct shopper needs) and the depth of assortment (the number of segments that fulfil the same shopping need and the number of single products).

In most cases, the retailer disposes of historical sales data that will guide in decision-making. If a brick-and-mortar retailer works with planograms for cereals with five different bay sizes it can calculate if the category sales level off when adding a bay and at which point further expansion of space does not result in more category revenue. The calculated revenue/square metre can thus be compared among categories to define an optimum balance. Similar thinking can be applied to online retailing but with so many more opportunities in terms of personalisation, measurement accuracy and speed of analysis.

Online and Brick-and-Mortar

Directly related to the amount of space and products is the question of where the shopper encounters the assortment offer. Strictly speaking this is a question of distribution; however, knowing where shopper demand occurs and how much space is allocated to each category is now closely connected to assortment decisions with the rise of online. Also, in terms of supply chain all sorts of combinations occur within the same category: Direct delivery from supplier warehouses, safety stock managed by third-party brokers, direct delivery by retailers to shoppers' homes. They allow category managers to carry an almost unlimited number of products. The questions that a retailer needs to answer are:

- Where does the shopper expect to buy the category, and what are the shifts: On the website, mobile device, brick-and-mortar store?
- What are the benefits of each phase of the customer journey such as product information search, payment and delivery for these three touchpoints?
- Will the retailer offer the same categories online and in brick-and-mortar store, or are they different? Why?

- Within each category what are the differences in number and in type of products sold between online and brick-and-mortar?

One jeans retailer may decide to focus on their assortment in brick-and-mortar stores and another jeans retailer may offer the same assortment through various touchpoints. Each retailer makes their own decisions on assortment as a result of shopper trends, competition and internal capabilities. The possibility to offer millions of products online is beyond the real understanding of any shopper or professional. Helping shoppers to understand what they are looking for might actually be the first step. Next, retailers can help navigate shoppers to specific formats of the retail brand; one of them could be online. This phase of assortment decisions should be rerun in an iterative way to ensure that the retail format takes on the right role for product discovery, comparison, buying, consumption and sharing.

Star Products

The definition of category roles steers the internal decision-making and in order to make sure it does not remain an internal, and potentially abstract, exercise, I think it is wise to single out certain products that will drive traffic to the store and/or are perfect examples of what the retail brand stands for. The selected products focus the communication to the shopper what the intended retail brand is and what assortment is offered. These are a few types:

- An icon. For fashion store Everlane, it could be a basic undershirt that is a symbol of the perfect, constant quality and values of simplicity the retail brand searches. For an organic food store, it could be an ugly but edible pumpkin that tells the trade-offs to be made in sustainability in one image. The icon product could be highly rotating, but it does not have to be, as long as it creates excitement and enhances the retail brand image.
- A traffic builder. Not necessarily the products that directly support the retail brand. Some products or categories are so-called traffic builders that are part of the typical offer shoppers find in that channel and drive people to stores with the help of promotions. For grocery stores it could be beer, bananas or chicken filet, for pharmacies this could be diapers, for online department stores this could be a summer dress. If the traffic builder belongs to the core assortment, the promotion will sponsor the retailer's price image. In case the retailer normally does not carry the category, the traffic builder has the sole function of letting people visit the store and sell other products than promoted.

- A Key Value Item (KVI). When shoppers buy significantly more of a product if the price is decreased the product is said to be price elastic. These products qualify to become key value items: Single products of which the shopper is both price aware and buys more of if the price is decreased. These are the products for which retailers scour the Internet to find out which price competition offers.

Brand Hierarchy

This represents the number and sort of brands that the retailer offers. The desired brand image will help answer questions on how many brands shoppers like and the quality level. Special attention should be given to the sourcing and development of private label as they reinforce the retail brand image, offer counter-balance towards suppliers of A-brands and often create high relative profit margins. Much like there is not one type of supplier brand, there are also different types of private label each with its own objective: Value brands competing with discounters, standard label targeted at supplier brands, premium private label ranges and specialty ranges such as organic or free from. Adding more complexity are national brands that are exclusively sold at the retailer.

Good Better Best

A helpful approach to start thinking about the assortment structure is to keep the rule of thumb of 'good better best' in mind and to find out at which pricing points shoppers obtain a different value perception from the product. For example, research may show that shoppers perceive wine below €3 as cheap, between €3 and €7 as standard and above €7 as excellent. With a clear image in mind of the type of shoppers retailers would like to attract, they determine the number of products and per price/quality range and type of brand. In a typical category, shoppers find one or a few products at entry-level pricing, the majority of the category offer at median price level (often with broad variety from national brands [NB] and the most favoured items copied by private label), and some premium-priced specialty products. When visualising this on two axes of price versus number of products, an onion-shaped figure appears, as shown in Image 7.6. Again, this is not a prescription but a helpful approach to start building assortment and to benchmark with competition. Retailers may choose to only operate on one pricing level such as discounters mostly do. Food discounters such as Aldi and Lidl are expanding their assortment with national brands so that some of their categories get a pyramid shape. All kinds of shapes may arise.

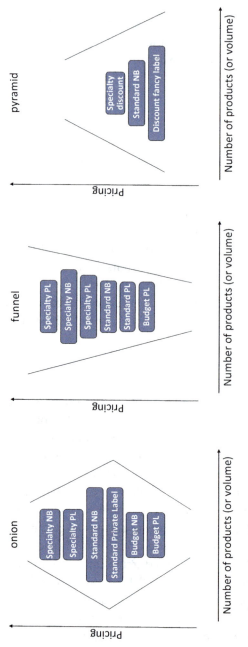

Image 7.6   Category brand hierarchies

When the retailer thinks the category is mature and does not wish to compete on price with competitors, it may choose to offer more variety on higher price levels. Investment in innovation may lead to exclusive variety in high-quality private label ranges. The visualised outcome looks like a funnel (Image 7.6).

Assortment Role Framework

Not all categories require private label. The assortment role framework helps retailers work out how many and which types of brands are needed for each category. The starting point is the assessment of the actual variety offered in each category as measured by the number of products, the number attributes and attribute levels. This drives the enjoyment of shoppers in the category. For them, the more variety the better as more shopping needs are potentially met, though preferably products are organised in a neat manner. Retailers could work with data from their existing assortment, which steers the allocation of resources across categories, or the retailer could work with data on a range of competitors and market channel data, which creates a vision of what the brand hierarchy could look like in the future. Apart from actual and desired variety, another important driver for a retailer to push more products and brands into a category is when more profits can be made. This could be measured through the added value per category: The average consumer retail price excluding VAT minus the net purchase price (as much as possible supplier conditions are considered as well). Plotting categories according to their level of variety and category value contribution delivers four quadrants, which is shown in Image 7.7.

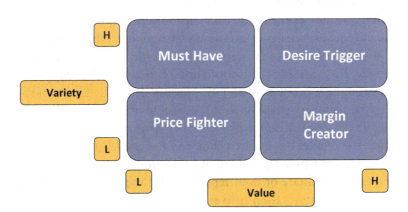

Image 7.7   Assortment role framework

The implications from the assortment role framework for the brand hierarchy are different by type of assortment role:

- Must Have: This category brings in little profit but as shoppers' need for variety is high, retailers are encouraged to expand private label in an effort to increase the category margin. Indeed, private label could be introduced on value, standard and premium level.
- Desire Trigger: The shopper finds a great offer of private label on all price levels here too. However, this is accompanied by many national (both A- and B-) brands. So total assortment size is substantial. What could also be different here is that the retailers are active innovators.
- Margin Creator: The retailer offers a limited number of A-brands. Private label is launched to compete against the leading national supplier brand.
- Price Fighter: Not much money is made here. One A-brand is sufficient and if the category is commoditised this could be replaced by a (value) private label. Retailers could also attempt to offer one A-brand and a more premium private label in order to gain more from this category.

Service Level

Some categories need more personal attention and communication than others either because the category comes with intrinsic shopping hurdles or because they promote the retail brand best. Take, for example, the bread category. A grocery store has the option of offering this through pre-packed bread in self-service, unpacked with self-service slicing machine, pre-baked delivered and sold over the counter, baked in-store and sold over the counter, vending machines outside the store and a combination of all of these. Depending on the desired image and capabilities, different service levels are possible. A footwear retailer could show a few models and deliver personalised service with qualified sales assistants or they could rely more on self-service, for example, by providing full information on shoes on the shopper's mobile phone, attaching a product label with product description to each shoe and ensuring the complete stock of sizes is available on shelf. Each mode has its own impact on shopper experience, category space and store profits. In other situations, the retailer has less of a choice, for example, prescription drugs in a pharmacy or the rental department in a DIY store. Through communication the retailer can facilitate or even replace staff: Product descriptions, reviews and other online information help shoppers search and get prepared for the actual in-store sales. Signage either with product information or inspirational messages should be considered at an early phase of the assortment and merchandising process as it influences the performance of products and impacts the number of staff needed either in call centres or in-store, and because any type of communication requires space online or on shelf. In summary, category managers decide on the service level by determining the level of personal attention and (online and in-store) communication. In order to reach that decision they work out three steps:

1. From a retail brand perspective: Describe the desired shopper experience and the actions performed by the shopper. What impression will the retail context leave on shoppers?
2. From a shopper perspective: Describe the actions performed by the shopper in the retail context. Is it pleasant and useful to perform them (here)? How much and what type of information does the shopper require, now or at a different moment?
3. From a retail employee perspective: Describe the actions performed by the employee in the retail context. Is it pleasant and useful to perform them (here)? How much and what type of information does the employee require, now or at a different moment?

Great Ways to Position the Retail Brand Based on Assortment and Merchandising

Mixing and shaping these decisions will define the assortment profile of the retail brand. And what that may look like has been described in an inspiring manner by Floor (2006). In his book *Branding a Store*, he provides a great framework for positioning retail brands. He makes a distinction among brands focused on range, price, convenience and experience. Brands can no longer afford to perform well on just one of these four positioning attributes. In fact, they need to compete at least on a qualifying level though preferably even better on a competitive, supporting or differentiating level. Retailers that choose range as their most important attribute open up several paths that they can tread. Each of these positioning paths has a distinct influence on assortment and merchandising:

- Merchandise brand: The retailer offers exclusive products with recognisable style that shoppers can probably not buy anywhere else. Examples: Lush, L'Occitane en Provence.
- Selection brand: The retailer differentiates itself either by an unusually broad range of product categories or by a narrow but very deep offer within one category. Examples: Specialty stores Tiffany's and Victoria's Secret,

super-specialist stores Swatch and Tie Rack, category killer Amazon, department store Hudson's Bay.

- Brand-mix brand: The retailer offers a unique combination of private and/or supplier brands. Examples: Marks & Spencer with private labels and Selfridges with a unique mix of supplier brands.
- Product-mix brands: Retailers combine a number of completely different product categories in a surprising manner though the shopper should see some logic and relevance. Examples: Office supplies retailer Staples offering insurances and other services.
- Target group brands: These retailers stand out from competition by focusing their entire range on one specific target group. Examples: Build-A-Bear Workshop, Mothercare.
- Speed brands: Retailers are faster than any other retailer in adjusting their range to shopper behaviour as trends and hypes spread quickly around the world. Examples: Zara, Tchibo.
- Ideology brands: Retailers are mainly led by their social ideology. Examples: The Body Shop, Ben & Jerry's.

Example Summary Assortment and Merchandising Plan

The assortment and merchandising plan is an inseparable part of the retail marketing plan. Each organisation will have their preferences of detail and format. To illustrate the relationship between the strategic input from the retail marketing plan into the assortment and merchandising plan, I use a fictitious example. The example in Table 7.4 is what the summary of the assortment and merchandising plan for the lunch category at a brick-and-mortar convenience store retailer called 'Go & Fresh' may look like.

Important Learnings from This Chapter

- A structured assortment and merchandising process is instrumental in shaping the retailer specific signature in an efficient way.
- A solid assortment and merchandising plan is built around six decisions: (1) Core and related categories, (2) Amount of space and products, (3) Online and brick-and-mortar, (4) Star products, (5) Brand hierarchy and (6) Service level.
- The assortment role framework helps decide retailers on type and number of brands per category based on (actual/desired) product variety and profit contribution.

Table 7.4 Summary assortment and merchandising plan

From retail marketing plan	
Mission	Provide food to people in a hurry
Summary overall objective	Increase share of spend in out-of-home market
Summary overall strategy	Compete directly with quick service restaurants in terms of location and time spent in-store
Brand personality	Modern, energetic, upbeat sense of humour
Brand benefits	Fast checkout
Shopper target group	Widely defined target group in terms of socio-demographics as many are looking for a convenient solution at times. Market research shows there are several types of shoppers: • Office workers aged 20–45 years • Foreign tourists • Neighbourhood families for late night dinner • Train travellers • School youth
Assortment and merchandising	
Shopper insight	Shoppers perceive hamburgers from quick service restaurants as fresher as they are prepared on demand. Space at Go & Fresh is limited and cost of staff is high so both aspects do not allow preparation on site. Fresh perception will need to be delivered through fresh, high-quality ingredients, mainly from sandwiches. Target shoppers want to enjoy the taste of freshness but at low cost.
Category role	Lunch is a destination category for Go & Fresh with which they want to meet shopper demands in many segments such as bread and fruit. Most products in the lunch category are price competitive with lunch deals at quick service restaurants, assortment variety is smaller versus city supermarkets and perception of freshness is lower compared to bakery stores. 50 per cent of product space is dedicated to lunch, 10 per cent to coffee & tea, 20 per cent to water and soft drinks, 15 per cent to ready-to-heat meals, 5 per cent to non-food necessities (batteries, oral care, female hygiene, etc.).
Stars	Icon product is a bag of cookies with a joke on the bottom of the bag. KVI list consists of ten items among which black coffee small size and a cheese sandwich.
Brand hierarchy	In the lunch category, all products are private labels with distinct sublabels: GoBudget (value label), GoFresh (standard label), GreenGo (organic premium), GoLive (the free from range with less salt and sugar and no allergens)

(continued)

Table 7.4 (continued)

Online versus brick-and-mortar	All products are visible online with full ingredients declaration. Go & Fresh is working on an app to let shoppers browse if the desired product is still available including expiry date in a store nearest to the shopper. Pilot whereby shoppers could pick up groceries from a full-service supermarket has been stopped due to lack of cooled storage room.
Merchandising	No furniture in the centre of the store should be wider than 2 metres and higher than 1.5 metres to allow fast navigation and quick search. Lunch is in centre of store with wooden-look. All other categories have merchandising with metal-look.

References

CVS Health. (2018). *Corporate Website*. [Online]. Retrieved June 20, 2018, from https://cvshealth.com/about/purpose-statement.

ECR Europe. (1997). *Category Management Best Practices Report*.

Floor, K. (2006). *Branding a Store: How to Build Successful Retail Brands in a Changing Marketplace*. Kogan Page.

Wall Street Journal. (28 June 2017). [Online]. Retrieved June 23, 2018, from https://www.wsj.com/articles/why-your-local-cvs-is-hiding-the-candy-and-tanning-oil-1498647600, author Sharon Terlep.

8

Universal Merchandising Guidelines

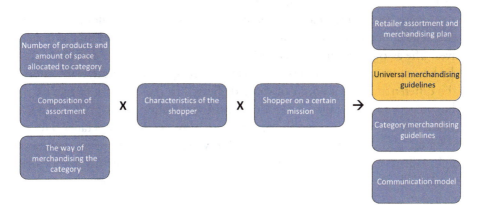

Image 8.1 Integrated assortment and merchandising model

Learning Objectives

- Apply five merchandising principles that make decisions on products from any assortment more pleasurable and efficient for shoppers.
- Describe common and differentiating principles for online and brick-and-mortar stores.
- Introduce style groups for fashionable and decorative categories.

The main purpose of merchandising guidelines is to remind retailers of the way shoppers like to browse and buy from the category. In everyday hassle, they may forget what is really important. The format of the guidelines could

© The Author(s) 2019
C. Berkhout, *Assortment and Merchandising Strategy*,
https://doi.org/10.1007/978-3-030-11163-2_8

range from a set of rules to a colourful story with images and stories that are shared with shoppers. When the retailer has clarity about what is needed to invest, they can start making trade-offs between different parts of the store and among categories. In an ideal situation, the guidelines promote the financial results and make the retail brand more competitive. The biggest reward for a visual merchandiser is when the way of organising becomes the signature for the retail brand. When thinking of two optical retailers in their local market, most shoppers perceive the assortments as more or less similar. However, service and merchandising could be very different from each other! One optical retailer may have neatly organised, self-service racks and in the other shoppers first experience a cosy seating area and coffee machine before getting to the pairs of glasses categorised by style group.

Universal principles should support the assortment and merchandising objectives that the retailer has selected in the areas of supply chain, finance, operations, shopper and retail brand. In theory, the universal principles are true for any retail context as they relate to generic shopper behaviour. However, each retailer constructs their own context based on the selected mix of objectives. The assortment and merchandising strategies provide the pair of spectacles how to interpret the shopper behaviour in the specific, commercial context. The difference in the amount of space dedicated to the category as a result of the category role at retailers will influence the application of the universal principles. Therefore, the universal principles are universal for one retailer. Here I focus on 'shopper truths' but the possible variation of type of guidelines is high. Whatever works for a retailer could be formulated as principles for this retailer. The wording of the principles reflects the perspective the retailer takes, such as:

- Supply chain: 'All products delivered to store should be placed completely on-shelf without back-store storage'.
- Financial: 'Percentage margin is twice as important as rotation'.
- Operational: 'It is always possible to stock 1.2 times the unit case amount'.
- Shopper: 'Place products in groups according to first split in the shopper decision tree' or more practical, universal principles such as 'Allow 6 cm of finger space to facilitate product picking'.
- Retail brand: 'Each aisle starts with one bay of private label products'.

Once a Format & Marketing Director at a large grocery retailer asked me to come up with one and only one universal guideline that could govern the merchandising of the store. And as much as I wanted to take on the assignment, I thought this was impossible and declined the offer to work with the retailer. I thought differences among shopper target groups and types of categories were too large. Fortunately, the Format & Marketing Director agreed to compromise to 'a few' guidelines and the challenge was on for me. My search started with a visit to eye experts that could tell me about the possibilities and limitations of human vision. Next, I zoomed in on the increasing number of studies on human decision-making from neuro-research and the behavioural science discipline. This set the foundation for me to validate these in retail practice and at the same time I tried to figure out the reason why some old retail wisdoms had appeared to be effective. In my quest for universal merchandising principles, I kept in mind that the evolution of the human brain and the human preference for routines and automatic responses dictate some generic truths no matter the retail context the shopper faces. This is not to say that webstores are effective with the same principles as brick-and-mortar stores or that one retail format can be as effective as another retailer applying the same principles. The preceding chapters gave insight into some general principles, such as more assortment results in more satisfaction with the variety but it also generates more complexity. Some principles are more applicable to one retail context than the other. For example, the filtering options found widespread application online but are occasionally used in brick-and-mortar stores such as in optical retail. Principles may take another name or shape, for example, webstore designers speak of white space when in brick-and-mortar retail they speak of space-to-product ratios.

Building on the academic findings and learnings from retail practice as highlighted in the preceding chapters I formulate here universal merchandising guidelines. In the descriptions, I attempt to be neutral with regard to online and brick-and-mortar retail. Often the illustrations refer to brick-and-mortar retail context, quite simply because these have a similar appearance: Tables, racks and checkout. For illustration purposes this makes it easier to explain the principle. Online offers so many more design options in terms of, for example, colour, images and personalisation that it is difficult to create the same starting point for the illustration. What I would like to share are some universal principles based on human biology and brains that are applicable in the widest sense, though they require creativity to adapt them to the specific format. This chapter closes with a summary of detailed principles that arose in previous chapters. All together they form a great starting point for formulating what retailers consider as most important. And they are also the diving board from where the next chapter discusses how to make a distinction among the characteristics and role of categories.

Five Important Universal Merchandising Guidelines

1. Start with the shopper decision tree.
2. Create visual clues.
3. Fill from left to right.
4. Make product visually available.
5. Place retailer favourite on eye-level.

Start with the Shopper Decision Tree

The shopper decision tree is a great starting point because in this way the shopper is in your mind from the beginning. The shopper decision tree symbolises the trade-offs that shoppers make in a certain assortment in order to fulfil their needs. Sometimes it is difficult to fully reap the benefits from this concept, for example, a convenience store with only one cola in the beverages assortment or a variety store that offers a limited assortment of all kinds of bicycle accessories. Still in such situations some products are more related to each other than others. The shopper likes to see the products that are complementary grouped together. Shoppers intuitively give names to the collections of products that are close. It is up to the retailer to keep the number of groupings around seven according to the Miller principle. For brick-and-mortar stores, this means that as much as possible segments are presented in a vertical manner whereby the dividers form the natural stop among the segments. As shown in Image 8.2, the shopper decision tree is translated into blocks of products that go together. The first split in the shopper decision tree corresponds with the first, vertical division of blocks of product. There should be a logical or an easily recognisable order, for example, prices go up from bottom to upper shelf. With the shopper target group in mind make sure the products are literally within reach. Online retailers often use images to catch the eye and illustrate what the segment is about. Next, shoppers drill down easily with filters on the left side of the screen. This is an important tool to translate the shopper decision tree in online formats.

When the first and most discriminating cut-off point from the shopper decision tree is divided into vertical blocks, the shopper finds all products within arm's reach. In comparison, a horizontal layout makes it difficult to see all products from the same segment together. Image 8.3 shows the difference between vertical and horizontal layouts. Shoppers are required to walk and compare

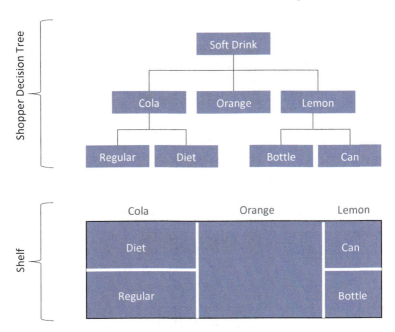

Image 8.2   Shopper decision tree reflected in shelf merchandising

along the bays. It is common practice in emerging economies to give suppliers the responsibility of merchandising shelves, and as a result, shoppers are often confronted with a category whereby each bay reflects the offering of one supplier. The question to ask is: Do shoppers walk into the store having a specific supplier in mind, or would they rather like to search by flavour, price or brand?

Placing the segments in a vertical way could also support navigation into the aisle. This is visualised in Image 8.4. If the segments are characterised by different shapes or colours, they offer diversion. With each step shoppers move to a new section and they perceive movement. Think of soft drinks where shoppers see black-coloured cola blocks, orange-coloured beverages and transparent bottles of lemon drinks. If merchandised horizontally, the aisle horizontal blocks seem never-ending stripes. If aisles are very long, the horizontal merchandising reinforces a 'tunnel feeling': Shoppers have a natural resistance to enter long, seemingly never-ending, closed paths, certainly when they are dark.

Create Visual Clues

Retailers apply all kinds of tools to attract the shopper's attention online or in brick-and-mortar stores such lighting, scents and images. Products themselves may play this role as well. And it is perhaps an even more preferable approach

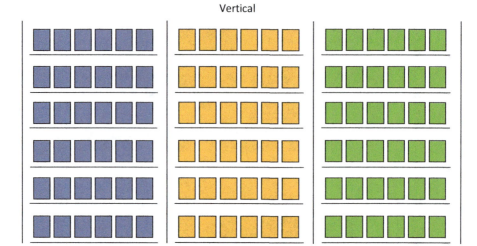

Vertical

Horizontal

Image 8.3   Horizontal versus vertical segment blocks

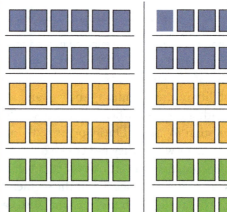

Vertical

Horizontal

Image 8.4   View into store aisle

because it is more cost effective and shoppers have less chance of feeling overwhelmed. The application of products to help shoppers navigate is called sign-posting. Sign-posts are either brands or product segments that have a uniform, very salient colour or shape. If they are brands, they have the highest top of mind awareness in the category. The most powerful sign-posts are also traffic builders, so not only the shopper's eyes are pulled towards the sign-post, but this brand or segment has the highest rotation in the category or belongs even to the best rotating store assortments. If the online store provides a wide range of options or if the grocery aisle is long, retailers are encouraged to apply various sign-posts that signal in a fast way to shoppers what the different parts of the assortment represent. This is visualised in Image 8.5. In a brick-and-mortar store, there are often several categories within one aisle and each category could benefit from a sign-post should this be available. First of all, a sign-post at the end of the aisle facilitates the search for a certain product when shoppers walk in the main aisle and scan the store to find out which aisle they should enter. Next, a sign-post in the middle of the aisle serves to make shoppers pay attention to the middle segment, but this also helps in another way. Shoppers have the unconscious hesitation to enter long aisles and a visual interruption which could be the sign-post, but also things like a protruding merchandising element or lighting, makes shoppers perceive the aisle to be shorter.

The order of the categories, in this case coffee, cake and tea, is determined by a mix of factors; however, my recommendation is to first interpret shopping behaviour. Starting with the segments that rotate most and following with the segment with the highest shopping affinity delivers maximum shopping convenience. Similar thinking could be applied online. When webstores started all too often they applied an alphabetical order to products. They too can start with the sign-post brand rather than let shoppers scroll to the bottom

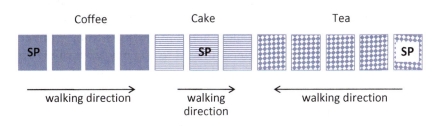

SP = Sign-post segment

Image 8.5   Aisle Management

of the page because the retailer presents first more margin-rich products or brands for which the retailer received a (temporary) financial incentive.

The concept of visual clue not only relates to sign-posts and building the order of categories but also when building the category itself. Shoppers should find the view on the online store or on the bay aesthetically appealing. Suggestions for laying out assortments are:

- Leverage contrasting colours. For example, when presenting 20 flavours of jam, shoppers experience less confusion when jars with a similar flavour and colour of berry are not presented next to each other.
- Keep the context free from clutter so that the shopper can focus on the product (image) and description/price tag.
- Use a principle that shoppers intuitively easily grasp when the category takes several bays or screens. For example, prices run up from left to right like numbers on a ruler.
- Make sure the view is consistent. For example, when the category consists of three bays, try to place the shelves at the same height in each bay. This principle also relates to the products offered. When building an assortment, I always try to imagine what name a shopper gives to a section of products (one or more bays/screen views). This could be as simple as a product name ('cheese') but could also be more goal-oriented ('kids' lunch'). On the one hand assortment within the section should be related, and on the other hand I try to keep the number of sections at a maximum of seven in accordance with Miller's suggestions.

This is also the moment to check whether shoppers appreciate the logic of the shopping decision tree, or if the creation of product blocks of similar colours and shapes makes it convenient and more satisfying to shop. For example, shoppers may select baby food based on age group but find it much easier to find the jar when the baby food is presented by brand. Reasons might be that the brands have very distinctive brand packaging or shoppers may be very loyal to one brand. From what people say, or even better through eye-tracking, retailers may obtain hints from shoppers as to how they search. Retailers are encouraged to test new ways of merchandising. This is much easier online where retailers can target the way of organising the assortment more specifically to shoppers. In case of brick-and-mortar planograms, retailers could test several scenarios including one planogram based on the shopper decision tree and one based on shopper hints on the visual search tree.

Fill from Left to Right

Once shoppers halt for the assortment where they think their target product most likely has been placed, the most convenient head movement for human beings is vertical. Should the assortment consist of distinct segments and there is not sufficient place to place them next to each other, shoppers like to see them placed either above or below the first line of products. A block could be a shelf or horizontal series of products, but it could also take up more space. Preferably there is some kind of logic in the vertical placement such as 'higher priced products are on top'. In an optimal situation within the bay or screen view each shelf or line of products belongs to the same block and transfers the same meaning to shoppers. Because products are placed on the same shelf or a line, shoppers intuitively think retailers send a message of similarity among these products. Therefore, as visualised in Image 8.6, shelves 1 and 2 deliver a more calm and convenient view than shelves 3 and 4, where the products belonging to the same segment are placed on different heights. If possible, there is a certain logic behind the vertical placement on one shelf or line in the screen view. In case the vertical blocks are based on flavour, this could offer the opportunity to build up price from left to right. If a brand has

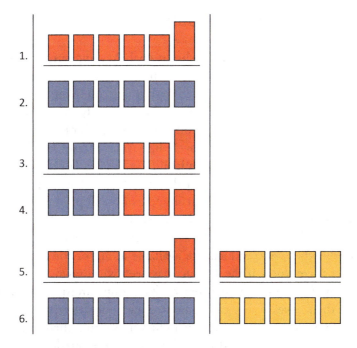

Image 8.6 Shopper-led shelf merchandising

two products of one type of flavour but in two sizes, placing the largest product on the right side could nudge shoppers to trade up, as some 90 per cent of people are right-handed. This is also one of the reasons some retailers like to place their private label alternative at the right side of the national brand product. This is demonstrated on shelf 1. On shelf 5, most products belonging to the same segment can be placed together; however, one has been placed in the next bay. This is confusing for shoppers as they consider the bay dividers as natural ends of a group of similar products. Retailers are strongly suggested to reduce the assortment with one product.

The suggestions work similarly for online. The horizontal display is much faster to absorb for shoppers as a result of the binocular vision. In addition, scrolling down takes more time and effort and this is risky when shoppers are too impatient. If the shopper searches more than one product such as groceries, they easily compare and select products on one horizontal line. If only one item is required, like a printer, more vertical scrolling of pages is convenient for the shopper. Shoppers start their search often in the middle. In some parts of the world such as Hong Kong, shoppers may read from right to left; however, as most read from left to right and because numbers on a ruler build up from left to right, this seems to be a natural order.

Make Product Visually Available

Often this is the primary merchandising goal: Making sure the product is available, even if everything else fails. When leading a team of space managers at a non-food retailer and confronted with a failed implementation of new space management software, this was my one and only focus: Availability of product in-store without consideration of shopper decision trees or quality of merchandising. For large global players like Amazon and locally dominant online stores such as BOL.com, availability is the fundament of their positioning. Products themselves are not different from what shoppers can find elsewhere, and therefore the fact that shoppers find all products always available is the primary driver to start the search with a diversified online retail store. Guaranteeing online product availability means that retailers communicate clearly whenever products are available at all, or for convenience for shoppers let them know if the product has been withdrawn. Online retailers that work with third-party vendors or have outsourced the warehousing should ask themselves if they can guarantee the same delivery times (and service conditions) across all products including those from their in-house managed warehouse, or if they end up making an online puzzle for shoppers to find out which service is connected to which product.

The fourth guideline explicitly states the term 'visually'. Aiming at availability is sometimes not sufficient in brick-and-mortar retail: Products might be so small that they are actually present on shelf but very hard to notice for shoppers. Therefore, retailers work with minimum stock levels to meet demand until next store delivery moment and to ensure visibility of the product. The number of facings could be driven partly by commercial objectives such as the practice to create double or more facings for private label no matter the rotation or stock loss. Space managers keep a close watch on the number of products in the (shipping) case unit. When store staff replenishes the shelf, it is more efficient for them to empty the complete case unit rather than return to the back-store storage with a half-filled tray. Therefore, space managers work with rules of thumb such as the minimum required availability equals the number of products in a case unit plus 2 (or multiplied by 1.2). In this way, space managers ensure that when the shelf is replenished with a new case unit, in principle there are always products visually present just before the moment of re-stocking. There is a risk in applying this rule of thumb. If rotation of the product is low or time between stocking moments long, high quantities on a case unit result in too many products on shelf. For example, let's say rotation of product A is 1 unit per week and the case unit contains 24 units. If only 5 units can be placed in 1 line (so 1 facing), the product requires 24/5 = 4.8 so at least 5 facings of the products. At a rotation of 1 unit per week, this results in almost half a year of stock in each store. Retailers are encouraged to tailor the case units they obtain from suppliers to their channel and preferably to their specific needs. Suppliers may purposely offer large sizes of case units. Some have found more creative ways to enlarge and enhance the visibility. Take the craft beer brand Noble Rey. They produce cans of beer that if stacked on top of each other connect heads and bodies of colourful beings together. This encourages specialty stores to give more and preferred space without Noble Rey asking or paying them to do so.

The minimum case rule helps staff to work efficiently. Another rule applied by the supply chain department is directed at optimal visual appearance. Replenishment might be set up such that it is very likely for shoppers to see one product per assigned space (facing). The rule may sound as simple as the number of products on shelf ('presentation stock') equals 1.5 times the number of facings.

Visual availability may be interpreted differently in food retail, non-food retail and online retail. While the packaging of the consumer unit makes the difference in grocery retail, non-food retailers selling, for example, consumer electronics or household goods like to display the consumer unit without packaging at eye-level and place the products in packaging alongside. This requires, first of all, the delivery of show models to all stores, but also emphasises the importance of creating packaging that is appealing rather than just perceiving these as containers for shipping. For online sales, retailers put in much effort in getting attractive, high-resolution product images, which often are a combination of the unpacked product, the product packaging and the product in use or consumption context.

Place Retailer Favourite on Eye-Level

The unconscious inference that products placed on top of the screen are better is important to remember. Shoppers zoom in first into the upper middle part of the screen, so this is where to place the favourites. For brick-and-mortar retail, there are more physical and spatial implications that need to be considered and therefore the fifth principle focuses on brick-and-mortar retail. The different vertical heights in ordinary grocery stores can be divided from bottom to top in zones for kneeling, bending, grabbing, viewing, stretching. A mix of retailer and category strategies determines what the favourite items are and how to measure this. As discussed before, products on viewing level have a better chance to be noted by shoppers and products on eye-level seem to deliver better value from a shopper perspective. Next, a shopper would rather grab or bend. The least favourite motion is to kneel as it requires the most energy, and unless retailers operate with protruding bottom trays or apply other visual merchandising elements, products on this level are hardly noticed. This brings me to two observations. Retailers like to advertise a lot out-of-store about their budget offering; however, in-store they prefer to hide them and seduce shoppers with more expensive products. A second observation is that shoppers dislike bending especially when they have the feeling other people are watching them or are nearby. Having observed shoppers for a day in a Shell petrol station, I concluded that especially female shoppers did not pick confectionery from the lowest level shelf that was built into the checkout desk. Male visitors hanging around in the coffee area may have had something to do with this. What's placed on eye-level depends on the objectives the retailer sets for the category. This might be an over-faced block of private label products to generate profits or to reinforce a favourable price image, or a national brand that works as a sign-post.

The different heights also play a role when there are different sizes of product available. Intuitively, shoppers like to see the heavier, larger shapes placed at the bottom so that they seem to carry the other products. This also avoids shoppers having to stretch their arms and lift heavy items from the top shelf. In recent years, retailers have come to understand that merchandising placed in the middle of the store should be kept low so that the shopper can easily navigate through the store. This solves the challenge for shoppers of not being able to reach products above their head but creates a challenge as there is less space available for the current assortment size. The low merchandising also redefines what is eye-level. The top-level shelf may very well become the most salient part of the merchandising gondola.

Style Groups

Special attention needs to be given to so-called style groups, a concept that is relevant whenever fashion trends play an important role. This is mainly relevant in non-food retail such as for clothing, home décor, home improvement, consumer electronics and household goods retail sectors, but could also be instrumental when selecting decoration styles on category level, for example, for the bakery category. Style groups describe a preference for a combination of design, material, consumption patterns and extrinsic characteristics such as colour. These are often obtained by showing a wide range of examples and asking what shoppers like and what will fit their personal tastes. For example, in clothing, a style group could be called 'expressionist' and appeal to shoppers that look for provocative, daring outfits that tap into the need for personal expression while another style group could be more conservative and quality oriented. Traditionally, marketeers segment the market in terms of socio-demographics such as age, income and profession. Segmentation by style groups is different and recognises that a certain style could attract people of all ages and incomes. The differences among style groups are driven by a combination of long-term values in society and cultural groups the shoppers belong to, personality traits and more domain- (category-) specific factors. In the fashion world, the domain-specific factor could be the importance shoppers attach to taking care of their appearance. Once shoppers are linked to certain style groups, they could be described with the help of variables such as category spend, online search behaviour, media usage and—if discriminatory—socio-demographics. The concept of style groups is important for non-food retailers for a number of reasons:

- They provide the opportunity to focus the retail brand on one or a few style groups. There should be a common theme in the selected styles.
- If the retail store carries more style groups, it gives direction to floor and space planning. A furniture store may create separate rooms per style. And

a home décor retailer may decide to present cushions, carpets and chairs by style group.

- Fashion trends will impact the colour and design; however, within the scope of the style group. Once you have identified the style group of your target group, fashion trends will drive the sourcing and collection activities.
- The style groups also form inspiration for advertising campaigns and promotional themes. Events such as Halloween may not play a role for the target group, while events like Christmas may be expressed in several themes each tailored around a target group.

When it comes to assortment merchandising, the challenge for style groups is twofold. Shoppers are often unconscious of the style groups that retailers have defined. They may state that they select a table based on price first, while the retailer observes that style group comes first, next size of the table followed by price. Dividing and ranking the assortment of tables by price may only confuse the shopper, though this corresponds with their claimed shopper decision tree. In these circumstances, retailers need to tailor their research efforts. The focus needs to be on identifying the style, for example, by asking them to state their style of preference from images or by assuming their favourite based on purchases in all kinds of different categories. The second challenge for working with style groups is that the way style groups come alive changes frequently, sometimes several times per year. Knowing what the fashion trend within each style group comprises of is often more art than science. Having professionals that are familiar with fashion and arts on board is pivotal. They may not always feel at ease in data- and results-driven cultures but making sure their involvement in assortment and merchandising is appreciated and applied contributes in large part to the success of non-food retailers.

Summary List of Merchandising Principles

The five universal merchandising principles are helpful in creating a pleasant and efficient shopping experience for shoppers no matter the type of category or retail context. On top of these broadly applicable principles, the academic studies discussed in previous chapters pointed to more useful pieces of advice to organise assortments. These are conveniently listed below supplemented with suggestions from my personal experience.

General Guidelines

- Shoppers need less time to look at all available options in the horizontal set-up which allows for an increased perceived variety and higher number of selected varieties.
- Impact on shoppers and therefore importance for retail decision-making of vertical placement is higher than horizontal placement.
- A higher number of labels that are more specific will drive satisfaction and assortment variety for shoppers that are unfamiliar with the category.
- For the preference constructor satisfaction and perceived variety is much lower if there is no categorisation. So, any category label is better than having none.
- In cluttered aisles especially when the products are small, building a block of products that have the same shape and/or colour may form a gentle start for shoppers browsing the assortment.
- If you let the shopper discover the assortment in steps, they feel encouraged to discover more.
- When products are presented by benefit, shoppers obtain a more abstract mindset, see more similarities among the options and are more satisfied, but as result of the higher perceived similarity among products, tend to select the less expensive ones (versus attribute grouping). Shoppers perceive more variety in an attribute grouping than in a planogram organised by benefit.
- Shoppers that are familiar with a category report higher level of variety if they shop an assortment congruent with the importance they attach to the product criteria. The difference between congruency and incongruency is not relevant if the shopper is unfamiliar with the category.
- Scarcer alternatives win preference because scarcity makes shoppers think the products are more popular and of higher quality. This is restricted to situations when shoppers think the product is truly unique (rather than incidentally out-of-stock) and as long as shoppers have no doubts about freshness and expiration date of the food product.
- Merchandising by complementarity gives shoppers a more positive assortment feeling though the breadth and depth of their search are more restricted than in case of substitution-based grouping. Indeed, the latter is perceived as less effortful while they view more unique options.
- Complementarity creates a more positive assortment perception for shoppers with a hedonistic shopping focus and/or that buy hedonistic products. Organisation by substitutes works better in terms of assortment perception for utilitarian products.

Guidelines for Online Stores

- Place positive wording on top of the screen.
- Place the target product in the horizontal centre as shoppers tend to look straight ahead and perceive the centre as landing spot for further exploration.
- A page with a large number of products is better presented with words than with images.
- By presenting the information in the shape of product characteristics and by seeking manners to actively engage shoppers, they get to know their preferences better and are more satisfied with the purchase in the end.
- In order to avoid fears of any type of contamination online, retailers should present any product as 'fresh' to the shopper and communicate its operating principles for returns online.

Guidelines for Brick-and-Mortar Stores

- When the store offers both products hanging on bars and products on shelves, it is visually more appealing to have products hanging on bars on top of products lying on shelves. This avoids the impression of empty space. In addition, there is no need of a shelf straight below the hanging products so that the products on shelf are immediately visible.
- Place target product on eye-level so that the shopper can notice these at a downward 15 degrees vision line.
- In order to avoid fears of contamination shoppers may select produce at the back of the crate so it could make sense for grocery stores to replenish produce starting with the first row.
- Create rules for space between shelf and the product on the shelf below. Actual heights vary by retail context. In grocery stores finger space of 3–6 cm could let shoppers conveniently observe and pick the product. However, this is not a fixed rule. Depending on the type of product and the vertical placement, more space between shelves is needed. For non-food such as shoes more space is better as a result of the product dimensions and attractiveness of the category. When shopping for small domestic appliances and electronic devices shoppers like to touch, open, test the products and show models placed above packed products should allow this 'working' space.
- Make sure that at least one case unit fits on shelf plus allow for additional products to avoid visual out-of-stock. Basket analysis shows how many

units of the same product are purchased. This is very important for product groups such as crockery and cutlery where shoppers typically buy several on one occasion.

- Maximum product height principles are necessary to allow shoppers to conveniently pick up products without help from staff. When working with tables and other low merchandising, products on the top shelf should not extend the height of the merchandising itself or maximum extensions should be in place in order to maintain open vision lines.
- Planograms for high wall gondolas cannot be copied immediately to those for low floor gondolas. First of all, because the floor gondolas offer less space, and secondly because the eye falls differently on this type of merchandising. For example, on floor gondolas the shopper's eye wanders often first to the top shelf. Therefore, it helps to stock larger, appealing products on the top shelf.

Agree on Fit and Healthy Merchandising

The merchandising principles are instructive in the phase of organising the assortment; however, they are also at the heart of the decision at the moment of signing off the assortment plan. This might be a moment when the category manager invites the Buying & Merchandising Director and other stakeholders to have a final look at the assortment built up in a pilot store, or when the category manager produces the test results of different website alternatives. I found it helpful to define upfront a set of rules that helped decide whether the assortment was ready to go live, in other words some guidelines that the organisation applies to decide if the assortment and merchandising are 'fit and healthy'. This could look something like this:

1. Meets all merchandising principles (and my suggestion is to list these briefly).
2. Offers products in at least three price brackets.
3. Contains all information a shopper requires to decide in the moment.
4. Contributes to the main financial objective in the category plan (profit, revenue, volume).
5. Makes a connection with shopper-related objectives (incidence, cross-selling, basket spend, basket size).
6. Ensures the share of space is more or less aligned with the shares of revenue, profits, volume (if not, good reasons for deviations are given).
7. Contains only products that are physically available when the planogram goes live.

8. Allows the target shoppers to easily observe and pick the products.
9. Offers products that actually belong in this category rather than another category.
10. Disperses traffic builders and sign-post brands throughout the aisle/page to enable several entry points into the category.

Practitioners are encouraged to define what best describes a fresh, crispy-looking assortment and merchandising in their organisations!

Important Learnings from This Chapter

- Five universal merchandising principles are helpful in creating a pleasant and efficient shopping experience for shoppers no matter the type of category or retail context.
- In fashion and other non-food retail style groups are more convenient and inspirational for shoppers than claimed decision trees.
- Starting the discussion on merchandising tactics based on facts and analysis sets the scope for the much-required creativity from visual merchandisers.

9

Category Merchandising Role Model

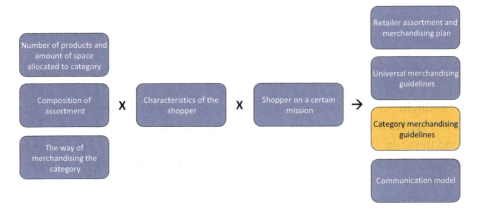

Image 9.1 Integrated assortment and merchandising model

Learning Objectives

- Understand how scoring categories on shopper decision aspects helps simplify decisions on the way of organising assortments.
- Apply the category merchandising role model based on frequency of purchase and complexity of decision-making to categories.
- Find ways to operationalise the model in a more tailored approach for the online retail and brick-and-mortar retail context.

© The Author(s) 2019
C. Berkhout, *Assortment and Merchandising Strategy*,
https://doi.org/10.1007/978-3-030-11163-2_9

The number of variables that practitioners can include in deciding what type of merchandising a specific category deserves is high: I have discussed variables such as number of products, types of product attributes and the shopping goals the category fits in. The findings of the academics in the first chapters are very important and helpful for making better assortment and merchandising decisions. However, the myriad of variables is so high and complex that it may stop retail practitioners from actioning on the insights. Therefore, I advise to implement a less sophisticated framework that focuses merchandising efforts, allocates investments across categories and is grounded on objectively measured data. The intrinsic nature of the category is one of the drivers of complexity. Recognising the differences among categories provides a basis for the retailer to then amend where they think it is necessary for the retail brand, the category role and the formats (channels) they operate in. One of such category frameworks that I found useful is to score each category on two factors, which are complexity of the category and frequency of purchase. The choice for these factors is further illustrated and the model is explained with an example from grocery retail.

Complexity

Simplifying merchandising decisions into a score on two dimensions is far from perfect because it fails to recognise outcomes of recent academic findings and the variability of day-to-day experiences from practitioners. However, the simplicity will encourage adoption with category managers that are time-stressed and often much more occupied with promotions and administrative jobs than they would wish.

The complexity factor in the category merchandising model represents the differences in complexity among product categories. For example, basic T-shirts form an easier choice than a suit for shoppers in a fashion store. The categories have intrinsic features that impact the complexity of the choice for the shopper. Here, complexity is the degree to which shoppers can take an easy and a fast choice from the category. It reflects the human need for finding a product that meets their personal needs and enables shoppers to feel different from others. In order to compare and score categories, this complexity needs to be operationalised. The complexity of a category is thought to be higher than other categories the retailer carries when:

- The number of products is higher.
- The number of attributes of the category is higher.
- The number of values that the attributes may take is higher.
- The consumer price is higher.
- The total basket spend of which the category forms part of is higher.

- The shopper needs more time to search and select.
- But also when the shopping trip is short and the shopper is time-stressed.
- The purchase is made for someone else or shared.
- The product has low price elasticity.
- The category comes with high involvement during the shopping and/or consumption.
- The shopper has not established habits and is not brand loyal.

I am the first to admit that these elements may impact each other in the mix and it is not always clear in the complex reality what cause and effect are. However, they provide direction for retailers to start measuring complexity. Which elements are measured depends on the availability of data and the sophistication of analytical tools available. The first three mentioned elements (the number of products, the number of attributes and the number of attribute values) reflect the variety of assortment options. Variety seeking is an intrinsic human need when comparing categories and retailers should seek to reflect this. As discussed, there is a difference between the actual variety and perceived variety and therefore in the complexity that the shopper experiences. Should the retailer be able to measure the perception by category this would be preferred of course, but this consumes much energy and cost to measure by category. In a few cases, I have been able to operationalise the perceived complexity with the help of time studies. Based on video-camera research and also with RFID tracking in supermarket trolleys I measured the time it took for shoppers to select products by category. Categories where the shoppers needed one or a few seconds were considered less complex than those where tens of seconds were spent browsing the category and assessing products.

Once the retailer has operationalised the complexity factor, the next question pops up immediately: Is the retailer comparing categories in the current assortment or the desired assortment? Indeed, the retailer may influence the end-score, for example, by reducing assortment size. My recommendation is to start with the current assortment, and to check if the assortment is aligned with the retail strategy. It is clear that the retailer has a choice. For example, if the retailer has just started up and is forced to keep the assortment small in actual numbers, it could use large images online or use labels to give the impression of a large assortment. This becomes the desired state of the retailer's ambitions. In exceptional cases there are no historical sales data available. Once I worked on the entry of a retail brand into an Eastern European country, so not only was historical data unavailable but market data from research companies such as Nielsen and IRI were still lacking. Instead, to determine the assortment, I visited two competitive banners and listed what they had on shelf.

A final remark is that more complex categories are often described as more emotionally driven, while less complex categories are purchased in a more functional manner. For example, when buying wine (a product which is often intended to share and therefore the perceived risk of making a mistake is relatively high), shoppers spend more time and get involved to know more about the varieties and flavours during the shopping process. In comparison, a pint of milk is a routine purchase and shoppers wonder more when next to replenish or if it fits the shopping bag less than the flavour or origin of the product.

Frequency

The second factor that determines the way differences are made in merchandising categories is the relative frequency of purchase of the categories in-store. Frequency mirrors the degree with which shoppers are familiar with the category in the retailer's store. For example, a winter jacket is purchased less frequently than a pair of jeans; therefore, it needs a more appealing merchandising in a fashion store. Preferably, the retailer works with the frequency of purchase for their own stores. However, a category could be purchased often in other channels and stores but not at the retailer itself. Therefore, shoppers could be more or less experienced with the category than what the retailers think they are based on the retailer's own data.

In my experience, the choice for frequency and complexity as factors for the category merchandising decisions makes sense, but again, is not perfect. The factors may not always be truly independent of each other, that is to say when shoppers visit the retailer's category more often they perceive this as less complex. In addition, the ambition of a retailer to make the category a prominent traffic builder influences the way it will build up the assortment. An alternative is working with the degree to which the category is purchased on impulse. Reminding shoppers of what they want but almost forgot to buy is certainly important to take into consideration for merchandising. I found it hard to measure the degree of impulse for each category for retailers such as department and grocery stores but replacing frequency as a factor by impulse might work for retailers with a low number of categories and where there is no issue of measurability. The value is found predominantly in the comparison of the categories, which then forms a basis for alignment to the brand positioning and strategy by the retailer. The complexity factor could be perceived as the ease of making choices in the category or shopper decision tree. The frequency factor reflects the ease of search and represents the visual search tree. In frequently purchased categories shoppers appreciate the convenience of large over-faced products or large images on the website, so that search time is reduced.

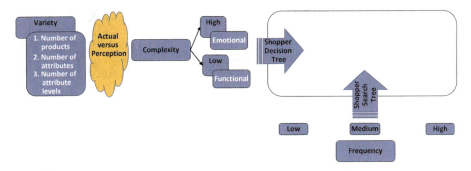

Image 9.2 Factors driving category merchandising role model

The process for building the category merchandising model is visualised in Image 9.2 below. Variety and the resulting complexity are assessed by the number of products, attributes and attribute levels. Ideally, the retailer would like to see perceptual values, but these might be challenging to measure for all categories. Depending on their availability other elements signalling complexity might be added. Shoppers absorb this information through a more cognitive process, the shopper decision tree. The other factor, frequency of purchase, is ideally constructed with the help of a loyalty card data, but could be assessed with market consumer panel data or conversion numbers from scanning data. The more frequently the category is purchased the more the shopper is looking for sign-posts and other visual elements with which the shopper is familiar.

This is an iterative process: If the outcomes are not desired, the retailer can actively change (perceived) variety, other elements of complexity and frequency. Scores on complexity and frequency lead to different merchandising strategies by category and I found it useful to work out six of them:

- Formula House
- Impulse
- Pleasure
- Formula Brick
- Routine
- Stock

Image 9.3 shows how these six merchandising roles relate to the level of complexity and to the purchase frequency of the category. Next, Image 9.4 suggests the merchandising strategies that belong to each of these six roles. Each of the roles brings with it highly practical and detailed suggestions to

H
Pleasure
Impulse
Formula House
Complexity
Stock
Routine
Formula Brick
L
L
H
Frequency

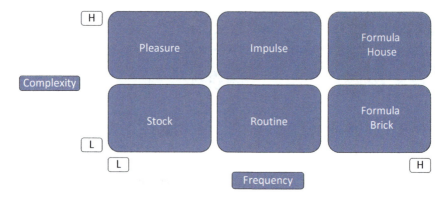

Image 9.3 Category merchandising role model

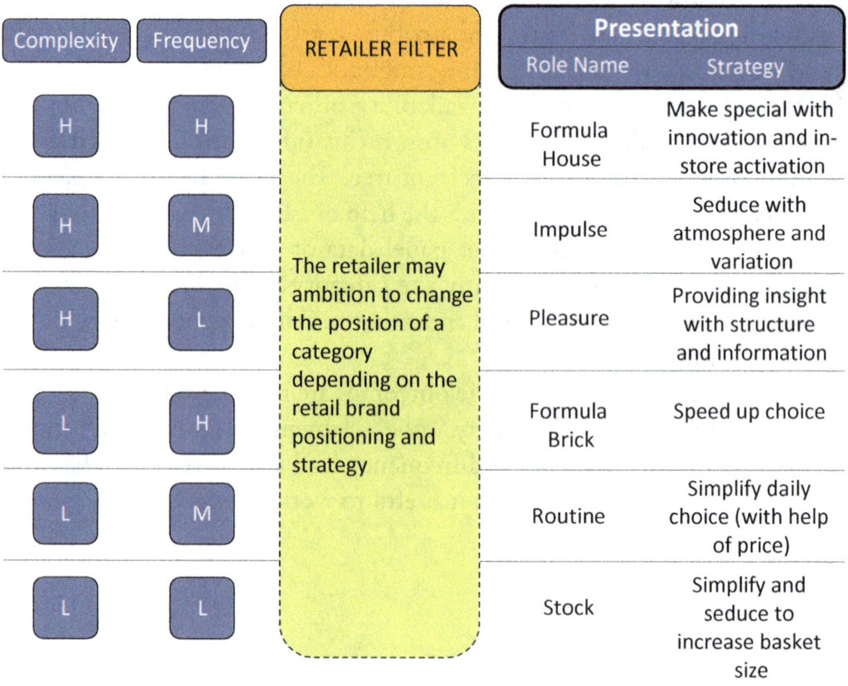

Complexity
Frequency
RETAILER FILTER
Presentation
Role Name
Strategy
H
H
Formula House
Make special with innovation and in-store activation
H
M
Impulse
Seduce with atmosphere and variation
H
L
Pleasure
Providing insight with structure and information
L
H
Formula Brick
Speed up choice
L
M
Routine
Simplify daily choice (with help of price)
L
L
Stock
Simplify and seduce to increase basket size
The retailer may ambition to change the position of a category depending on the retail brand positioning and strategy

Image 9.4 Strategy by merchandising role

merchandise the category. I will illustrate this through an example for a fictitious brick-and-mortar grocery store. Image 9.5 shows what a summary of the merchandising roles could look like in the retail marketing plan of a grocery retailer.

Complexity	Frequency	example	Presentation		
			Role Name	Strategy	Implementation
H	H	Fruit, meat	Formula House	Make special with innovation and activation	Low furniture Mood board
H	M	Chocolate, ready made meal	Impulse	Seduce with atmosphere and variation	Lighting Colour and shape of shelf (sticker)
H	L	Fresh herbs, wine	Pleasure	Providing insight with structure and information	Coloured dividers Reco on card Video
L	H	Milk, bread	Formula Brick	Speed up choice	Price segment first On wheels
L	M	Cola, coffee, pilsner	Routine	Simplify daily choice (with help of price)	Split by price Red bin
L	L	Pet food, canned food	Stock	Simplify and seduce to increase basket size	2pack sealed Permanent deal

Image 9.5 Example category role model for grocery retailer

Formula House

Though shoppers know this category well as they visit this on a very frequent basis, the Formula House obtains special attention. This is partly driven by the fact that the often large offer makes people feel confused; however, the main reason is that the retailer wishes to give their shoppers a warm welcome. The Formula House serves the retailer brand positioning and is often one of the destination categories. If retailers wish to transform some of their store into a theatre, these are the categories where shoppers wish to be entertained. The store becomes an inspiring environment. People spend time here because they want to be here. The variety is intrinsically large, each product seems unique, suppliers have their own preferred production methods and there is so much to tell about the products and their heritage. The retailer chooses to emphasise the differences, make the category more unique through innovation and seeks ways to activate shoppers through, for example, games, trials and entertainment. Despite the high purchase frequency, the shopper has new experiences in each visit by discovering new varieties and learning more on the category. In a supermarket context categories like fruit and meat are candidates for Formula House. Merchandising could take all kinds of shapes:

- Low furniture to open the view on all products
- Images to create ambiance
- Prominent location for private label on eye-level and/or as separate block as this reinforces the association with the retail brand
- Protruding shelf elements
- Fashionable colours
- Trendy and innovative use of materials
- Warm lighting
- Sampling
- Live cooking in mobile floor-kitchen on the weekend
- Production and cultivation in-store
- Self-service and re-use of packaging for better environment
- Extensive information on category available online

Impulse

These categories have a medium level of purchase frequency but there always seems to be a good reason for the shopper to increase purchase rate and get a new one. The complexity could be driven by a huge number of flavours or sizes of packaging. It is up to retailers to gently bring these to the attention of shoppers. Retailers try to seduce shoppers with ambiance and highlight the large variety in communication. This is perhaps counter-intuitive but by making sure that people switch products regularly, they stay in the category, though there may also be a trusted, safe option in the shopper's evoked set. It is the perfect balance between trust and surprise. Typical impulse merchandising categories in a supermarket include salty snacks and chocolate, but also ready-made meals. Examples of merchandising for Impulse categories in the category merchandising model are:

- Additional spot lighting
- Playing with the colour or shape of the merchandising
- Events or temporary products that tap into seasonality
- Limited editions to create sense of urgency
- Shelf sign with divergent shape and colour
- Second placement through displays
- Depicting the consumption context in all sorts of social contexts
- Regular amendments through mobile merchandising or by allocating frequent planogram changes in the annual calendar

Pleasure

These categories are not purchased often and because of their complexity they require the full attention of shoppers. The way the retailer facilitates the choice through merchandising and communication is crucial for the shopper enjoying the shopping process. The shopper is largely unaware of relevant dimensions in this category and is looking out for help. The kind of support looked for is providing clear insight with the help of structured presentation and information that enables the shopper to get to know the category and become enthusiastic. In some countries, wine has a low penetration and qualifies as Pleasure merchandising category. Other supermarkets see specialty beers and more recently fresh herbs as Pleasure categories. There are a number of merchandising techniques that help retailers obtain the maximum value from these categories:

- Videos, preferably with the help of touch screen to stimulate interaction
- Preparing shoppers online before the actual purchase is made (either online or in brick-and-mortar store)
- Coloured shelf dividers
- Signs praising specific products
- Poster telling the forgotten heritage and probing curiosity through 'did you know' facts
- Products sorted in colour blocks and according to style trends
- Reviews by other shoppers
- Sign indicating the top 5 products sold or 'the chef's favourite'
- Pre-selected items on a table, perhaps ranked with the help of numbers

Formula Brick

The Formula Brick merchandising category is often purchased and therefore very important for the retailer's traffic into the store and their store revenue. These categories form the foundation of the retail brand, and hence the name Formula Bricks. They generate the required cash flow, while at the same time the retailer works on innovation in other categories to enhance the retailer brand image. The high frequency has an impact on shopping behaviour: Shoppers have come to associate the retailers with these categories. In combination with the (perceived) low complexity, this also means that shoppers appreciate an efficient shopping time with merchandising techniques that accelerate the selection process. Indeed, they come here often and do not require much information and will become annoyed when entertainment disturbs the shopping act. An example of a Formula Brick could be milk. In many Western countries, milk has become a commodity as a result of a process where milk from hundreds of farms is mixed and ends up in the same type of carton packaging. Without intervention by the retailer, bread is a Formula Brick as well. Though I do not want to hurt the feelings of bakers, for many shoppers bread is a choice between white and multigrain. Retailers could choose to bring back value for the shoppers by emphasising the organic heritage of ingredients, placing slicing machines in-store to guarantee maximum freshness, producing reduced salt options, baking in-store and creating fresh bread scents. What Formula Bricks need in terms of merchandising is:

- Bulk presentation
- Shelf-ready packaging so that there is no hurdle to have products replenished quickly
- The bay itself placed on wheels so that empty merchandising is moved out quickly and replaced by full ones from the back storage
- Pallet presentation
- Entry of category with large value offer
- Prominent placement of private label
- Wide gondola paths to allow maximum movement for incoming and outgoing shopping trolleys

Routine

The Routine categories do not offer much of a challenge to shoppers: They are low in terms of complexity and more or less frequently purchased. Shoppers have their favourite that they can find blind folded, and therefore become very annoyed when retailers change the planogram, the location in-store or any part of the merchandising. Unfortunately, retail organisations like to allocate these categories to junior category managers who are ambitious to leave their footprint. Instead, all they should do is leave Routine categories alone in terms of merchandising and focus on price negotiation with suppliers, promotion management and supply chain management. Retailers should attempt to facilitate a frequent, sometimes daily choice with the help of clear price signals. Pilsner and cola could be such Formula Bricks in a supermarket. Coffee could be another example though retailers could also opt to enlarge the perceived variety in this category, for example, by organising trials, creating space for small suppliers and featuring events with baristas. If they emphasise the efficiency, the Routine merchandising categories are presented as follows:

- Easy comparison of standard national brands and private label
- Sorting and ranking by price
- Self-service to emphasise the commodity nature and entry pricing
- Bins with loose products, possibly in red, to raise attention for value pricing
- Double-facings for the highest rotating products

Stock

Some categories just do not need any merchandising support other than perhaps a gentle reminder so that they are not forgotten. Both complexity and their purchasing frequency at the retailers' stores are low. First of all, retailers should seek to simplify the offer and merchandising tools. Once the shopper is getting ready to make a choice, attempts could be made to let the shopper buy more because the retailer does not know if and when the shopper returns to the category: The additional quantity is offered as a service and reminder to the shopper. They are named Stock merchandising categories as shoppers could easily hoard up on this category at home. Examples are canned food and paper towels. Though pets are considered part of the family and the consumption context is emotional, actually the shopping process of pet food is predominantly habitual and functional. Therefore, merchandising investment could be kept low and attention could shift to developing several sizes of packaging and temporary packaging with additional volume. This is what the merchandising of Stock categories could look like in supermarkets:

- Permanent promotional deals, possibly printed on-pack
- Products sealed together in one bag
- Packaging with additional volume
- Sign telling shoppers 'do not forget …'
- Double-facing of private label
- Small descent of shelf so that products are 'self-replenishing' when product in front of shelf is picked up
- Low number of brands

The example of the category merchandising model has been applied to a (Western) grocery store that works with some 80 categories. The same structure could be applied to other types and sectors of retail including fashion, home décor and online department stores. The names and strategies of the category merchandising roles remain the same, but the application of merchandising techniques will take a different shape. For example, for a fashion store a seating area with coffee might be relevant, a home décor retailer may create a workshop space and online department stores will do more with augmented reality, videos and online communities.

Important Learnings from This Chapter

- Simplifying merchandising strategy into visual frameworks encourages adoption with category managers that are time-stressed and often much more occupied with promotions and administrative jobs than they would wish.
- Scoring categories on complexity and frequency of purchase gives clear direction to the type of merchandising required for shoppers. The complexity aspect represents the degree of difficulty when making a decision according to the shopper decision tree. The frequency aspect reflects the degree of search fluency and represents the visual search tree.
- The Category Merchandising Role Model suggests six distinct roles for categories (Formula House, Impulse, Pleasure, Formula Brick, Routine and Stock) each with its own merchandising objectives and tactics.

10

Communication Model

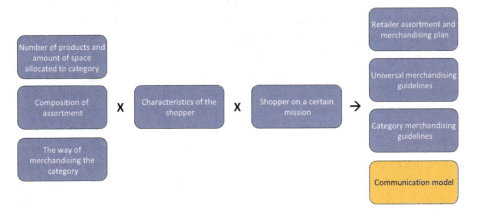

Image 10.1 Integrated assortment and merchandising model

Learning Objectives

- Understand that some categories require more communication as a consequence of shopper needs and/or retail brand positioning.
- Fine-tune communication to shoppers by considering the way stimuli are processed in Systems 1 and 2 and the relevant timing in the shopping journey.
- Identify appropriate online and in-store media for the communication model.

© The Author(s) 2019
C. Berkhout, *Assortment and Merchandising Strategy*,
https://doi.org/10.1007/978-3-030-11163-2_10

When retailers make decisions about what type of assortment they put on offer, they will be more successful if they consistently connect these with the other marketing mix instruments such as staff and price. For example, people expect prices to go up from the bottom to the upper part of the website or in-store bay. And the perception of variety is not only an outcome of the way retailers organise the assortment but also if shoppers are assisted by store staff that recommends them new varieties. In the retail assortment and merchandising plan, these interrelationships come together. Throughout the book the focal point has been the way shoppers select a product and how retailers respond with appropriate assortment and merchandising strategies. Still one marketing instrument needs more attention though without having the pretension to cover this in any manner completely, that is, communication. The main reason for this is that the product itself is an information carrier mostly in the shape of its packaging, but also through its intrinsic qualities such as size and shape. The second reason is that the product itself may not express the quality or technical details sufficiently and additional communication is required. In addition, in my consulting practice I observe retailers struggling with keeping the various shapes of assortment communication consistent with the retail brand and with the allocation decision as to which categories actually need more communication than the product and packaging already offer. Sometimes I feel there are too many signs and together with the product variety they lead to an overload of information. And at other times I miss a sign telling me about the heritage of the product which makes the product so much more interesting and unique. Interestingly, any communication displayed by retailers is assumed to be relevant to shoppers. Though so much other information is completely missed when shoppers are on their shopping trip, they try to understand the message as they make their selections.

The collection of information could be a conscious effort or not, happen fast or slow, occur in one or more trips and is part of a larger customer journey. The purpose of the shopping trip might be purely the collection of information the shopper thinks is necessary to make a good choice. For example, they learn which attributes are relevant for making a choice among laptops by browsing through online stores. A visit to a car dealer informs them which kind of car falls within budget. At other times the shopper makes the product choice in one trip and searches and applies all information at hand, either from the store or real-time online search.

When assortments are large, a retailer may feel the necessity to add information in order to facilitate the search process for shoppers. However, more information and visual features make the retail context more crowded. More products, more merchandising materials, more shoppers, more communication: Each of these has an impact on the perceived information density. The first priority is to let the product packaging speak for itself and next step is to structure the assortment in such a way that the derived information cues become more digestible. In the case of a small assortment, adding signage and digital features create more excitement and entertainment but they could easily lead to choice stress in case of large assortments.

Traditionally, retail communication focused on features and coupons to convince people to visit the store and in-store media such as displays and posters to convince them to buy the product. The communication landscape for retailers has changed significantly as a result of the proliferation of media options, the increased strength of retail brands, the shopper demand for tailor-made solutions and of course the rise of online as information source, search engine, shopping mall and electronic wallet. It is up to the retailer to take all communication options into consideration given the selected target group and in consistent alignment with the communication objective. Retailers should avoid a selective focus on media carriers, for example, by adding more content and images when operating as online player and hanging another ceiling card when they have physical stores. What makes more sense is starting with the shopper in mind and exploring what communication and carriers are most optimal along the shopping journey. Retailers should enable communication along the complete journey including the consumption moment; however, when it comes to product selection two stages are crucial: Before and in the moment of purchase. The before moment is when the shopper recognises the shopping needs, orientating on various product and channel alternatives and searching for information. In the moment describes the situation when the shopper is about to decide. The difference in time between the two moments could be a matter of seconds when a shopper transfers from the price comparison site to the shopping cart of a certain retailer, or it may be months of sorting out the technical details of a consumer household appliance before it gets to an actual decision.

As seen in Chap. 2, the messages sent by the retailer are either processed in the more automatic System 1 that turns them into impressions and emotions without much effort by the shopper or they are processed in System 2, the more cognitive and considerate part of the brain that makes balanced trade-offs in a careful manner. When grouping retailer marketing communication according to the moment in the shopper journey and the way shoppers process these, a framework for structuring the type of shopper messages and their carriers arises. This applies both to the marketing communication on retailer brand level and on the lower level when the retailer promotes categories and brands. This framework helps to keep the information for a product choice focused and consistent with the retail brand. The framework is shown in Image 10.2.

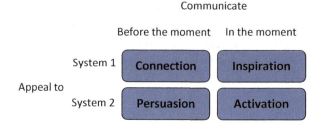

Image 10.2 Effective communication to shoppers

Connection

Some categories become relevant only infrequently or even once in a lifetime: Think of buying a mortgage or kitchen oven. Still brands want to make sure they are part of the evoked set once the shopper is getting involved. Apart from the creation of brand awareness they aspire to build up a positive emotion towards the brand. More frequently purchased brands seek cues that automatically connect them to a specific (destination) category or shopping trip. The objective of the Connection phase is that retailers continuously tell and show what the retail brand stands for. Examples of messages and media that fit the Connection classification are:

- YouTube and TV commercials that tell about the values of the retailer
- Images at the entrance of the store with founder and history of the retail brand
- Brand pages in online department stores
- Welcome mat at entrance
- Service and returns desk
- Colours and style of clothing of store staff, perhaps with text
- Faces and names of online helpdesk employees
- Retail brand website that tells about the brand's approach to sustainability

Persuasion

How much conscious effort shoppers exert in preparation for the moment of purchase depends on the involvement of the shopper and the benefits and risks that shoppers expect to obtain. Some categories need more of this than others: Buying a new car poses a higher financial risk and comes with a more complex set of attributes for consideration than buying a cup of coffee. These messages are meant to first of all inform and provide all relevant decision criteria for the category purchase. Perhaps existing category attitudes and behaviours need to be changed, or the shoppers are not even aware they have a certain need. Next, retailers strive to convince shoppers based on arguments which brand or product best fits their needs. The types of messages and media that fit Persuasion moments are:

- List of reviews displayed next to the product image
- Informative stories about the production areas and types of olive oil
- Support of price comparison websites by providing product and price information accurately and in time
- Temporary website with specific content to explain a promotion or product
- Educative brochures for pick-up alongside the category
- Workshops for do-it-yourself jobs
- In-store cooking classes
- Enabling online communities and product forums

Inspiration

The shopper is open to buying the category and the retailer moves shoppers into the right mood to buy. For example, the shopper is browsing in a shoe store and they are familiar with the retail brand and are aware of their preferences. At such moments, the retailer could speak to the shopper emotions, in this example by showing how the pair of shoes would fit different styles of dresses or telling them that the shoe manufacturer provides a fair pay to their employees, which takes away any feeling of guilt with the shopper. The inspiration could be a matter of seconds, or it takes more time when the shopper plunges into browsing and pure enjoyment of shopping itself. Inspiration is offered in various ways:

- Online demonstration videos
- QR code on shelf where the shopper can find more information on the way the product is produced
- Card with product story on shelf
- Display windows, showrooms, decorative tables in brick-and-mortar stores
- Pop-up stores
- Live cooking sessions
- Show consumption moments and people that shoppers can relate to

- Thematic campaigns
- Event area in-store
- Discovery of product through augmented reality either online or in brick-and-mortar store
- Interactive fitting rooms where shoppers can see themselves with a new dress without changing clothes
- Digital in-store media that change the message dependent on weather, time of day or shopper characteristics

Activation

The main purpose of this step is to get people into immediate action. This could be comprised of the actual selection and payment of the product or the action consists of another significant step in the purchasing process such as making an appointment with a mortgage advisor or inviting shoppers to try on a dress in a fashion store. The question is how prepared (the majority of) the shoppers come to the act of purchase. Are they informed sufficiently? And if not, are they willing to pause and make such inquiries that they select the product based on the retailer's arguments? Indeed, these shoppers would probably like more Persuasion type of communication. When people are (almost) ready to decide, they appreciate both transactional and promotional information that each requires a different communication style:

- Quiet, background style for transactional information:
  - Navigation telling where to find categories
  - Shelf sign with regular price and/or functional information about what product can do
  - Paid search results for the combination of category brand in combination with the search term 'coupon'. The retailer may choose to pay for all types of search combinations with the retailer brand name with terms such as 'feature' and 'opening time' to avoid others stealing away store traffic
  - Availability of stock in-store, in other stores or estimated time from order to delivery
  - Good visibility of retail brand locations including opening times and contact details on Google Maps

- Eye-catching, urgent promotional messages:
  - Display advertising whereby the retailer launches an online campaign on news sites, social networks (Facebook) and price comparison sites that link to the retailer site
  - Search engine advertising of iconic or promotional traffic builder products through Google AdWords and Google Shopping
  - Promotional and everyday low price tags
  - Promotion leaflet at display
  - Shelf signage regarding clearance sales department
  - Temporary change to home page according to theme of promotion
  - Window poster
  - Promotional offer on shopper's smartphone based on geographical catchment areas

Where the Model Helps

With the positioning of the retail brand comes a series of choices on logo, colour, tone of voice and other communication elements. When applied consistently, the shopper recognises the brand easily and the shopper plays back the desired brand benefits. However, shoppers are in all types of shopping phases, may have different needs by category and not all shoppers have the same needs. Therefore, retailers are encouraged to work out communication tactics that tap into the different needs of Connection, Persuasion, Inspiration and Activation, while maintaining a consistent retail brand communication across media carriers. For each quadrant the retailer selects images, typography, copy and colours that are specific to the quadrant but are still related to each of the others. For example, the communication guidelines may prescribe that the same corporate retailer colour yellow is used for all stages, and red is used as support colour in Activation communication.

A second area where the communication model helps is in the allocation of communication budget across categories. In theory, it is possible to tell an inspiring story about each of the retailer categories; however, budget is not unlimited as are the information-processing skills of shoppers. Impulse categories might benefit more from Activation messages and Wine from inspirational stories about wine tours in Italy.

Thirdly, much of retail effort is directed at generating traffic and creating volume that, multiplied by low percentage profit margins, results in large and profitable businesses. And as the relationship between a promotional sign and sales is more measurable than between a product video and sales, retailers may find out that their communication spend across the four types in the communication framework is not in balance. What happens if the retailer finds out that 80 per cent of the communication budget is allocated to Activation? Will the retailer be able to inspire and connect with the shopper in the long term?

The framework is designed for shopper decision-making on products in retail. In retail, the communication around a certain category or specific product cannot be separated from the sender, the retail brand. This is different for suppliers with consumer brands such as Maggi and Swiffer. Therefore, in retail information about the sender is more important. The communication challenge becomes more complex when the retailer banner name is the same as the corporate organisation name such as for Tesco. In such cases, the framework needs to be aligned with the corporate communication model. A retailer like Albertsons in the US may run the communication for their retail banners Safeway, Vons, Jewel-Osco, Shaw's, Acme and others separate from the corporate communication, while more alignment needs to occur with regard to the communication for their Albertsons banner that holds the same name. Finally, focus on shopper decision-making with regard to products also implies that separate attention needs to be given to the design and look and feel of service messages such as on navigation signs to bathrooms, opening times and store addresses.

It might feel frightening from a retailer perspective that shoppers bring with them their communication devices, smartphones, into the stores. While seconds away from a potential purchase, they enable shoppers to check assortment and prices of products offered by competition. Brick-and-mortar players will need to find ways to reassure shoppers of the best price, for example, through price guarantees and money-back policies. A more practical approach is push self-scanning as Albert Heijn does so that shoppers have no hands free for the phone, to offer interactive experiences like inspirational tables in fashion stores or let shoppers use the phone for the retailer's benefit like Hema in China where shoppers scan products for more detail and pay with their smartphone. For online players, competition is a click away and they need to invest in better understanding of the shopper journey. Analysis of online visits is needed where shoppers walk away and which approaches such as offer of online assistant could help.

Important Learnings from This Chapter

- To control information density, shoppers like the product packaging to speak for itself and derive information from the way the assortment is organised.
- Structuring marketing communication according to the way the messages are processed and the moment in the shopper journey presents the

opportunity to communicate in a more selective and targeted approach. Messages and media carriers could assume four roles: Connection, Persuasion, Inspiration and Activation.

- Retailers are encouraged to work out communication tactics that tap into the different needs of the four phases, while maintaining a consistent retail brand communication across media carriers.

11

Path to Shopper Delight

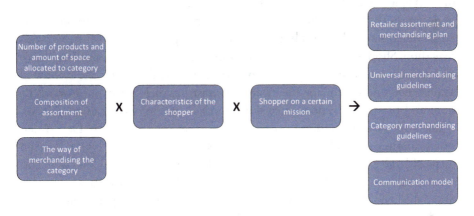

Image 11.1 Integrated assortment and merchandising model

Learning Objectives

- Learn how differences between online and brick-and-mortar retail contexts disappear as a consequence of shopper expectations and the environment such as sustainability impact.
- Prepare for nearby future developments that change the way shoppers make assortment decisions and challenge the retailer competencies and current ways of making decisions on assortment and merchandising.

© The Author(s) 2019
C. Berkhout, *Assortment and Merchandising Strategy*,
https://doi.org/10.1007/978-3-030-11163-2_11

The task of the shopper is to make a choice among various alternatives. During the performance of this task, they may need to cross several hurdles: They may not have full information on the attributes, have not (yet) established preferences for certain attributes or attribute values, have a dislike for working out the numbers, have no idea what the relevance of the attribute is and may enter the decision process with conflicting goals. Sometimes the products are not even from the same category, for example, when shoppers decide whether to spend their bonus on a car or a vacation. This is a good reason for luxury car brands to present themselves at boat shows, as suddenly the cars seem to be inexpensive. Marketing professionals have slowly come to realise that shoppers do not make their decisions fully rationally due to restrictions in the way they process information. Much of what they do is dependent on the context. This means retailers have a great influence on and responsibility for shopper choice. For retailers and suppliers that want to know and understand shopper behaviour, the challenge does not stop here: Even if the retailer controls the context and understands the relationship with shopper behaviour, it is difficult to predict the actual outcome, as shoppers learn more about the product and themselves while they shop. Shoppers are not actors who come completely prepared to the film set and speak the text lines they learnt by heart. In fact, they enter the scene with some beliefs and may shape their role and construct their behaviour towards the store and product selection while the camera is on. So, what can retailers do? Retail formats of today have no guarantees of success tomorrow. Department stores dominated retail sales around the 1900s pushed forward by the development of large cities and railroads. Hypermarkets and mass merchants were considered invincible in the 1970s when large building sites became available, disposable income grew fast and rise in car ownership made shoppers fully mobile. Today, much of the attention of practitioners is—justly—directed towards website and mobile shopping. At the same time, Eataly opens Fico in Bologna where shoppers learn about ingredients and the craftsmanship of authentic Italian products in 40 factories, obtain preparation advice from experts during daily workshops, explore the diversity of Italian cuisine by tasting and eating in over 40 restaurants, and finally get a chance to take the best home from more than 100 stores. I can only conclude that there are no dominating retail formats. Retailers need to operate in several channels at the same time to catch the shopper on different shopping trips and meet the requirements of different groups of shoppers.

The difference between online and brick-and-mortar retailers will be reduced to the decision on the proportion of products sold through these distribution points. The two types of retail will integrate and originally pure players from both sides will meet somewhere along the road. On the one hand, online sales across retail sectors will rise, even for categories such as cars, do-it-yourself and groceries, to meet shopper demand. In addition, originally pure players such as

Amazon and Alibaba have already opened brick-and-mortar stores. Good reasons for this could be the assurance to shoppers the retailer is there to stay, the possibility to enrich the retail brand image with new elements such as entertainment and to offer new services related to the category or generic customer service such as for returns. Personally, I see the need to deal with our planet in a sustainable manner as a primary reason the two channels blend with each other. Brick-and-mortar stores already offer a mix of self-selection, on-site eating and drinking and pickup of online ordered products and the latter will become more important. The explosive growth of delivery of small parcels to individual households will become too much of a burden on the environment due to energy consumption and additional packaging requirements. In addition, most retailers suffer significant losses on home delivery. Rates for delivery will most likely go up but this will not be sufficient to cover both the cost price set in a traditional manner (petrol, labour, depreciation of truck, etc.) and added with environmental cost (CO_2 pollution). Retailers are expected to come up with smart combinations of online and brick-and-mortar shopping. For example, DIY retailers may decide to deliver large and heavy products such as bags of mortar and garden fences only directly and focus on services such as workshops and smaller items at physical locations. Some retail players like Zalando accept a returns rate of more than 50 per cent, which means the environmental impact is even greater. There comes a point that all interests of shoppers and the environment are respected and the full price for such online orders is paid.

Realising shopper behaviour is fickle and difficult to predict when it comes to the assortment and merchandising arena, there are several ways retailers can prepare themselves, sharpen their skills and build their capabilities:

1. Incorporate new technology to leverage retailer data.
2. Integrate merchandising aspects into assortment decisions.
3. Reset the merchandising function in pursuit of shopper.
4. Become more international.
5. Assess the shopper emotion.
6. Apply voice-based search and assistance.

Incorporate New Technology to Leverage Retailer Data

The first step to better performance is making more informed decisions rather than relying too much on gut instinct. Better decisions are fed by the ability to collect, process and apply data in business decisions on a continuous basis. This sounds intuitively right; however, sometimes practitioners need the evidence and numbers to actually start working on this. Fortunately, a study by Brynjolfsson and colleagues (2011) did just this. They showed that organisations that apply 'data-driven decision-making' increase their productivity by 5–6 per cent. They also have a higher market value which is directly related to the level of IT investment the organisations make. Van Nierop and colleagues (2006) showed that data-modelling delivered 6–20 per cent more profits than application of best rules of thumb.

Assortment and merchandising practices have not kept up with the growing complexity of the category manager's responsibilities and fast development of technology. While masses of assortment data are flowing ever faster, lack of automation still leads to human error in data collection and processing. Retailers should embrace advanced tools to diagnose the data and that allow to devote more time to business understanding and driving solutions. The playing field of the category managers expands each time new players, new products and substitutes enter the game. Highly unexpected newcomers may be online stores with people and servers thousands of kilometres removed that suddenly set the new price benchmark in the retailer's local market. In addition, retailers have started to mix their offering with packaged food, non-food, dining and services resulting in more diverse competition. It is up to category managers to not only spot shopper trends early on but also to respond to and prepare for a widening competitive field. Shoppers become more aware of their shopping opportunities and more demanding towards retailers as standards rise through technology. Missing products or failing to notice competition that undercuts the retailer's pricing policy leads to immediate loss of revenue. Only some 30 years ago, retail professionals were waiting every 2 months for research agency Nielsen to provide paper reports with market trend numbers. Category managers of today rightfully require a fully integrated view on their assortment and merchandising that enables them to capture shopper trends based on internal and external data, build assortments for a wide variety of store formats and merchandising including online and amend fast by store. Pure online players have the advantage of applying the right tools from the start. Too often I see traditional brick-and-mortar retailers struggling to integrate all their internal data and spend too much time on software development rather than investing in off-the-shelf technology in order to service the shopper across channels and media. New technology should bring category managers the following answers:

- What happened in the past? Reporting of the performance of the assortment including description of trends, outliers and comparison between performance and budget, previous years, targets, competition.

- What happens now? Real-time monitoring of important performance indicators such as out-of-stock and promotions in order to take immediate action.
- Why did it happen? Deeper understanding of the performance drivers by applying advanced analytical tools to a mix of internal and external data. This deeper understanding is grounded not just in correlation but also in causality between drivers and performance. This is where category managers experience 'aha' moments of insight.
- What will happen? Predicting the shopper response, organisation performance and competitive action and giving clarity to the opportunities ahead.
- What could possibly happen? Drawing alternative scenarios of the retail landscape and simulating various assortment and merchandising actions. Like the previous benefit, the category manager looks ahead in the future; however, this time the category managers remind themselves that yesterday's drivers of success are not necessarily the ones that deliver success tomorrow.
- Prescription of actions that category managers should take to optimise their assortment. The software learnt so much about the retailer's assortment and merchandising that it will tell category managers what to do or, when instructed to do so, execute the right assortment and merchandising actions. This is called artificial intelligence when smart systems make decisions independently (regardless of whether there is little or much data). If these systems do not 'just' detect patterns, understand the causalities, calculate the probabilities but also learn from their mistakes and correct their actions, data scientists speak of machine learning. The future is more nearby than retailers think. A chat bot, which combines the words chat and robot, is a common feature to assist shoppers online. And when the assistant is called on the shopper's smartphone the chat bot may also become available in brick-and-mortar stores such as through Macy's on Call that helps shoppers navigate through the store when staff support is not available … or wanted.

Integrate Merchandising Aspects into Assortment Decisions

Imagine a screen or website with tablecloths and apart from the colour there is little difference. The retailer offers several blue products, two white ones and a pink one. The shopper's eyes will be drawn to the pink tablecloth, rest there for a few moments and next wander off. Most likely shoppers will buy the blue or white option that can be used throughout the year and seems a safer choice when it comes to feedback from guests. The pink tablecloth has low sales and may end up on the product elimination list at the end of the season. However, a smart category manager recognises the sign-post function of this salient product that will stay low in sales but promotes total category value. For a similar reason, DIY retailers have many odd paint colours in stock though they are aware most revenue originates from a few white colour types. The large frame with colour samples in DIY stores is a bit illusionary: In order to make a visually attractive colour scheme, colours are added that retailers know will have no or few sales. One of the reasons why product rationalisation based on sales fails in practice is that practitioners do not take into consideration the visual aspects of products and the function of a product in total category sales.

When space managers have a say in the development of product packaging, they can advise the most optimal way the product will come to live on shelf. For example, by turning the text direction by 90 degrees, the front view and the numbers for length, width and height could be changed in such a way that more of the product fits the shelf. The condition is that space managers are made co-responsible for the product packaging and merchandising material.

The way the assortment is organised is likely to have a bigger impact on sales than the space the products occupy. It may seem a hard challenge for non-food retailers like department or DIY stores that work with long order and delivery times due to overseas production; however, defining the assortment cannot be executed without knowing if space is available, and what type. All too often I observe non-food category managers who order high quantities in China only to find out months later the products do not fit the space available. The result is often a presentation that is less attractive and less easy to process for shoppers. I worked with a non-food retailer that approved the final assortment four weeks before space was assigned in the merchandising plan, which encouraged category managers to buy more products the store could carry.

Reset Merchandising Function in Pursuit of Shopper

Before the emergence of the category management concept in the 1990s, buyers focused on negotiating at the best possible margin, but the conversion to this new concept made the CEOs responsible for managing the flow of goods in their categories from sourcing to merchandising in-store. Managing the complete category P&L meant the attention of category managers was allocated not just to cost of goods but also to costs of warehousing and store operations and to new performance measures such as category growth. Today, category managers need to make a mental reset again and are required to move their focus from the category to shopper behaviour. New channels have popped up, retail banners assume functions from different formats and channels, and shoppers experience less transaction costs when switching. Of course, digital plays a big part in the current retail changes. A Deloitte (2016) report on digital shopping experience in the US shows that the percentage of revenue with the help of any digital device for the purchase in a brick-and-mortar store went up from 14 per cent in 2012 to 56 per cent in 2016. When the pure online experience is included some 60 per cent of all US retail sales are under digital influence. Thirty-seven per cent of brick-and-mortar retail sales in 2016 were influenced by mobile devices. Today, category managers need to understand the complete shopper journey and how shoppers interact with the channel and media touchpoints when choosing a product. This starts with having the shopper target group in mind. Some shoppers complete their journey fully online: They let Pinterest determine what they need and Google search curate where and which product to buy. At the other end of the spectrum I know of a brick-and-mortar household and electronics retail brand that experiences an uplift in a category where most sales now occur online: Consumer electronics. There is still a group of shoppers who start and complete their purchase of products like a water cooler or iron in a brick-and-mortar store. This retailer experiences an increasing demand that they attribute to the ageing population in their Western markets that prefer personal assistance and the fall-out of competition due to the shift to online sales.

Advancements in technology make new store formats possible. It is up to brand format managers to identify the needs of shoppers along the journey and describe the operational processes and tools to fulfil those. For example, the moment of payment is automatically linked to the end of the shopping trip. What happens if the retail model changes to payment in advance like subscription? Or automatic cashless payment like Amazon Go? In the same manner the finished product is assumed to be ready, but shoppers can already design their running shoes before any production has taken place. New technologies such as 3D printing exceed imagination and redefine where and how the functions of design, production, search, selection and payment take place.

When following or even predicting shopper behaviour, the merchandising responsibilities need to be reset. Rather than selecting products, category managers make the product available that is subsequently recommended to shoppers. Analysing when shoppers are open to buying a category might be more helpful knowing than relying on traditional events such as Mother's Day when there is a lot of competition around. Establishing partnerships could help category managers to meet the demands of the shopper quicker. In summary, the category manager's role becomes more creative, more experimental, more data-driven, more analytical, more technology-driven and more strategic. Sounds like the combination of a chef and a rocket scientist. As a result, the performance indicator moves from supplier-focused percentage margin to shopper-focused satisfaction ratings and from market share to partnership alliance growth.

Become More International

According to Deloitte's (2018) report on global retailing, 67 per cent of the top 250 retailers operate internationally in approximately 10 countries. Some 23 per cent of their revenue is accrued abroad. The initiative to grow abroad may come from many perspectives. This could start as a defensive move against competition. Sales through websites and mobile devices accelerate the speed at which retailers face competition from other countries. In addition, the large online players such as JD, Amazon and Zalando generate disruption because their business models seek market share dominance rather than high profit margins and operate with the newest technology for information search, product selection and payment.

The drive for more internationalisation may also come from the wish to restore a distorted supplier power balance. Large suppliers that historically already have a vast footprint abroad double their efforts. They seek ways to counter-balance the power from the likes of Alibaba, Amazon and Walmart. First of all, they strengthen their brands and seek cost reduction by focusing on fewer but large brands. An example is Reckitt Benckiser's Powerbrands strategy for more efficiency. Suppliers also attempt to mitigate their dependency on large customers by shifting trade spend investments from traditional service supermarkets such as Kroger and Delhaize towards growing retailers like the discounters Aldi and Lidl. This may also include a push on the online share of their own sales as Unilever's acquisition of the Dollar Shave Club shows. It is not sales, not even long-term profits, that could be the major advantage of such strategy. The suppliers build knowledge on behaviour based on the way shoppers search and interact. This allows suppliers to regain control on shopper traffic and in this manner they can steer shoppers to their own e-commerce offer. Alternatively, they reward those (dual or pure online) retailers by steering some of those shoppers to preferred retail partners. An example of a large supplier that makes large investments in online shopper expertise is Procter & Gamble that sets up online communities like Vocalpoint and BeingGirl.

The international expansion of suppliers, both on the ground and online, offers a threat to retailers in terms of negotiation power and this is reinforced by a new trend: Some large vendors have amended their business model in such a way that individual countries are no longer kept accountable for a certain profit level but this responsibility rests with clusters of countries or for one category across all countries. This relieves the pressure in negotiation with local retailers and as such is an impulse for retailers to operate more internationally. Internationalisation could also be the outcome of the recognition that (some) shoppers have the same needs across the globe. The retailer's business model might actually be partly based on this: Fashion retailers Zara, H&M and Uniqlo require only five weeks from spotting a British Princess with a new dress and offering the dress to women around the world. No longer do suppliers have the exclusive privilege of launching products fast and in a coordinated manner in several countries. International presence allows retailers to pick local trends and take them to other countries. And if the retailer does not execute on the trend, the shoppers themselves will find a way to get the product over. Even if retailers do not cross borders with their own brand, they could join large buying alliances. For example, the leading Belgian retailer Colruyt is a member of AgeCore that represents a retail market revenue of some 140 billion euro. The bundling of efforts pays itself in lower prices from suppliers. The products sold by large retailers mostly come from abroad and taking presence internationally may actually increase the product expertise and buying position of finished products or ingredients. For example, a Chilean grocery retailer could bundle its fruit purchases from Chile and source their own coffee from Columbia and sell these in grocery stores across the five South American countries it operates.

Assess the Shopper Emotion

In the good old days of mom and pop stores, the shopkeepers knew their customers well. When my aunt, tante Trui, who ran a small grocery store in Arnhem, the Netherlands, saw somebody was sad or stressed, she took the time to console and offered help. If she really liked the customer, preferential loan rates were part of her retail marketing programme. Assessing shopper emotions is still the best way to connect and seek to understand. Tools have changed: From facial recognition cameras that recognise universal human emotions to shoppers who leave likes or smileys at electronic screens or online. Retailers find it easier to approach shoppers in a rational way: Giving shoppers economic discount through promotions, telling shoppers the retailer has the fastest delivery time or informing them they have the widest assortment. However, a crowded environment, stress from work or just human laziness makes shoppers act less rational. They steer on automatic pilot and let decision heuristics do the work. Ideally, for each trip the retailer identifies the mood the shopper is in. If a shopper enters the store angry, even if the cause is completely unrelated to the store and might be the result of a missed bus, what would be nicer than calming scents or sounds from a forest in the landing zone to cheer up the shopper? The spectrum of emotions is wide and there is no consensus under academics on the types of emotions and underlying factors that exist. Personally, I find the Tomkins model (2018) very useful for understanding shopper emotions. Tomkins makes a distinction among affect, feeling and emotion. According to his theory, an affect is an innate response to firing of neurons. This affect leads to certain feelings and a feeling combined with the memory of such feelings in the past is an emotion. What I find really interesting is that all humans are born with nine affects that are expressed on, for example, their face and skin and can be measured increasingly better. The nine affects are distress-anguish, interest-excitement, enjoyment-joy, surprise-startle, anger-rage, fear-terror, shame-humiliation, disgust and dissmell. In addition to accommodating to shoppers on individual trips based on these emotions, they work refreshingly as a retail-positioning model. Traditionally, retailers look for range, price, convenience, experience and service as grounds for strengths on which to compete. They could also try a more emotional approach. For example, Trader Joe's could be described as a discount grocery store with friendly staff and lots of organic foods. To me the affect they tap into is that of anguish of people with high education but low on money who are first of all concerned about their personal situation but also their health and about where the world is going if people eat too much meat and retailers carry genetically modified food. Trader Joe's knows how to cheer them up with Fearless Flyers, catalogues of seasonal products, hand-painted store-signs and staff in Hawaiian shirts. For too long, practitioners have been talking about 'bringing experience to the store' as a way to compete, especially in the context of brick-and-mortar stores competing with online players. This is too vague for me: I encourage practitioners to be more precise with which shopper affect or emotion they wish to connect. The end-goal is a happy, delighted shopper. Not always is this happiness linked to pleasure and fun. For some shopping trips and some retailers, the objective might be to bewitch a smile on the shoppers' faces and to let them mumble 'wow'. Think of retailers like Victoria's Secret or Tiffany & Co. At other times completing the mission, getting the work done is more important. Dolan (2014) describes that achieving purpose is another route to happiness in life. This corresponds more with the needs that are fulfilled in an ordinary stock-up trip in a grocery store on Saturday or the re-stocking of pet food from the shopper's favourite online store.

Apply Voice-Based Search and Assistance

Shoppers of today rely much on their vision to make their way through large assortments that are organised in all sorts of ways. They may need to prepare the shopping trip, study attributes, compare alternatives and calculate if the price is right. What if all of that is no longer required and voice-based interaction takes away all the restraints from our vision and cognitive processing? Here are the personal assistants Alexa, Siri, AliGenie and Assistant developed by respectively Amazon, Apple, Alibaba and Google. Shoppers do not need to care about where they find the product or which brand is best equipped to meet the shopper demands when the shopper can ask about any product from a voice-based system. In addition, shoppers can have a conversation with them to navigate through the assortment and avoid any choice stress. The assistants operate on devices like smartphones or specially designed smart speakers that rapidly find new shopper homes. According to market research agency Canalys (2018), the number of installed smart speakers will amount to 100 million units in 2018, 2.5 times more than the year before. They expect that more than 300 million households will have access to smart speakers in 2022. Voice-based shopping will certainly tap into real shopper needs; one only has to think of the blind or visually impaired. Getting answers to any question from these mobile encyclo-paedias of retailers and products feels sexier than looking for store employees and reading reports about the pros and cons in product test magazines. Shoppers can quiz the smart speaker on 'the cheapest water cooler' or 'fashion worn by Rihanna', hopefully receive the right answer and instruct the payment to be made. However, more technology advancements and data might be required. Giving predefined instructions sounds easy and fast but a multitude of questions might be required before the shopper feels ready to decide. When inter-acting with the voice-assistants the order in which the product suggestions are made has a large impact: Will the shopper stick to the first mentioned product option or will only the last suggestion stick in the shopper's memory? Or will the voice-assistant give only one product option? It will be impossible to offer the complete variety, so the question arises if the selection of product sugges-tions is based on past purchases, profiling in comparison with other shoppers or anything that the retailer considers good for the shopper. It is matter of experi-mentation how shoppers develop trust in the suggestions from retailers. In addition, the algorithms need to make sense for each culture. To reach global adoption the algorithms require translation into the shopper's own native lan-guage, a process which may go slower than expected. The smart speakers are helpful in day-to-day chores and dealings such as opening the curtains, check-ing the local weather and ordering a taxi. When it comes to shopping, smart speakers might be most handy for categories when shoppers are uninvolved, brands matter less and routineously made shopping decisions. Not surprisingly, Alexa is built into refrigerators. Most of value for Amazon might not come from the e-commerce sales but from the knowledge that technology companies build on the way shoppers live, consume and make shopping decisions.

Time to Relax

So much of this book rests on academic evidence and data-driven experiments because I firmly believe that retailers have still so much to gain from a faster adoption of academic findings into their way of working in the field of assortment management. As available data grow, the retailer should break away from their legacy systems and data silos to make sure the category manager has access to data points along the shopping journey fed by both internal and external sources. This will allow category managers to respond to sudden shopper demand changes, pre-empt competitive moves and create category value through innovation. The good news is that intelligent systems and process maps are available that orchestrate the workflow and decision-making from conception of products to evaluation and forecasting. It is not just a numbers game. Selecting the right products is as important as the visual design of the assortment and telling the story. Therefore, category managers are encouraged to work closely together with visual merchandisers and communication teams to communicate a consistent message to the shopper (and internal stakeholders). This is a huge responsibility for category managers. Aided by technology developments, individual shopping paths become fluid and difficult to predict. When overlaid with types of categories and stages of the shopping journey the data look messy. Technology is there to help and retailers need to apply this more in assortment and merchandising management. It is the task of the category manager to identify the right moments to engage with shoppers. It is for management in retail to ensure the category manager has as much time for spreadsheets as time to relax, to let their thoughts wander off, to collect anecdotal observations on shoppers, to make mistakes, to visit own and competitor stores, to experiment, to enjoy!

Important Learnings from This Chapter

- Retailers have a great influence on and responsibility for shopper choice as many shopper decisions are dependent on the context.

- Retailers need to operate in several channels at the same to catch the shopper on different shopping trips and meet the requirements of different groups of shoppers.
- Inclusion of the costs on the environment will drive a further blended model of online and brick-and-mortar retail.
- Retailers are encouraged to increase their capabilities in order to meet shopper needs in assortment and merchandising:

  – Incorporate new technology to leverage retailer data.
  – Integrate merchandising aspects into assortment decisions.
  – Reset the merchandising function in pursuit of shopper.
  – Become more international.
  – Assess the shopper emotion.
  – Apply voice-based search and assistance.

- Assortment and merchandising practices have not kept up with the growing complexity of the category manager's responsibilities and fast development of technology.

References

Brynjolfsson, E., Hitt, L., & Kim, H. (2011). *Strength in Numbers: How Does Data-Driven Decision-Making Affect Firm Performance?* [Online]. Retrieved July 4, 2018, from https://papers.ssrn.com/sol3/papers.cfm?abstract_id=1819486.

Canalys. (July 10, 2018). *Bret Kinsella*. [Online]. Retrieved July 18, 2018, from https://voicebot.ai/2018/07/10/smart-speakers-to-reach-100-million-installed-base-worldwide-in-2018-google-to-catch-amazon-by-2022/.

Deloitte. (2016). *The New Digital Divide, the Future of Digital Influence in Retail.* [Online]. Retrieved July 29, 2018, from https://www2.deloitte.com/insights/us/en/industry/retail-distribution/digital-divide-changing-consumer-behavior.html.

Deloitte. (2018). Global Powers of Retailing 2018. *Transformative Change, Reinvigorated Commerce.* [Online]. Retrieved July 29, 2018, from https://www2.deloitte.com/insights/us/en/industry/dcom/global-powers-of-retailing.html.

Dolan, P. (2014). *Happiness by Design, Finding Pleasure and Purpose in Everyday Life.* Penguin Group.

Tomkins. [Online]. Retrieved August 4, 2018., from http://www.tomkins.org/.

Van Nierop, E., Fok, D., & Franses, P. H. (2006). *Interaction Between Shelf Layout and Marketing Effectiveness and Its Impact on Optimizing Shelf Arrangements.* Erasmus Research Institute of Management, ERS-2006-013-MKT.

Index

© The Author(s) 2019
C. Berkhout, *Assortment and Merchandising Strategy*,
https://doi.org/10.1007/978-3-030-11163-2